Radical Islam
Understand, Prepare, Defend

by Joseph Lumpkin

Radical Islam
Understand, Prepare, Defend

Fifth Estate Publishing, Blountsville, AL 35031

Cover Designed by An Quigley

Printed on acid-free paper

Library of Congress Control No: 2016905729

ISBN: 9781936533817

Fifth Estate, 2016

Table of Contents

Joseph Lumpkin

Preface

On the morning of Tuesday, September 11, 2001 the United States was changed forever. An Islamic terrorist group calling itself al-Qaeda (The Base) commandeered four separate commercial planes and declared war on the U.S. and the western world. Two of the planes were flown directly into the Twin Towers of the World Trade Center complex in New York City. A third plane targeted the Pentagon and the fourth plane was flying toward Washington, D.C. when passengers overpowered the hijackers causing the plane to crash near Shanksville, Pennsylvania. The act was to herald a decade and a half of increasing violence and hate by a growing group of Muslims aimed at the destruction of the non-Muslim world. Their rage and bloodlust would expand and become more distilled and dangerous, as groups break away from the previous body to form a more fundamental and violent force. From the local militia fighters of the Mujahedeen to the Taliban, al-Qaeda, and now ISIS, the violence and determination to kill and destroy have increased with every incarnation of Islamic fundamentalism. Even more disturbing is the push to expand territory in order to form an ever-growing Islamic nation. But why? What is driving the growth of these groups? What do they want? Where did they come from? What are their goals? How can a faith touted as a religion of peace give rise to such barbarism, hatred and carnage?

These are the questions I began to ask almost two years ago. With each period of research I uncovered more about Islam, the Quran (Koran) and the underlying socio-political structure of the religion that made the development of these terrorist groups possible. This book is the result of personal research aimed at answering the questions regarding Islam, the Quran, and the resulting terrorists groups emanating from the religion. Indeed, it may not be entirely fair to call Islam a religion if it is practiced in the way Mohammed (Mohammed) instructed. Islam, as it turns out, is not what we have been led to believe, but revealing more would spoil the book.

Since this book is based on pure research, it will contain quotes and articles cited from a wide variety of sources. This is a condensed summation given to the reader to answer the basic questions based on historical, religious, and political sources.

7

It must be stressed that not all Muslims adhere to the fundamentalist doctrine or literal views described in this book. Just as many Christians do not approach the Bible literally, there are Muslims who do not approach the Quran as a command to do violence to non-believers. Those who wage jihad today consider these moderate or liberal Muslims apostates. In the minds of the Jihadists (those who claim to fight a holy war), there are no "moderate Muslims". There are only Muslims and infidels. It is ironic that the future of Islam and its standing in the world will depend on these "apostate" Muslims to bring Islam out of the 7th century and into the world as an enlightened religion, as it was once viewed.

A great number of sources were used in the research of this book. English was not the primary language for many of these sources. Since we are attempting to stay close to the original words of the sources, decisions had to be made regarding correcting punctuation, spelling, and sentence structure to make the quotes more understandable. We decided to make corrections when the idea was obscured or lost within the errors; otherwise we let the quote stand as it was written.

As often as it was possible, the source, author, and date or publication were cited with the quote. Words and names are transliterated from Arabic to English as phonetically accurate as possible but sources may use slightly different spelling. In addition a list of the major sources is in a bibliography. The bibliography contains the books and websites recommended for further and more in depth research, or if one is curious regarding the exact wording or punctuation of the Arabic sources.

Above all, keep in mind that although the number of radicalized Muslims may be quite high, not all Muslims are radical or fundamentalists. Those who are not radicalized must help contain Muslim violence by identifying terrorists and those who wish to harm others. Otherwise, if the violence continues, one day no Muslim will be trusted. Silence implies consent.

Section 1

Understanding Radical Islam

The History and Goals of Radical Islam

Islam

Islam is a socio-political system founded on a religion. Its laws are a set of irrevocable and unchanging legal, social, and religious commands written in the 7th century in a book called the Quran (Koran) by the prophet and warlord, Mohammed (Muhhammad). Out of approximately 7 billion people inhabiting this world, between 1.2 and 1.6 billion are Muslim.

Beginning as the faith of a small community of believers in Arabia in the seventh century, Islam rapidly became one of the major world religions. The core of this faith is the belief that Mohammed (c. 570-632), a businessman living in Mecca, a commercial and religious center in western Arabia, received revelations from God. These revelations have been preserved perfectly and without error in the Quran. The heart of the revelations is that "there is no god but Allah (The God), and Mohammad is the messenger of God." The message is one of monotheism meant to guide the believer back on to the path of the great religious forefathers, Abraham, and Jesus.

Jesus, or Isa, is mentioned 59 times in the Quran. 25 times by name, 11 times as messiah, and 23 as son of Mary. Abraham (Ibrahim) is mentioned 69 times, Moses is mentioned 136 times. Mohammed is mentioned 4 times in the Quran.

The term Islam comes from the Arabic word-root s-l-m, which has a general reference to peace and submission. Specifically, Islam means submission to the will of God, and a Muslim is one who makes that submission. But do not confuse the idea of submission to god and the peace this submission is expected to bring with the idea of peace toward one's fellow man. There is a great difference between these two ideas.

This submission or act of Islam means living a life of faith and practice as defined in the Quran and participating in the life of the community of believers like oneself. This homogenous belief system becomes important when one understands there are various branches of Islam, somewhat like the different denominations within Christianity and like Catholics and Protestants of the past, the various branches of Islam are now at war and killing one another.

Muslims believe that Islam is the same monotheistic faith proclaimed by Abraham, the prophets and Jesus, down through history. The Quran is thought to provide the complete and final record of the message from Allah, which began with Abraham and was passed down to Jesus through the earlier prophets, ending with Mohammed. Islam begins with Mohammed in the city of Mecca.

The first and most important thing to realize is that Islam is not like any other religion. The Quran is not read or interpreted like the bible. The bible is a number of books collected into a single volume written by many authors, all bringing individual viewpoints. Christians are told when interpreting the bible to do so, "line upon line and precept upon precept." That is to say, balance and integrate the various knowledge, wisdom, and points of view of the included authors and arrive at a reasonable position on various subjects. It is also understood that the bible represents two distinct eras or dispensations consisting of the Old Testament, where there is a legalistic and punitive period and the New Testament, which focuses on love, mercy, and forgiveness.

Muslims believe the Quran is a single book, written by a single author, containing shifting points of view as Mohammed experienced life and its obstacles. We will see later that this belief is not based in fact. Muslims are instructed that although there may be different instructions and viewpoints presented in the Quran, whatever Mohammed last spoke regarding a topic is the final and lasting edict. This is the most important piece of information to remember when attempting to understand Islam. It is called, "The Rule of Abrogation".

All laws (Sharia Laws) and the moral, ethical, and social codes held in Sharia Law, issue from the Quran and the example set and shown by the life, teachings, and words of Mohammed, who preached in the beginning of the 7th century C.E. The morality, ethics, and religious codes and laws reflect the outlook and understanding of a 7th century Middle Eastern culture and the

example set by Mohammed, who practiced murder, pedophilia, polygamy, slavery and other horrific acts. Owing to the staunch belief that the Quran is perfect and timeless, the laws cannot be changed, updated, or altered. Sharia Law places the followers back into the bloody, violent time of the 7th century where women had no rights, slavery was a way of life, the spoils of war included people, and sex was forced upon anyone who was taken captive.
There is never separation of church and state in Islam because Islam is a self contained legal, political, and religious system. To live in a perfect Islamic state, such as that which ISIS is attempting to craft, is to covert or be killed or made a slave.

Islam is built upon five principles or Pillars. The Five Pillars of Islam are:
Declaration of faith, Obligatory prayer, Compulsory giving, Fasting in the month of Ramadan, Pilgrimage to Mecca.

Because Mohammed began preaching Islam in Mecca as a peaceful and tolerant man, teaching a religion of monotheism and tolerance, and ended his life as a warlord preaching death to infidels and conversion by the sword, and because the Quran is not written in chronological order it would be easy to misunderstand Islam and its intent but it is only the final stage and position that matters, and this position is one of violence and forced conversion by the sword or death to those who refuse to convert. This means the pious Muslims, those who attempt to follow the teachings of Mohammed as closely as possible, must seek to carry out his last commands. Essentially, this is the reason ISIS and al-Qaeda believe it is their obligation to conquer and kill.

What drove Mohammed to change from a man who married one woman and preached peace, monotheism and tolerance to a man who became a warlord and a polygamist who married a six-year-old girl, we may never know. The differences between the mythical life of Mohammed and the historical life of Mohammed have grown so divergent over time it is difficult to discern the truth. But before we plunge headlong into the religion of Islam it would be good to try to learn about the man behind the movement.

Islam and the Golden Rule

"In religion and politics, people's beliefs and convictions are in almost every case second-hand, and without examination, from authorities who have not themselves examined the questions at issue but have taken them at second-hand from another."
Mark Twain

In 1949, Karl Jaspers, the German psychologist and philosopher, published "The Origin and Goal of History," and coined the term, "The Axial Age", to describe the period from 800 BCE to 200 BCE. During this span of time, which in relation to the age of humanity was the blink of an eye, revolutionary religious and spiritual awakenings appeared in synchronicity around the world, with major hubs in China, India, and throughout the Middle East.
Anatomically modern humans arose in Africa approximately 200,000 years ago. Modern behavior was established only 50,000 years ago. Spiritually, humans may have come into their present stage only 3000 years ago. This is a single grain of sand in the archeological hourglass.

Jaspers saw in the recent shift of religious and philosophical thought, similarities that could not be accounted for without direct transmission of ideas between regions, and there was no evidence of "cross-pollination" of ideas or concepts to be found.
Jaspers argued that during the Axial Age "the spiritual foundations of humanity were laid simultaneously and independently."
In Karen Armstrong's book, "The Great Transformation," Armstrong expands on Japers' thesis, stating that the insights representing liberal religion occurred almost simultaneously and independently about 2500 years ago in four different areas of the world: China, India, Greece, and the Middle East.

Religion can be broadly understood as a system of beliefs and practices concerned with sacred things, rituals and/or symbols uniting individuals into a single moral community. The religious laws, rituals, and beliefs form a cohesive moral structure. If "religions" did specifically relate to the sacred, one could use the same definition for governments. Moreover, religions can become governments unto themselves. Therefore, a "religion" does not require a supernatural being as the object of worship, but it does have to represent a commitment to a particular moral or ethical code.

In the pre-Axial Age, religion always revolved around a deity. After the Axial Age, some religions, such as Buddhism, did not revolve around a god, but involved an inward journey toward deeper self-awareness.

Armstrong further suggests that the history of the last two and a half millennia is seen as a continuous struggle between those who acknowledge and value the newly evolved spiritual insights and those who may have a much older and more restrictive concept of the nature of religion.

There will be religions based on the old concepts of laws, judgment, punishment, blood, animal sacrifice, cruelty, judging and killing in an attempt to please God. There will be religions based on grace, love, peace, meditation, and a mystical interior journey to commune with God. Spiritually, for religious systems and for each person, these are our choices and this sets the stage for conflict, both internally and externally on a global scale.

There is no way to know the number of mystics or progressive religious thinkers that influenced any changes in the ancient world's religions, but archeology shows us that changes were molded mostly, if not totally, by migrations to and from adjacent regions, mixing cultures and gods.

This does not answer the nagging questions of why we persist in "structured" religions, and why all major religions carry the same moral or ethical imperatives. Jesus, among others, so beautifully summed up these imperatives: "Love God and love your neighbor as yourself. That is to say, treat all others as you want to be treated." The rest is commentary.

Until the Axial Age, the focus of religion was external, particularly on rituals and ceremony intended to influence or control a god or gods to protect the family or tribe, bring rain, guarantee success in battle, and so on.

During the Axial Age, this changed and an internal search for god began. There may have been several influences driving this evolution. The world became smaller with migrations and the advent of transportation via horseback. Cities grew and developed, continuous warfare mixed gods as the conquered tribe adopted the beliefs of the victor, considering their gods as more powerful. The amalgam of tribes and formation of armies began the demise of tribalism and the splitting of families through death and conscription into military service. The shattering of tribes and families brought about the rise of individual focus. Previously, consequences or punishment from actions of one individual or tribal member affected the entire family or tribe. With individuals separated from families and tribes, the perpetrator carried the consequences alone.

Continual hardships of war, disease, and changes in societies caused people to question the efficacy of their traditional god and religious practices prompting them to look for alternatives.
In China, India, Greece, and Israel, the spirit of humankind awakened in a flash. Wise men, shamans, sages, prophets, philosophers, and scholars independently articulated their insights. The religious traditions they created or influenced are alive in the major religions of today. Confucianism, Taoism, Hinduism, Buddhism, philosophical rationalism, and monotheism arose as though they were orchestrated and coordinated by a single hand.
The insights common to all religious enlightenment of the Axial Age include the ideas of reciprocity, compassion, love, altruism, and the individual's mandate to end the suffering of others. The ideas of compassion and reciprocity are summed up in the actions of treating others justly and as you wished to be treated. Judaism would go on to embody these values in their laws. In turn, the newly awakened Judaism translated that ideal, which has evolved into a monotheistic religion in which members seek communion with God.

16

In the years centering around 500 BCE, great advances in religion, philosophy, science, democracy, and many forms of art occurred independently and almost simultaneously in China, India, the Middle East, and Greece. Today, humanity still uses the spiritual foundations laid in that ancient time. In those times of social upheaval and political turmoil, spiritual and religious pioneers became the standard-bearers of a new religious, cultural, and social order. Great religious leaders rose up in various areas of the world attracting many followers, thereby changing many sociological, cultural, economic and spiritual beliefs.

In China, many individual thinkers, such as Confucius, Lao-Tse, and Mo Tzu, began to reflect on the ethical and spiritual implications of human existence. In time, their teachings became known throughout the world. Confucianism, Taoism, and Jainism are only a few religions to be founded or affected by them.

In India, the authors of the Upanishads expanded the scope of their explorations to include metaphysical thinking in the search for the ultimate truth and the meaning of life and death.
India experienced a dramatic social and intellectual transformation, and produced the teachings of the Buddha and Mahavira. Like China, new teachings ran the whole gamut of philosophical schools of thought, including skepticism, materialism, and nihilism.

In Palestine, the prophets Elijah, Isaiah, and Jeremiah made their appearance. Although the law and moral code of the Israelites dates back before this age, and may have been influenced by the code of Hammurabi of 1750 BCE, the prophets reached beyond the law and called believers into a relationship with Yahweh. In Mesopotamia, cultural and art developed but the concept of an omnipotent and omniscient creator God did not exist.

In Greece, developments were more philosophical than spiritual. Greece witnessed the appearance of Thales, Xenophanes, and Heraclitus who regarded all existence to be in a state of flux, exemplifying his concept by stating, "one cannot step in the same river twice." Parmenides commented on the nature of permanent "being" as opposed to the impermanent phase of "becoming".

Democritus devised the first atomic theory of nature, which later gave way to the scientific nature of matter and atoms.

These philosophers influenced the minds of Socrates, Plato, and Aristotle. They examined the very nature of existence, life, and thought, itself.

Each philosopher and thinker forced his or her culture to question and reinterpret previously devised cosmologies. Until that point in time, every cosmology was a cosmology put forth by a religious myth and none were based in reason or science, even though the scientific method was lacking.

Even as philosophers were dividing science from religion, mystics were emerging from crystallized religions of old to seek the real internal world that lay beyond the senses.

Buddhism propagated the preaching of the eight-fold path. Right View and Right Intention are the wisdom factors of the Noble Eightfold Path. Right Speech, Right Action, and Right Livelihood address ethical conduct. Right Effort, Right Meditation, Right Concentration address mental cultivation. The wisdom factors continually effect ethical conduct and mental cultivation.

This leap became the source of major and lasting cultural traditions enduring to the present time, giving way to a secondary stage or influence of spiritual transformation in which religions such as Judaism spawned the world's two major religions of Christianity and Islam.

The almost simultaneous changes in China, India, Greece and Palestine in the Middle East seem too remarkable to be accidental; especially considering the lack of influence one movement could have had on another, seeing the countries are widely separated from each other. The only example of intellectual communication among these countries appears to be the conjecture that in the 6th century BCE the Greek poet Alcaeus may have known the prophecies of Isaiah.

Religions began to influence and build on each other within different countries. Some religions became opposed to killing, while others expanded this concept to value all life. Ideas and beliefs of Jainism influenced a newly developing Hinduism and the new religion of Buddhism. The dualistic idea of good and evil contained within Zoroastrianism would influence the Jewish ideas of good and evil and the notion of Satan. The new face of Judaism would give way to Christianity and Islam. Christianity could be seen as an offshoot of Judaism whose direction is toward the newly developing selflessness and internal struggle embodied in the Axial Age. Islam can be seen as a religion, which chose to stay rooted in pre-axial age convictions of legalism and external power structures.

An internal or post-Axial Age religion seeks a relationship with the source, God, or inner self that deepens ones compassion, humanity, and connection with one's source, god, and fellow man. One seeks to connect personally with, god or inner self in such a way as to know within one's soul what is right, and to treat all others in accordance with that universal love and respect. .

An external or pre-Axial Age religion is one that follows a set of rules and laws precisely in order to please a punitive, angry, and judgmental god and stay his judgment or glean his favor. Another important mark of a pre-Axial Age religion is the idea that the believer should kill for their god, as if their god needed men to defend god's honor or word. Islam is among a very few religions that continue to do animal sacrifice, cutting the throats of animals and performing rituals to evoke the blessings of their god. Prayers, alms, rituals and sacrifice are all part of being Muslim. Killing in the name of Allah places those radical believers firmly in the pre-Axial Age position. Although they are not the only modern religion that demands the death of innocent animals as well as non-believers, they are among a small and vanishing number.

Islamic Text on the Golden Rule

The Quran:
"Serve God, and join not any partners with Him; and do good- to parents, kinsfolk, orphans, those in need, neighbors who are near,

neighbors who are strangers, the companion by your side, the wayfarer (ye meet), and what your right hands possess [the slave]: For God loveth not the arrogant, the vainglorious" (Q:4:36)

(In fact the Quran goes beyond saying the Golden Rule by stating in more than four places that "Return evil with Kindness." (13:22, 23:96, 41:34, 28:54, 42:40))
Other quotes are found in Sahih Muslim, a collection of hadith compiled by Imam Muslim ibn al-Hajjaj al-Naysaburi (rahimahullah).

 "None of you have faith until you love for your neighbor what you love for yourself" (Sahih Muslim)
"Whoever wishes to be delivered from the fire and to enter Paradise" should treat the people as he wishes to be treated." (Sahih Muslim)
"None of you truly believes until he wishes for his brother what he wishes for himself"(Forty Hadith-Nawawi)

(The Hadith is a collection of teachings from Mohammed, which came down by hearsay. It is a collection of statements recording what people supposedly heard the prophet say.)

"None of you is a believer if he eats his full while his neighbor hasn't anything." (Musnad)
"Do unto all men as you would wish to have done unto you; and reject for others what you would reject for yourselves." (Abu Dawud)
"Hurt no one so that no one may hurt you." (Farewell Sermon)
"There should be neither harming nor reciprocating harm." (Ibn-Majah)

The above statements depict the golden rule in Islam, and if Mohammed would have died within this time frame Islam may have become a force of peace in the world, but sadly this is not how events transpired.

In order to attract followers Mohammed taught things that people like and could easily identify as good. Once he became accepted as a prophet and spiritual leader he began to change his teachings. Due to the Quran being interpreted through abrogation, that is the rule that says whatever the prophet utters last supersedes everything that was said before, it was easy to change the golden rule to the rule of law.

The difference between a true spiritual teacher and a despot is in their consistency of selflessness and compassion. The problem with the good teachings of Mohammed is that they are reserved for fellow Muslims. When the hadith says "None of you [truly] believes until he wishes for his brother what he wishes for himself,." it is talking about the fellow Muslims. The brotherhood in Islam does not extend to everyone. The Quran (9:23) states that the believers should not take for friends and protectors (awlia) their fathers and brothers if they love Infidelity above Islam. That is to say if a friend, guardian, lover or parent is an infidel (non-believer) you should leave them behind and not count them as part of your life. In fact there are many verses that tell the Muslims to kill the unbelievers and be harsh to them. A clear example that Islam is not based on the Golden Rule is the verse (48:29): "Mohammed is the messenger of Allah; and those who are with him are strong (harsh) against Unbelievers, but compassionate with each other."

In "Islam and the Golden Rule" Robert Spencer writes:
    "The Quran tells Muslims to slay the unbelievers wherever they find them (2:191), do not befriend them (3:28), fight them and show them harshness (9:123), smite (cut off) their heads (47:4), etc. "These teachings, because they came later in the life of Mohammed, take precedence and authority over previous more compassionate verses and are not compatible with the Golden Rule. According to Muslims it is not the Golden Rule that defines what is good or bad, but the words or deeds of Mohammed that defines good and evil and what is compatible with the deeds or words of Mohammed is defined as good. Islam is the only doctrine that calls upon its believers to do evil to others for the simple fact that they do not believe as Muslim believers. They believe that what is good for Islam is the highest virtue and what is bad for Islam is the ultimate evil. This is the definition of good and evil in Islam.

An example of this reversal of tone can be found between the following chapters:

Verse 41:34 is a Meccan verse where Mohammed and his followers were greatly outnumbered and the religion was just getting started. In this verse Muslims were the underdogs. Here he preached patience and said repel evil with good so your enemy becomes a friend. These orders changed when Mohammed came to power. In Medina Mohammed banished and massacred entire populations just because he suspected that they might not be friendly to him. 28:54 is a repetition of 23:96 and 42:40 says whoever forgives and amends, he shall have his reward from Allah. However, Mohammed never forgave those who mocked him. Oqba used to mock Mohammed when he was in Mecca. When Oqba was captured in the Battle of Badr, Mohammed ordered his decapitation. When asked why Mohammed was going to do such a thing Mohammed replied, "Because of your enmity to God and to his prophet." "And my little girl!" cried Oqba, in the bitterness of his soul, "Who will take care of her?" — "Hellfire!", "and persecutor! Unbeliever in God, in his prophet, and in his Book! I give thanks unto the Lord that has slain you, and comforted mine eyes thereby." And with that Oqba was decapitated."

These action and words should be compared to those of Jesus when he was slighted, beaten, mocked, and killed. His dying words were, "father forgive them. They do not know what they are doing..."

How do you reconcile the claim that Mohammed in his farewell sermon said, "Hurt no one so that no one may hurt you." With the fact that on his deathbed he said, "No two religions are allowed in Arabia" and ordered the forced conversion, expulsion or ethnic cleansing of the Jews and Christian and the murder of Pagans?

The Golden Rule does not exist unless it is applied equally throughout the family of mankind, without respect to gender, race, or religion.

In "Islam and the Golden Rule" Robert Spencer writes:

"The chapter (sura) 9, which are among the last words of Mohammed, is a manifesto of discrimination and human right

22

abuses. Mohammed declared non-believers to be the worst of all creatures, worthy of eternal punishment and with these words he diminished the humanity of non-Muslims to a point incompatible with the Golden Rule, which relies totally on the idea of equality and universal love of mankind. Sura (chapter) 9 is referred to as the Verse of the Sword. The words were uttered so late in the life of the prophet and were so contrary to previous teaching they set aside in part or totally over 100 verses and rewrote the attitude of Islam into a violent and warlike religion. It deserves repeating that the Quran cannot be read in its entirety and synthesized, as one would read the Gita, Tao Te Ching, Bible, Dhammapada or other holy books.

The rules of interpretation for the Quran are simple.
1)   Find out what timeframe each verse was written in.
2)   Read and understand the verses and what they are dealing with.
3)   On each subject and belief, the last word stands uncontested.
Even though the attitudes, laws, rules, and beliefs are based on 7th century ideas, they cannot be altered or adapted. These are the rules that Islamic fundamentals live by."

The "Verse of the Sword" Quran 9:5
SAHIH INTERNATIONAL
And when the sacred months have passed, then kill the polytheists wherever you find them and capture them and besiege them and sit in wait for them at every place of ambush. But if they should repent, establish prayer, and give zakah, let them [go] on their way. Indeed, Allah is Forgiving and Merciful.

Here is another translation of the same verse.

Quran 9:5
But when the forbidden months are past, then fight and slay the Pagans wherever ye find them, and seize them, beleaguer them, and lie in wait for them in every stratagem (of war); but if they repent, and establish regular prayers and practice regular charity, then open the way for them: for Allah is Oft-forgiving, Most Merciful.

For 1400 years Islam has been at war. At first, they killed non-believers. Then they began killing other Muslims over differences in leadership and prayers. Now Islam is at war with the western world, blaming Christians, Jews, and western society for their woes. Fundamental Muslims blame the United States for their sins and lack of progress, although the U.S. has existed for only a little over two hundred years. We are not the ones causing them to cut off the hands of their people nor are we causing the stoning or beating of believers.. We are not the ones raping their women and children. Yet, like some great scapegoat or ancient sin eater, all sin is conveyed upon the west and upon Israel. Now they must kill us in a misguided attempt of propitiation to free themselves of the violence still living inside the Islam of fundamentalist and terrorists. It is a violence and evil uncontained and uncontrolled.

Finding the Baseline

According to a Pew Research Center, June, 2013 study, "There are an estimated 1.6 billion Muslims around the world, making Islam the world's second-largest religious tradition after Christianity, according to the December 2012 Global Religious Landscape report from the Pew Research Center's Forum on Religion & Public Life.
Although many people, especially in the United States, may associate Islam with countries in the Middle East or North Africa, nearly two-thirds (62%) of Muslims live in the Asia-Pacific region, according to the Pew Research analysis. In fact, more Muslims live in India and Pakistan (344 million combined) than in the entire Middle East-North Africa region (317 million)."

The Washington Examiner, February 13, 2016 reports,
Of the 1.2 billion Muslims they estimate as a world population, "Not all of them are radicals! The majority of them are peaceful people. The radicals are estimated to be between 15 to 25 percent, according to all intelligence services around the world. That leaves 75 percent of them peaceful people.
But when you look at 15 to 25 percent of the world's Muslim population, you're looking at 180 million to 300 million people dedicated to the destruction of Western civilization. That is as big [as] the United States.
So why should we worry about the radical 15 to 25 percent? Because the radicals are the ones who kill. Because it is the radicals that behead and massacre."

According to counterjihadreport.com, January 2016, Matt Barber wrote,
"We need only look to the many polls to affirm the alarmingly high percentages of Muslims (hundreds-of-millions in number) who seek, through the most violent means imaginable, Islamic world domination. Again, here are but a few:
83 percent of Palestinian Muslims, 62 percent of Jordanians and 61 percent of Egyptians approve of jihadist attacks on Americans. World Public Opinion Poll (2009).

1.5 Million British Muslims support the Islamic State, about half their total population. ICM (Mirror) Poll 2015.

Two-thirds of Palestinians support the stabbing of Israeli civilians. Palestinian Center for Policy and Survey Research (2015).

38.6 percent of Western Muslims believe 9/11 attacks were justified. Gallup(2011).

45 percent of British Muslims agree that clerics preaching violence against the West represent "mainstream Islam." BBC Radio (2015).

38 percent of Muslim-Americans say Islamic State (ISIS) beliefs are Islamic or correct. (Forty-three percent disagree.) The Polling Company CSP Poll (2015).

One-third of British Muslim students support killing for Islam. Center for Social Cohesion (Wikileaks cable).

78 percent of British Muslims support punishing the publishers of Mohammed cartoons. NOP Research.

80 percent of young Dutch Muslims see nothing wrong with holy war against non-believers. Most verbalized support for pro-Islamic State fighters. Motivation Survey (2014).

Nearly one-third of Muslim-Americans agree that violence against those who insult Mohammed or the Quran is acceptable. The Polling Company CSP Poll (2015).

68 percent of British Muslims support the arrest and prosecution of anyone who insults Islam. NOP Research.

51 percent of Muslim-Americans say that Muslims should have the choice of being judged by Sharia courts rather than courts of the United States (only 39 percent disagree).The Polling Company CSP Poll (2015).

81 percent of Muslim respondents support the Islamic State (ISIS). Al-Jazeera poll (2015)."

On July 7, 2005 four suicide bombers with rucksacks full of explosives attacked central London, killing 52 people and injuring hundreds more. It was the worst single act of terrorism on British soil to date. The bombers, Mohammad Sidique Khan, 30, Shehzad Tanweer, 22, and 18-year-old Hasib Hussain then fled the scene and met their fourth accomplice, 19-year-old Germaine Lindsay. The four terrorists headed to the capital by train. In London they detonate four devices. Three were on the Underground and one was on a double-decker bus. A large number of the British Muslim population cheered the acts of murder and declared them to be justified under Sharia law. Soon following the bombings the Muslim community of the UK was polled for their thoughts and reactions. The results sent a cold chill down the spine of the majority non-Muslim population.

ICM Poll: 20% of British Muslims sympathized with 7/7 bombers. http://www.telegraph.co.uk/news/uknews/1510866/Poll-reveals-40pc-of-Muslims-want-sharia-law-in-UK.html

NOP Research: 1 in 4 British Muslims sid 7/7 bombings were justified. http://www.cbsnews.com/stories/2006/08/14/opinion/main1893 879.shtml&date=2011-04-06 http://www.webcitation.org/5xkMGAEvY

Channel Four (2006) Britain: 31% of younger British Muslims say 7/7 bombings were justified compared to 14% of those over 45. http://www.policyexchange.org.uk/images/publications/living% 20apart%20together%20-%20jan%2007.pdf

Britain is not the only nation being targeted by Islam. All western powers are under attack.

People-Press: 31% of Turks support suicide attacks against Westerners in Iraq. http://people-press.org/report/206/a-year-after-iraq-war

World Public Opinion (poll and research): 83% of Egyptians approve of attacks on American troops.
26% of Indonesians approve of attacks on American troops.
26% of Pakistanis approve of attacks on American troops.
68% of Moroccans approve of attacks on American troops.
90% of Palestinians approve of attacks on American troops.
72% of Jordanians approve of attacks on American troops.
52% of Turks approve of some or most groups that attack Americans (39% oppose)
A minority of Muslims disagreed entirely with terror attacks on American troops.

About half of those opposed to attacking Americans were sympathetic with al-Qaeda's attitude toward the U.S. http://www.worldpublicopinion.org/pipa/pdf/feb09/STARTII_F eb09_rpt.pdf

The Polling Company CSP Poll (2015): 25% of Muslim-Americans say that violence against Americans in the United States is justified as part of the "global Jihad (64% disagree). http://www.centerforsecuritypolicy.org/wp-content/uploads/2015/06/150612-CSP-Polling-Company-Nationwide-Online-Survey-of-Muslims-Topline-Poll-Data.pdf

Israel stands as a lighthouse of democracy in the midst of Islamic theocracy. It is considered a western proxy by Islamic nations. Israel is the most hated nation by a the Muslim world.

YNet: One third of Palestinians (32%) supported the slaughter of a Jewish family, including the children: http://pajamasmedia.com/tatler/2011/04/06/32-of-palestinians-support-infanticide/ http://www.ynetnews.com/articles/0,7340,L-4053251,00.html

PCPO (2014): 89% of Palestinians support Hamas and other terrorists firing rockets at Israeli civilians. http://www.jihadwatch.org/2014/08/poll-89-of-palestinians-support-jihad-terror-attacks-on-israely

In the United States, there is a growing Islamic movement to replace the constitution and our corpus of law and Jurisprudence with Sharia Law. The movement is gaining ground with Muslims, both within the U.S. and outside the U.S. Almost 1 in 5 of American Muslims want to make Sharia Law the law of the land.

The Polling Company CSP Poll (2015): 19% of Muslim-Americans say that violence is justified in order to make Sharia the law in the United States (66% disagree). http://www.centerforsecuritypolicy.org/wp-content/uploads/2015/06/150612-CSP-Polling-Company-Nationwide-Online-Survey-of-Muslims-Topline-Poll-Data.pdf

The Rubic Center Research in International Affairs, February 13, 2016 estimated probable conflict intensity in connection with Islamic State terrorism (IS, formerly known as ISIS and ISIL). Based on Pew data, covering 2/5 of the global Muslim population, it is estimated that 17.38 percent of Muslims worldwide openly express terror sympathies (there were five terrorism support indicators used). Quantitative estimates on terror support rates for a number of additional countries are also provided, based on European Social Survey (ESS) data and their statistical relationship to Pew data.

The number of radical Muslims appears to be anyone's guess. While the Rubic Center placed the percentage at about 17 percent, Representative Loretta Sanchez of California thinks as many as 20 percent of Muslims want to establish an Islamic caliphate by any means necessary. Sanchez added that this 5 to 20 percent "are willing to use and they do use terrorism."

Speaking on PoliticKING With Larry King, the Democrat asserted: "We know that there is a small group, and we don't know how big that is — it can be anywhere between 5 and 20 percent, from the people that I speak to — that Islam is their religion and who have a desire for a caliphate and to institute that in any way possible."
President Barack Obama has repeated his guess several times, saying 99 percent of Muslims are peaceful people. It is a guess that most people dismiss outright as false.

Applied to the global Muslim population of over 1.6 billion, Loretta Sanchez's estimate of 5 – 20 percent of radicalization would imply a pro-caliphate, pro-terrorist contingent of 80 - 320 million people worldwide.

Sanchez did not give a source for these figures, other than "the people she speaks to." A recent Pew survey found minorities of Muslims supporting ISIS in several countries (including 20 percent of Nigerian Muslims, the highest figure), though in Lebanon, for example, ISIS' unfavorable status stood at 100 percent.

In the midst of all of this hatred and killing, where are the "Moderate Muslims"? Some believe there really is not such a person. Islam demands what Islam demands and a Muslim believing otherwise is not a true Muslim. They are apostate, cowards, lukewarm, westernized, or have simply sold out to the west. This is the rhetoric radicalized Muslims - or devout Muslims, as they would label themselves – are spewing against those Muslims who would interpret the Quran and Islam in a peaceful light.

USA News and World Report, December 18, 2015, in the article, "Pressing a Muslin Reformation", Mary Kate Cary wrote,
      "A small group of Muslim men and women launched the Muslim Reform Movement here in Washington. Led by Dr. Zuhdi Jasser, who is a medical doctor and a former U.S. naval officer, the group held a press conference at the National Press Club, issued a statement of their principles, and – in a move reminiscent of the famous "95 Theses" that Martin Luther posted on a church door in 1517, sparking the Protestant Reformation – affixed their precepts to the door of the Islamic Center in the heart of D.C.'s Embassy Row.

• "We reject interpretations of Islam that call for any violence, social injustice and politicized Islam. We invite our fellow Muslims and neighbors to join us.

• "We reject bigotry, oppression and violence against all people based on any prejudice, including ethnicity, gender, language, belief, religion, sexual orientation and gender expression.

• "We are for secular governance, democracy and liberty.

• "Every individual has the right to publicly express criticism of Islam. Ideas do not have rights. Human beings have rights.

• "We stand for peace, human rights and secular governance. Please stand with us!

This is exactly what we've all been waiting to hear. But while The Washington Post reported beforehand that the event would be taking place, once it did, the Post didn't even send a reporter. Instead, the Post editors ran a Religion News Service report and only posted it online – it didn't make the regular paper. As far as I can tell, The New York Times didn't run a story at all. Neither did the evening news broadcast that night on ABC, NBC and CBS."

The obvious problems are that their types of groups are too few, too quiet, and too small. There is a greater and more immoveable issue, it is one of perceived legitimacy. Even clerics have denounced the ongoing killing and radical movements. Some of these are high-ranking clerics. But, the problem with fundamentalism in any religion is that if anyone, no matter their station or rank, disagrees with them, that person is considered in error, apostate, sinful, and hell bound. It is a closed loop. Those who agree unite and fight. Those who do not agree are labeled apostate and fought against. The logic is inescapable and the minds are closed.

What does that mean? Assuming the worst-case numbers, simply put, there are 1.6 billion Muslims on earth and 300 million are would be terrorists seeking to bring down western civilization and they are not listening to alternative beliefs. The only thing that will stop them are moderate Muslims who are willing to find them and report them before Islam itself is declared an enemy of the free world.

The media and the Muslim communities attempt to chastise the wary U.S. public for being "Islamophobic," but if the information regarding the numbers and percentages of radical or fundamental Muslims is true, then out of every ten Muslims in the world, one or two will seek to destroy any society that is not based on Islam and kill anyone who is not Muslim. It seems foolish to be blind to such disconcerting odds. If a game of chance had a one in ten chance of ending in death, would you place a bet or spin the wheel?

So, how did this all start? Who was the man that founded such a faith? What do we know about him? How did Islam get to this point?

Mohammed

Mohammed was born 570 AD in the town of Mecca in Arabia. His father Abd-Allah, from the tribe of Hashim in Mecca, died before he was born. His mother Amina, from the tribe of Naggar in Medina, died five years later. Mohammed lived in Mecca with his pagan father's parents and was cared for by an Ethiopian Christian woman named "Baraka," whom he called his "Mom". From childhood, Mohammed suffered epileptic seizures. "The Hadith (Islamic tradition) describes the half-abnormal ecstatic condition with which Mohammed was overcome." (The Shorter Encyclopedia of Islam by Cornell University)

At age ten Mohammed began working on a caravan for his uncle, Abu-Talib. He traveled in Israel and Syria on trading missions. On his journeys, Mohammed enjoyed talking to Christian Monks in the monasteries that were located in Arabia along the route of the caravans. The monasteries served as "Rest Areas" on the route of caravans. (The Detailed Encyclopedia in the History of Arabs Prior to Islam by Dr. Jawad Ali, published by The Iraqi Scientific Association)

At age 25, Mohammed worked on a caravan owned by Khadija, a forty-year-old Christian widow. Mohammed was attracted to Khadija, and her help gave him status in the community. They married and Mohammed went to live with her. Khadija's cousin, Waraka Bin Nofel, was the priest of a Christian sect called the Ebionites -- founded in Arabia in the 7th century. The Ebionites believed that the Messiah was just a prophet, not God manifested in human flesh. Islamic sources indicate that Bin Nofel was working on an Arabic translation of a book, The Hebrew Gospel of Matthew. The translation is lost to history, but its traces can be found in the Quran.

After marrying Khadija, Mohammed was exposed to and studied Ebionism for 15 years. Ebonites do not believe in the godhead, divinity, or virgin birth of Jesus, but they do believe Jesus was a prophet. It is this heretical Christian sect that may have formed the basis of Islam.

There is ample evidence that Mohammed began having Temporal Lobe Epilepsy based on descriptions of witnesses. At times he would become catatonic, immovable, and unresponsive. Other times he would fall to the ground and break out in huge drops of sweat. His head and neck would tremble. He would become anxious, fearful and troubled. He would see light and hear bells. He would forget or imagine things. His personality and appearance would change. These things are reported in Bukhari 1,2,6,7,9, and 22

Sahih al-Bukhari is a collection of hadith compiled by Imam Mohammed al-Bukhari (C. 870 AD). His collection is recognized by the overwhelming majority of the Muslim world to be the most authentic collection of reports of the Sunnah of the prophet Mohammed. It contains over 7500 hadith (with repetitions) in 97 books.

By putting together the accounts, a list of anomalies is revealed:
He hallucinated, seeing an angel or a light and hearing voices.
He experienced bodily spasms and abdominal pain and discomfort.
He was overwhelmed by sudden emotions of anxiety and fear.
He had twitching in his neck muscles.
He had uncontrollable lip movement.
He sweated even during cold days.
His face flushed. His countenance was troubled.
He had rapid heart palpitation.
He had loss of memory. (There is a tradition that states Mohammed was bewitched and used to think that he had sexual relations with his wives when he actually had not.)

We can compare the above episodes with a partial list of symptoms of a Temporal Lobe Seizure.
TLE common symptoms are:
Hallucinations or illusions such as hearing voices when no one has spoken, seeing patterns, lights, beings or objects that aren't there,
Rhythmic muscle contraction,
Muscle cramps are involuntary and often painful contractions of the muscles which produce a hard, bulging muscles,
 Abdominal pain or discomfort,
Sudden, intense emotion such as fear,

Abnormal mouth behaviors,
Abnormal head movements,
Sweating,
Flushed face,
Rapid heart rate/pulse,
Changes in vision, speech, thought, awareness, or personality,
Loss of memory (amnesia) regarding events around the seizure (partial complex seizure).
Muscle twitching (fasciculation) is the result of spontaneous local muscle contractions that are involuntary and typically only affect individual muscle groups. This twitching does not cause pain.

We see the list of outward signs during his revelations match the symptoms of TLE. This may also explain why Mohammed had shifted so dramatically from a peaceful prophet into a killer in such a short time, as brain trauma may have occurred.

One may ask how it could be said that Mohammed may have suffered from TLE and the apostle Paul did not. It is because Paul reported only one incident wherein he had a religious experience connected with a flash of light and a voice. It was reported that Mohammed suffered episodes from a young age and separate from religious experiences. That said, it should be stressed that information is sparse and not completely reliable.

Mohammed had a vision that frightened him greatly. He felt he had encountered a demon. His wife convinced him it was not a demon but it was the angel Gabriel. He would accept this interpretation of his vision and move forward to be a religious leader.

When he was 40, Mohammed felt himself selected by God to be a prophet, based on a vision he had revealing that there was only one God. Up to this pint the Arabs, unlike other nations, had no prophet. In the cave of Mt. Hira, north of Mecca, he had a vision in which he was commanded to preach. Throughout his life he continued to have revelations, many of which were collected and recorded in the Quran.

The central points of his message were,
There is one God; people must submit to Him; nations have been and will be punished for rejecting God's prophets; heaven and hell are real and they are waiting; the world will come to an end with a great judgment. He included as religious duties frequent prayer and almsgiving, and he forbade usury (making money on loans).

In his first years Mohammed was preaching in Mecca, a city of Jews and polytheists. The polytheistic people of the city and the surrounding area saw their gods as protectors and the reason their city was prosperous. Much of the city's revenues depended on its pagan shrine, the Kaaba, a huge cube-like structure in the center of town that displayed as many 360 pagan gods. An attack on the existing religion was an attack on the prosperity of Mecca. The system worked and the people had no reason to change. Certainly the Jews were not going to change. They held to their religion and enjoyed the fruits of the trade route, which Mecca was on. Still, Mohammed preached. He made few converts but many enemies. His first converts were Khadija, Ali (who became the husband of Fatima, Mohammed's youngest daughter), and Abu Bakr, a man who would become a driving force in Islam, after Mohammed's death.

Mohammed continues to preach and push the idea that he was the last prophet in the line of Abraham and Jesus. His message was rejected and from about 620 AD on, Mecca became actively hostile.

For 12 years, from 610 AD to 622 AD, Mohammed tried to gain followers in Mecca. He was so frustrated that he resorted to deception to try to convince people to follow him. He claimed that the djins / jinns (genies) and fairies, who Arabs believed inhabited the trees, rocks and water of Arabia, believed in him. (See Quran 72)

72. Surah Al-Jinn (The Jinn)
In the Name of Allah, The Most Gracious, Most Merciful

1. Say (O Mohammed): "It has been revealed to me that a group (from three to ten in number) of jinns listened (to this Quran). They said: 'Verily! We have heard a wonderful Recital (this Quran)!

2. 'It guides to the Right Path, and we have believed therein, and we shall never join (in worship) anything with our Lord (Allah).

3. 'And exalted be the Majesty of our Lord, He has taken neither a wife, nor a son (or offspring or children).

4. 'And that the foolish among us [i.e. Iblis (Satan) or the polytheists amongst the jinns] used to utter against Allah that which was wrong and not right.

5. 'And verily, we thought that men and jinns would not utter a lie against Allah.

6. 'And verily, there were men among mankind who took shelter with the masculine among the jinns, but they (jinns) increased them (mankind) in sin and disbelief.

7. 'And they thought as you thought, that Allah will not send any Messenger (to mankind or jinns).

8. 'And we have sought to reach the heaven; but found it filled with stern guards and flaming fires.

9. 'And verily, we used to sit there in stations, to (steal) a hearing, but any who listens now will find a flaming fire watching him in ambush.

10. 'And we know not whether evil is intended for those on earth, or whether their Lord intends for them a Right Path.

11. 'There are among us some that are righteous, and some the contrary; we are groups each having a different way (religious sect, etc.).

12. 'And we think that we cannot escape (from the punishment of) Allah in the earth, nor can we escape (from the punishment) by flight.

13. 'And indeed when we heard the Guidance (this Quran), we believed therein (Islamic Monotheism), and whosoever believes in his Lord shall have no fear, either of a decrease in the reward of his good deeds or an increase in punishment for his sins.

Mohammed's teaching was failing in his hometown but it was faring better farther way. In the town of Yathrib, Islam was gaining a foothold. As it would turn out, Islam would live or die in Yathrib.

As Mecca begin to turn against Mohammed and people began to whisper about killing the trouble maker he began to fear for his life. In the summer of 622 AD Mohammed fled from Mecca as an attempt was being prepared to murder him. He and his followers escaped the city in the night and made his way to Yathrib. From this event, the flight, or Hegira, of the prophet (622), the Islamic calendar begins. There was a reason Mohammed chose Yathrib as his destination. He had been in negotiations with the leaders of the town to come there as a type of judge or arbitrator. The city fathers of Yathrib could not seem to settle disputes by bickering factions, which threatened to tear the town apart. It was not a pleasant task but Mohammed had little to lose.

Mohammed spent the rest of his life at Yathrib. That city is now called Medina, the City of the prophet. At Medina he built his model theocratic state and from there ruled his rapidly growing empire. It was Mohammed's harsh judicial methods and decisions at Medina over the next 10 years that set in place the laws of Islam.

Medina sits on the caravan and trade route north of Mecca. Caravans were constantly making their way to and from, carrying goods and money. Mohammed would send his men to raid the caravans and steal what they could. They tormented the Meccans. The Meccans could not tolerate the fact that Mohammed's men were plundering the caravans and planned to fight back. Skirmishes occurred on a regular basis but a major battle occurred at Badr between Mohammed's men and the Meccans. The Muslim raiders were victorious. Since the Muslims were of an inferior force from the poorer city and won over the men of Mecca, the Muslims claimed it was divinely inspired and thus they gained prestige in southwest portion of Arabia. A year later Muslim raiders were active in the Eastern Empire, in Persia, and in Ethiopia.

Mohammed had become absolutely convinced that he was the successor of Abraham and Jesus and was the last in the line of prophets. Mohammed expected the Jews and Christians would agree and accept his position and revelations. It was not to be.

Medina had a large Jewish population and the Jewish history was replete with stories of Jews withstanding conversion. The Jews were not about to give up their ancient faith. They controlled the wealth of the city and they stood in unity against Mohammed. But Mohammed was empowered by his position in Medina. After heated discussions, from which Mohammed left unsatisfied, he simply took their property by force. He then turned to one of the nearest Jewish enclaves and begin to exact his anger on them. In 628

Mohammed and his men raided and conquered the mostly Jewish city, the oasis of Khaibar. The Christians were no easier to convince of his calling and they too refused to convert. Mohammed became equally resentful and distrustful of Christians.

His renown increased, and he made a pilgrimage to Mecca.

Amidst growing fame as a warlord and religious leader, in 629 he returned to Mecca with an army to conquer the city. He did so without interference. Once in Mecca, he pulled down all of the idols and statues of the pagan gods, including a moon god referred to as Allah. Allah is a general name for god, probably indicating it was the main god of the area. This could very possibly be the origin of the term used for the Islamic god and for the symbol of the moon used in Islam. The pagan gods were displayed on the top of a black cube, called the kaaba. Karen Armstrong speculates there were 360 statues on the top of the Kaaba, one god for every day of the year. The kaaba still stands and all Muslims performing the hajj or pilgrimage to Mecca circle this same kaaba and kiss it. Mohammed would later tell his followers the kaaba was rebuilt by Abraham. Stories differ as to its origins. Some say angels and some say Adam built it.

In Mecca Mohammed won valuable converts, including Amr and Khalid (who had fought him at Uhud). In 630 he marched against Mecca, which fell without a fight. Arabia was won.

Myth and miracle are mixed with fact, so it is notoriously difficult to know details about the founder of a world religion. In the case of Mohammed, Muslim literary sources for his life only begin around 750-800 CE, some four to five generations after his death, and few Islamicists (specialists in the history and study of Islam) these days assume them to be straightforward historical accounts.

There is no doubt that Mohammed existed. His neighbors in Byzantine Syria got to hear of him within two years of his death. A Greek text written during the Arab invasion of Syria between 632 and 634 mentions that "a false prophet has appeared among the Saracens" and dismisses him as an impostor on the ground that prophets do not come "with sword and chariot". It thus conveys the impression that he was actually leading the invasions and the occupants did not accept a warlord as a prophet. An Armenian document probably written shortly after 661 identifies him by name and gives a recognizable account of his monotheist preaching. Sources dating from the mid-8th century preserve a document drawn up between Mohammed and the inhabitants of Medina (Yathrib), which is accepted as authentic.

Mohammed's death is normally placed in 632, but there is the possibility that it should be placed two or three years later. The Muslim calendar was instituted after Mohammed's death, with a starting-point of his emigration (hijra) to Medina ten years earlier. Some Muslims, however, seem to have correlated this point of origin with the year which came to span 624-5 in the Gregorian calendar rather than the canonical year of 622.

We can be reasonably sure that the Quran is indeed a collection of sayings uttered by Mohammed as he believed Allah revealed them to him. The book does not preserve all the messages he claimed to have received. We have evidence from several witnesses that indicate verses were lost, forgotten, and not remembered correctly. To add to the confusion regarding the Quran, the arrangement of the verses is not in the order they were revealed or dictated by Mohammed. They were collected after his death, and seem to be arranged from largest to smallest.

Even though the Quran is constructed by verses uttered by Mohammed, it cannot be used as a historical source. The source does not reveal much about the historical Mohammed and the language used to write the earliest versions of the Quran is too "fluid." There are also unresolved questions as to how the Quran reached its present, codified and classical form. The earliest versions of the Quran offer only the consonantal skeleton of the text. No vowels are marked and no diacritical marks, so that many consonants can also be read in a number of ways. This is reminiscent of Hebrew before the vowel marks were used. It was essentially a written language with no vowels.

Modern scholars usually assure themselves that since the Quran was recited from the start, we can rely on the oral tradition to supply us with the correct reading. But there is often considerable disagreement in the traditions. To prove the point, the disagreements usually have to do with vowelling, but sometimes involving consonants as well and always over the correct way in which a word should be read. This rarely affects the overall meaning of the text, but it does affect the details that are so important for historical reconstruction. There were, in the very beginning, at least four versions of the Quran written down from several reciters and none of them were exactly the same.

Sometimes the Quran uses expressions that were unknown even to the earliest exegetes. There are words that do not seem to fit in some sentences, so the meaning must be inferred or guessed. Sometimes it seems to give us fragments detached from context making the meaning vague or uncertain.

The prophet could have formulated his message in the liturgical language in which he grew up and was adapting and imitating ancient texts such as hymns and prayers, which had been translated from another Semitic language.

Patricia Crone was professor of Islamic history at the Institute for Advanced Study, Princeton until her death in July 2015.
In the June 2008 publication Open Democracy, Patricia Crone wrote, "The Quran does not give us an account of the prophet's life. It focuses on his psyche as God is speaking to him, telling him what to preach, how to react to people who poke fun at him, what to say to his supporters, and so on. We see the world through his eyes, and the allusive style makes it difficult to follow what is going on. Add to that the fact the Quran is not in chronological order so verses must be artificially placed in a sequence in which they were assumed to occur." (The allusive style refers to expressions designed to call something to mind without mentioning it explicitly.)

Crone continues, "Events are referred to, but not narrated. Disagreements are debated without being explained. People and places are mentioned, but rarely named. Supporters are simply referred to as believers; opponents are condemned as unbelievers, polytheists, wrongdoers, hypocrites, all with only the barest information on who they were or what they said or did.

One thing seems clear however, all the parties in the Quran are monotheists worshipping the God of the Biblical tradition, and all are familiar – if rarely directly from the Bible itself – with Biblical concepts and stories. This is true even of the so-called polytheists, traditionally identified with Mohammed's tribe in Mecca. The Islamic tradition says that the members of this tribe, known as Quraysh, were believers in the God of Abraham whose monotheism had been corrupted by pagan elements. Modern historians would be inclined to reverse the relationship and cast the pagan elements as older than the monotheism, but some kind of combination of Biblical-type monotheism and Arabian paganism is indeed what one encounters in the Quran. "

Those who hold to the monotheistic Abrahamic God, such as Jews and Christians are called, "Children of the Book." Although, it seems the jury is now out on Christians. Due to the doctrine of the Trinity, some Muslims now consider Christians polytheists.

Most polytheists in Arabia believed in one creator God who could be approached through prayer and ritual. These gods usually had helpers and messengers such as angels, and even though Islam holds fast to their belief in jinns or genies, which are themselves supernatural creatures, Mohammed denounced all of these religions as totally polytheistic. One highly respected Islamic source named Ibn al-Kalbi cast the pagans as "naive worshippers of stones and idols of a type that may very well have existed in other parts of Arabia."

Crone continues, "What then are the big issues dividing the prophet and his opponents? Two stand out. First, time and again he accuses the polytheists of the same crime as the Christians – deification of lesser beings. The Christians elevated Jesus to divine. The polytheists elevated the angels to the same status and compounded their error by casting some of them as females. Just as the Christians identified Jesus as the son of God, so the polytheists called the angels sons and daughters of God, apparently implying some sort of identity of essence. "

Indeed, it is the main source of division and killing of Christians by Muslims today that some Muslims consider Christians to be polytheists because of the Christian doctrine of the Trinity. Much of the vitriol of Muslims toward Christians comes from the misunderstanding of the Trinity and a refusal to entertain the possibility of any other expression of God in any other form since this would lead to a type of polytheism. Thus the concept of a single God being expressed as a Father image, and /or a messiah, and/or a spirit led Muslims to label Christians as polytheists, which in turn, according to the Quran, gave Muslims permission, if not the command, to kill Christian as they were wont to do with any polytheist who did not convert to Islam. This continues to be part of the battle cry by fundamentalist Muslims today that all polytheists and all those who will not convert must be destroyed. It was the first purpose of Islam and will likely be its last that only those fitting a fixed theological and monotheistic mold should be allowed to live.

The polytheists further claimed that the angels were helpers and messengers between god and man. Christians also saw angels as messengers and helpers. To Christians, Jesus was the only intercessor between God and man. Mohammed took exception to this since to him it spoke of Jesus having a shared power or essence as God.

The angels were seen by some pagans as manifestations of God himself rather than simply his servants. Christians see Jesus as the manifestation of God on earth in the form of the Son of God. All of the above opens these non-Muslims up to accusations of polytheism. This flew in the face of the primary message of Islam, that God is one and alone, without children and shared in his divinity, essence or power with no one.

Muslims believe in the resurrection of the dead. Mohammed preached of a bodily resurrection, after which they would be judged. Many sects of pagan did not agree with him. Some saw the end as a spiritual resurrection. Some did not believe the dead would come back in any form. The Quran speaks to this subject.

"Verily, those who believe Our Signs and treat them with arrogance, for them the gates of heaven will not be opened, and they will not enter Paradise until the camel goes through the eye of the needle. Thus do We recompense the criminal sinners." (Quran 7:40)

"And the Trumpet will be blown, and all who are in the heavens and all who are on the earth will swoon away, except him whom God wills." (Quran 39:68)

"And the Trumpet will be blown (the second blowing) and behold! From the graves they will come out quickly to their Lord." (Quran 36:51)

"As We began the first creation, We shall repeat it." (Quran 21:104)

In the verses above we see, in the comments about trumpets being blown and "a camel passing through the eye of a needle", a Christian or New Testament influences. Islam also has an obvious Old Testament influence. Moses is mentioned in the Quran more than any other person. Israelites are mentioned 43 times. Like Judaism, Islam has a body of laws. Both have oral and written traditions.. Other sources likely contributed but are difficult to pinpoint due to the limited historical information about Mohammed or his exposure to other religions. Religions are blended and terms are redefined for the purpose of Islam but little of this process is recorded or described. Adding to the problem of having no direct history of Mohammed's life is the fact that the place where Islam originated was somewhat inaccessible. There were trade routes within the area in which goods and money flowed, but the center of the Arabia peninsula was not easily accessible, leaving many of the exact towns and places mentioned in the Quran open to interpretation.

Patricia Crone wrote, "Inhabitants of the Byzantine and Persian empires wrote about the northern and the southern ends of the peninsula, from where we also have numerous inscriptions; but the middle was terra incognita. This is precisely where the Islamic tradition places Mohammed's career. We do not know what was going on there, except for what Islamic tradition tells us.

It yields no literature to which we can relate the Quran – excepting poetry, for which we are again dependent on the Islamic tradition. Not a single source outside Arabia mentions Mecca before the conquests. In sum, we have no context for the prophet and his message. It is difficult not to suspect that the tradition places the prophet's career in Mecca for the same reason that it insists that he was illiterate, to drill home the fact that out of nowhere God raised up an illiterate man to be his prophet and so everything he knew or said came from God. Mecca was supposed to be a virgin territory; it had neither Jewish nor Christian communities. The facts seem to be quite different. The area had both Christian and Jewish inhabitance. And there is a very great chance Mohammed knew how to read and write, due to the fact that he ran a business and was married to a well to do older lady, who would not have married a man who was illiterate.

The suspicion that the location is doctrinally inspired is reinforced by the fact that the Quran describes the polytheist opponents as agriculturalists who cultivated wheat, grapes, olives, and date palms. Wheat, grapes and olives are the three staples of the Mediterranean; date palms take us southwards, but Mecca was not suitable for any kind of agriculture, and one could not possibly have produced olives there.

In addition, the Quran twice describes its opponents as living in the site of a vanished nation, that is to say a town destroyed by God for its sins. There were many such ruined sites in northwest Arabia. The prophet frequently tells his opponents to consider their significance and on one occasion remarks, with reference to the remains of Lot's people, that "you pass by them in the morning and in the evening". This takes us to somewhere in the Dead Sea region."

Sources say that the Quraysh traded in southern Syria, Yemen, Iraq, and Ethiopia. The Quraysh were a powerful merchant tribe that controlled Mecca and its Ka'aba (Kaaba). They traded in leather goods, wool, and frankincense for which they exchanged for goods from India and South Asia. Routes and journeys of the caravan are part of biblical and quranic stories. It was within these caravans and trade routes that converts spread Christianity and Islam.

Hidden Context

One of the most perplexing problems in understanding the Quran is that the stories and people are spoken of without context or background. The early expansion of Islam is a patchwork of snapshots seen outside firm context, due to a lack of historical knowledge of the time and place Mohammed lived and preached. We attempt to glean knowledge from the Quran, the hadith, and from archeology.

The Quran, like many religious texts, is slanted in its historical depiction and silent regarding stories which paint the religion in a negative light. It is practically silent when it comes to the details of the life of its prophet and tends only to reveal certain qualities of his thought process and disposition.

To learn about Mohammed and to place things in context we must rely on outside or second hand sources. Two of these are the hadith and the sira.

The sira literature includes a variety of materials, containing stories of military expeditions undertaken by Mohammed and his followers. The stories are intended as historical accounts and used for veneration. The fact that they were written to be used for veneration tells us they cannot be fully relied on as historically accurate.

The sira also includes a number of written documents, such as speeches, sermons, and political treaties, such as the Treaty of Hudaybiyyah or Constitution of Medina. They also include military enlistments, assignments of officials and document to and from foreign rulers. The version or collection of sira by Hassan ibn Thabit is considered the most accurate, or authentic.

The hadith are a collection of second hand reports of the words and deeds, and ideas of Mohammed. They are reports from other people claiming to quote what the prophet Mohammed said verbatim. They can be on any matter or idea of law or theology. The term comes from the Arabic meaning, "report", "account" or "narrative".

Hadith is hearsay and would not hold up as evidence in court but they are second only to the Quran in developing Islamic jurisprudence. They are regarded as important tools for understanding the Quran and commentaries (tafsir) on it. Many important elements of traditional Islam such as the five salat prayers are mentioned in hadith but not the Quran. A salat is a very ritualized prayer used in Islam.

Muslims regard various hadith with different levels of importance, although all variants emphasize the Sunnah (the record of teachings, deeds and sayings of Muhammad). They can be second hand reports, such as a reliable person who claims the prophet said something on a particular occasion about a particular matter. Most of the early sources for the prophet's life, as also for the period of his immediate successors, consist of hadith in some arrangement or other. The closest modern corollary would be the Doctrine and Covenant of the Mormon Church, where the book of Mormon is considered scripture and the teachings contained within the D & C are held up as teachings used for clarification.

Because the Hadith are oral reports that have been written down, they could have been easily fabricated or misunderstood. They were usually short phrases and as such did not contain the context in which the statement was made. The purpose of such reports was to validate Islamic law and doctrine. Some reports seem to contradict others and so they testify to intense conflicts over what was or was not the true teachings of Islam in the period up to the 9th century, when the material was collected and codified

The hadith literature is based on spoken reports that were in circulation in society after the death of Mohammed. Unlike the Quran itself, which was compiled under the official direction of the early Islamic State in Medina, a central authority did not compile the hadith reports. Hadith were evaluated and gathered into large collections during the 8th and 9th centuries, generations after the death of Mohammed, after the end of the era of the "rightful" Rashidun Caliphate, over 1000 km from where Mohammed lived.

Each hadith is based on two parts, a chain of narrators reporting the hadith and the text itself. By "chain of narrators" it is meant that is it reported that each person who passed along the story is recorded. Each of these individuals must be found honest and the chain must be confirmed. Each hadith is classified by Muslim clerics and jurists into three categories: authentic, good, or weak. The problem is that the clerics do not always agree. If the hadith agrees with their personal view they are more likely to accept it as authentic. If a statement does not align with the teaching or belief of a group is would be easy to classify that hadith as "weak". This means that certain groups may tend to rely on certain collections of hadith.

The hadith could be used to bolster a faulty interpretation of the Quran since clerics were in the habit of taking lines of the Quran out of context and reinterpreting them in isolation or in light of some event in the prophet's life the verse had nothing to do with. Text without context is not only error but can be so tortured by lack of logic and context it can be made to say anything.

By keeping the Quran and Mohammed's teachings in context the rise of Islam can be related to developments in the world of late antiquity and understood in the correct light.

Logical interpretations of the Quran and the hadith should be combined with data collected via research and archeology to form a more informed picture of Islam. No interpretation of the Quran can be accurate unless historical interpretation succeeds and that will take the correct context and perspectives. Oddly, this is something most clerics seemed disturbingly unconcerned about.

So, we are left with lack of verifiable information regarding the life and times of Mohammed.

David Wood of North American Missions Board sums up the life of Mohammed like this:
    "The Hadith are collections of sayings and deeds of Mohammed, usually arranged topically. The goal of the writers was to describe what

Muslims should do in a given situation, based on the example set by their prophet. The Sira literature was quite different. Sira writers often attempted to write complete accounts of the life of Mohammed, and these writings are therefore quite similar to modern biographies. The two genres of historical writing employed slightly different methodologies, and Muslims today favor Hadith over Sira.

The sira literature includes a variety of heterogeneous materials, containing mainly stories of military expeditions undertaken by Mohammed and his companions. These stories are intended as historical accounts and used for veneration. The sira also includes a number of written documents, such as political treaties (e.g., Treaty of Hudaybiyyah or Constitution of Medina), military enlistments, assignments of officials, letters to foreign rulers, and so forth. It also records some of the speeches and sermons made by Mohammed, like his speech at the Farewell Pilgrimage. Some of the sira accounts include verses of poetry commemorating certain events and battles. Some of which are considered to be of a lesser quality and lacking authenticity, but the most serious of those are the ones by Hassan ibn Thabit.

The primary Hadith collections were written more than two centuries after Mohammed's death, and even the earliest extant Sira work (Ibn Ishaq's Sirat Rasul Allah) comes from more than a century after the life of Mohammed. Muslims themselves typically reject this source. We therefore have no detailed historical source written within a century of the prophet of Islam, and no source trusted by the majority of Muslims within two centuries. Such a time gap calls much of Mohammed's life into question, and some scholars hold that we can know virtually nothing about him.

*Even pictures of Mohammed are virtually nonexistent. **Of course strict Muslims do not believe in having pictures of anyone, especially Mohammed, since it is said to promote idol worship.** The Quran does not explicitly forbid images of Mohammed, but there are a few hadith which have explicitly prohibited Muslims from creating visual depictions of figures. It is agreed on all sides that there is no authentic visual tradition as to the appearance of Mohammed, although there are early legends of portraits of him, and written physical descriptions whose authenticity is often accepted. Many visual depictions only show Mohammed with his face veiled, or symbolically represent him as a flame; other images, notably from* *before about 1500, show his face. With the notable exception of modern-day Iran, depictions of Mohammed were rare, never numerous in any community or era throughout Islamic history, and appeared almost exclusively in the private medium of Persian and other miniature book illustration. Visual images of Mohammed in the non-Islamic West have always been infrequent. In the Middle Ages they were mostly hostile, and most often appear in illustrations of Dante's poetry."*

Adding to the list of documents and ideas shaping Islam, beside the Quran, Hadith, and Sira, is the idea of the fatwa. A fatwa is simply a judgment rendered regarding a subject by a cleric. In 2001, Egypt's Grand Mufti issued a fatwa stating that the show "Man sa yarbah al malyoon? "– Literally "Who will Win the Million?", modeled on the British show Who Wants to be a Millionaire?, was un-Islamic. The Sheikh of Cairo's Al-Azhar University later rejected the fatwa, finding that there was no objection to such shows since they spread general knowledge.

The Fatwa on Terrorism is a 600-page Islamic decree against terrorism and suicide bombings released in March 2010. This fatwa is a direct refutation of the ideology of Al-Qaeda and the Taliban. It is one of the most extensive rulings, an "absolute" condemnation of terrorism without "any excuses or pretexts" which goes further than ever and declares terrorism as kufr (blasphemy, impiety) under Islamic law. It was produced in Canada by an influential Muslim scholar Dr. Mohammed Tahir-ul-Qadri and was launched in London on March 2, 2010. Dr Qadri said during the launch "Terrorism is terrorism, violence is violence and it has no place in Islamic teaching and no justification can be provided for it, or any kind of excuses or ifs or buts." According to CNN experts, the fatwa was seen as a significant blow to terrorist recruiting. They were most definitely wrong. This is the nature of a Fatwa. It is one man or one group's view on a situation and carries no weight except to be a viewpoint posted by a particular cleric.

On July 2, 2013 at Lahore (Pakistan) 50 Muslim Scholars of the Sunni Ittehad Council (SIC) issued a collective fatwa against suicide bombings, the killing of innocent people, bomb attacks, and targeted killings declaring them as Haram or forbidden. The problem here is that each individual or group gets to decide who is innocent. In the view of many pious Muslims there are no innocent infidels (non-believers).

On March 11, 2015, Syed Soharwardy, the founder of the Islamic Supreme Council of Canada, and 37 other Muslim leaders of various Islamic sects from across Canada gathered in Calgary and issued a fatwa condemning followers of the Islamic State (ISIS) as non-Muslims. Soharwardy cited capturing opponents and beheading them, killing Muslims who disagree with ISIS's actions, destroying mosques, burning enemy soldiers alive and encouraging Muslim girls to join ISIS, among others, as acts by ISIS that violate Islamic law. Under this fatwa, anybody who even wishes to join the group will be "excommunicated from the Muslim community" and no longer considered Muslim. Fatwas do not matter to those who hold an opposite position and are convinced of their correctness.

Fatwas go from a plea for peace to an order to kill. One man's preacher is another man's Satan and fatwas reflect this. In an interview given on September 30, 2002, for the October 6 edition of 60 Minutes, American Southern Baptist pastor and televangelist Jerry Falwell said: "I think Mohammed was a terrorist. I read enough by both Muslims and non-Muslims, [to decide] that he was a violent man, a man of war." The following Friday, Mohsen Mojtahed Shabestari, an Iranian cleric, issued a fatwa calling for Falwell's death, saying Falwell was a "mercenary and must be killed." He added, "The death of that man is a religious duty, but his case should not be tied to the Christian community." I suppose Sheabestari proved Falwell's point about the violence of Mohammed and his followers.

Fatwas are meant to be issued by a religious/legal scholar, not by any political entity, but since Islam represents a political and religious state the separation of who speaks from a religious, political, or legal point of view is limited and often mixed. Generally, any given case may have many fatwas (legal opinions) written by the scholars of the region at the time. The fatwa backed by the State is the one with legal power if the state agrees to make it part of their body of law. Fatwas are useful only to the followers of the cleric that articulates them. The more important the cleric or the more people who follow him, the more weight the fatwa will have.

A Brief History of Mohammed

According to PBS.org "Mohammed: Legacy of a prophet" a general timeline of the life of Mohammed can be summed up as follows:

570   Mohammed's Birth and Infancy
Mohammed was born in the year 570 in the town of Mecca, a mountain town in the high desert plateau of western Arabia. His name derives from the Arabic verb hamada, meaning "to praise, to glorify." He was the first and only son of Abd Allah bin Al-Muttalib and Amina bint Wahb. Abd Allah died before Mohammed's birth and Mohammed was raised by his mother Amina, who in keeping with Meccan tradition entrusted her son at an early age to a wet nurse named Halima from the nomadic tribe of the Sa'd ibn Bakr. He grew up in the hill country, learning their pure Arabic.

575   Mohammed Becomes an Orphan
When Mohammed was five or six his mother took him to Yathrib, an oasis town a few hundred miles north of Mecca, to stay with relatives and visit his father's grave there. On the return journey, Amina took ill and died. She was buried in the village of Abwa on the Mecca-Medina Road. Halima, his nurse, returned to Mecca with the orphaned boy and placed him in the protection of his paternal grandfather, Abdul Al-Muttalib. In this man's care, Mohammed learned the rudiments of statecraft. Mecca was Arabia's most important pilgrimage center and Abdul Al-Muttalib its most respected leader. He controlled important pilgrimage concessions and frequently presided over Mecca's Council of Elders.

578   Mohammed in Mecca in Care of an Uncle
Upon his grandfather's death in 578, Mohammed, aged about eight, passed into the care of a paternal uncle, Abu Talib. Mohammed grew up in the older man's home and remained under Abu Talib's protection for many years. Chroniclers have underscored Mohammed's disrupted childhood. So does the Quran: "Did God not find you an orphan and give you shelter

and care? And He found you wandering, and gave you guidance. And he found you in need, and made you independent" (93:6-8).

580-594   *Mohammed's Teens*
As a young boy, Mohammed worked as a shepherd to help pay his keep (his uncle was of modest means). In his teens he sometimes traveled with Abu Talib, who was a merchant, accompanying caravans to trade centers. On at least one occasion, he is said to have traveled as far north as Syria. Older merchants recognized his character and nicknamed him El–Amin, the one you can trust.

594   *Mohammed is a Caravan Agent for Wealthy Tradeswoman, Khadija.*

In his early twenties, Mohammed entered the service of a wealthy Meccan merchant, a widow named Khadija bint Khawalayd. The two were distant cousins. Mohammed carried her goods to the north and returned with a profit.

595-609   *Mohammed's Marriage and Family Life*
Impressed by Mohammed's honesty and character, Khadija eventually proposed marriage. They were wed in about 595. He was twenty-five. She was nearly forty.

Mohammed continued to manage Khadija's business affairs, and their next years were pleasant and prosperous. Six children were born to them, two sons who both died in infancy, and four daughters. Mecca prospered too, becoming a well–off trading center in the hands of an elite group of clan leaders who were mostly successful traders.

610   *Mohammed Receives First Revelation*
Mecca's new materialism and its traditional idolatry disturbed Mohammed. He began making long retreats to a mountain cave outside town. There, he fasted and meditated. On one occasion, after a number of indistinct visionary experiences, Mohammed was visited by an overpowering presence and instructed to recite words of such beauty and

force that he and others gradually attributed them to God. This experience shook Mohammed to the core. It was several years before he dared to talk about it outside his family.

613   Mohammed Takes his Message Public

After several similar experiences, Mohammed finally began to reveal the messages he was receiving to his tribe. These were gathered verse by verse and later would become the Quran, Islam's sacred scripture. In the next decade, Mohammed and his followers were first belittled and ridiculed, then persecuted and physically attacked for departing from traditional Mecca's tribal ways. Mohammed's message was resolutely monotheistic. For several years, the Quraysh, Mecca's dominant tribe, levied a ban on trade with Mohammed's people, subjecting them to near famine conditions. Toward the end of the decade, Mohammed's wife and uncle both died. Finally, the leaders of Mecca attempted to assassinate Mohammed.

622   Mohammed and the Muslims Immigrate to Medina

In 622, Mohammed and his few hundred followers left Mecca and traveled to Yathrib, the oasis town where his father was buried. The leaders there were suffering through a vicious civil war, and they had invited this man well known for his wisdom to act as their mediator. Yathrib soon became known as Medina, the City of the prophet. Mohammed remained here for the next six years, building the first Muslim community and gradually gathering more and more people to his side.

625-628   The Military Period

The Meccans did not take Mohammed's new success lightly. Early skirmishes led to three major battles in the next three years. Of these the Muslims won the first (the Battle of Badr, March, 624), lost the second (the Battle of Uhud, March, 625), and outlasted the third, (The Battle of the Trench and the Siege of Medina, April, 627). In March, 628, a treaty was signed between the two sides, which recognized the Muslims as a new force in Arabia and gave them freedom to move unmolested throughout Arabia. Meccan allies breached the treaty a year later.

630   The Conquest of Mecca
By now, the balance of power had shifted radically away from once-powerful Mecca, toward Mohammed and the Muslims. In January, 630, they marched on Mecca and were joined by tribe after tribe along the way. They entered Mecca without bloodshed and the Meccans, seeing the tide had turned, joined them.

630-632   Mohammed's Final Years
Mohammed returned to live in Medina. In the next three years, he consolidated most of the Arabian Peninsula under Islam. In March, 632, he returned to Mecca one last time to perform a pilgrimage, and tens of thousands of Muslims joined him.

After the pilgrimage, he returned to Medina. Three months later on June 8, 632 he died there, after a brief illness. He is buried in the mosque in Medina. Within a hundred years Mohammed's teaching and way of life had spread from the remote corners of Arabia as far east as Indo-China and as far west as Morocco, France and Spain.

The Meccan Period

Writing in the article, "Chronology of prophet Mohammed's Life" for the publication "Answering for Islam", Ehteshaam Gulam presents the following timeline for the periods of Mohammed's in Mecca and in Medina:

570 C.E. Mohammed is born in Mecca

595 C.E. Mohammed marries Khadija, who later becomes the first Muslim

610 C.E. Mohammed was in a cave on a religious retreat. Mohammed receives what he comes to believe is his first visitation from the angel Gabriel and revelation from Allah.

613 C.E. Mohammed begins preaching Islam publicly in Mecca

615 C.E. Friction with the Quraysh causes some Muslims to leave Arabia for Abyssinia

619 C.E. Khadija dies

620 C.E. The Night Journey prophet Mohammed is carried from Mecca to Jerusalem and then travels to the heavens and meets the previous prophets (Adam, Noah, Abraham, Moses, Jesus, etc).

622 C.E. The Hijra: Mohammed and the Muslims flee from Mecca to Medina

The Medinan Period

622 C.E. The Hijra: Mohammed arrives in Medina

624 C.E. The Nakhla raid. These raids were not solely designed to exact revenge from the people who had rejected the prophet who had arisen among them. They served a key economic purpose, keeping the Muslim movement solvent.

624 C.E. The Battle of Badr: the Muslims overcome great odds to defeat the pagan Meccans

624 C.E. Mohammed and the Muslims besiege the Jewish Qaynuqa tribe and exile them from Medina

625 C.E. The Battle of Uhud: the pagan Meccans defeat the Muslims

625 C.E. Siege and exile from Medina of the Jewish Nadir tribe

627 C.E. The Battle of the Trench: the Jewish Qurayzah tribe betrays Mohammed

627 C.E. Sa'd Ibn Mutab executes males of the Qurayzah tribe and enslaves the women and children.

628 C.E. Mohammed concludes the Treaty of Hudaybiyya with the pagan Meccans

628 C.E. Mohammed and the Muslims besiege the Khaybar oasis and exile the Jews from it.

630 C.E. Mohammed and the Muslims conquer Mecca

630 C.E. The Muslims prevail in the Battle of Hunayn and conquer Ta'if; Mohammed becomes the ruler of Arabia

631 C.E. The Arabian tribes remaining outside Islamic rule accept Islam

631 C.E. The expedition to Tabuk

632 C.E. Mohammed dies in Medina on June 8, 632 CE

We shall begin with Mohammed's call and revelation.
His experience is recounted in the writings of the eighth century Muslim, Ibn Ishaq, in his Sirat Rasul Allah:

When it was the night on which God honored him with his mission and showed mercy on His servants thereby, Gabriel brought him the command of God. "He came to me," said the apostle of God, "while I was asleep, with a coverlet of brocade whereon was some writing, and said, 'Read!' I said, 'What shall I read?' He pressed me with it so tightly that I thought it was death; then he let me go and said, 'Read!' I said, 'What shall I read?' He pressed me with it again so that I thought it was death; then he let me go and said 'Read!' I said, 'What shall I read?' He pressed me with it the third time so that I thought it was death and said 'Read!' I said, 'What then shall I read?' – and this I said only to deliver myself from him, lest he should do the same to me again. He said:

'Read in the name of thy Lord who created,
Who created man of blood coagulated.
Read! Thy Lord is the most beneficent,
Who taught by the pen,
Taught that which they knew not unto men.'

So I read it, and he departed from me. And I awoke from my sleep, and it was as though these words were written on my heart."
    Ibn Ishaq Sirat Rasul Allah (The Life of Mohammed), translated by A. Guillaume, Oxford University Press, 1980

At this point in his life is it possible that Mohammed had neither spiritual discernment nor an idea as to his purpose. The confusion is summed up by a quote from the Muslim scholar, Ibn Ishaq

"Mohammed was terrified by what happened to him. He believed that he had encountered a demon, and he became suicidal. His wife Khadija and her cousin Waraqah, however, convinced him that he was a prophet of God, and that he had met the angel Gabriel in the cave.

Mohammed spent the next twelve years preaching in Mecca, first only in private, then in public. During these early years, Mohammed preached a peaceful message. He called for religious tolerance, but he told people that they needed to turn to Allah. In general, the polytheistic Meccans hated him. The persecution eventually got so bad that Mohammed accepted an invitation to move to another city."

In 622, Mohammed and most of his followers moved nearly 300 miles north to Medina. The reasons for his move seem to be many. He was no longer welcome in Mecca. There were plans afoot to kill him. The polytheists were concerned about holding on to their religion and power. The town's folk were concerned that abandoning the old gods would upset Mecca's prosperity.

Mohammed was beginning to develop a reputation for being a holy man, so the people of Medina invited him to be a judge and arbitrator in their city, where there was growing tension between factions.

It's difficult to overestimate the importance of the move. It was in Medina that Mohammed began to define the Muslim community politically. The laws established here would become central to Islam.

Having been rejected by Mecca, Mohammed carried a grudge. We know that Mohammed took Mecca in what one could consider a war of revenge, but there were other factors at work, such as the persecution of the Muslims at the hands of the polytheists. Whatever the subtleties of reasoning for Mohammed's assault on the city of Mecca, this is considered to be his first Jihad

Most observant Muslims accept jihad as an integral part of Islam. It should be understood, however, that there are many kinds of jihad. Jihad may be internal or external. In Arabic language, the word jihad literally means striving and working hard for something. In Islamic terminology, it retains the literal meaning in two different dimensions, which are expressed by "major jihad" and "minor jihad".

In his article Peace and Jihad in Islam, published by Al-Islam, Sayyid Mohammed Rizvi writes:
"The major jihad is known as the spiritual struggle, a struggle between two powers within ourselves: the soul and the body. The conscience is in conflict with the bodily desires. This spiritual conflict is an ongoing jihad within each one of us. Islam expects its followers to give preference to the soul and the conscience over the body and its desires.
The fasting in the month of Ramadhan is an example of training personally for the major jihad.
The minor jihad is the armed struggle. However, that does not automatically mean unjustified use of violence. It is the external or minor Jihad that is the struggle of the sword, which has come to be known simply as jihad. "

Magnus Nilsson comments in his book, "Just War and Jihad:
A Cross-cultural Study of Modern Western and Islamic Just
War Traditions" that most modern day Muslims view jihad as their equivalent of the Bush Doctrine, where he gives the US the right to strike when attack seems unavoidable. In this position, paranoia would drive one to attack when there was no real aggression. Further, if one viewed a disagreement regarding religion or culture as an attack there would be no end to wars. This seems to be where we are today.

In Islam, war is justified and approved by God as a "holy war" if it is a response to oppression and aggression, or if it is to correct injustice. Of course, the problem here is that the injustice may be based on what is accepted or demanded under Shiriah Law as opposed to what western laws or cultures deem just or correct.

The Quran supports the idea that war ought to be waged in self-defense and the moment some cleric declares that the west is the enemy of Islam or goes against Islamic values he has fulfilled the idea of defending Islam and in this light, however dim it might be, jihad is condoned.

The question arises, however: does the sira (biography) of the prophet Mohammed support such a view? Mohammed waged history's first jihad when he and his army stationed in Medina attacked the Quraysh of Mecca.

Did Mohammed wage a war against Mecca simply because the people there were infidels? Was he waging war out of revenge, or was he waging a war of self-defense? His motivations would be instrumental in formulating Islam's views of war and peace.

Mohammed was in Mecca when he was called and there he preached his message peacefully for over ten years, but his message was one that demanded change and the people did not want to change. He was seen as a troublemaker so the leaders persecuted him and his followers. The early Muslims suffered and some were killed. The persecutions reached a level Muslims were forced to flee.

Mohammed's uncle died and Mohammed was left with no tribal connections and thus no protection. This left him vulnerable to enemies within the city. But when he fled the city to Medina, 300 miles away, there was no reason to fear. He was no longer in harm's way. There was no reason to go back and kill anyone in Mecca. Here we must conclude that anger and revenge drove him to war, and not holy appointment.

Many on the Medina city board accepted Islam and promised to protect Mohammed. They secretly met Mohammed while he was still in Mecca, and took two solemn oaths to protect him, known as the First and Second Pledge at al-Aqaba. Under the cover of night, waves of Muslims began to flee Mecca to find refuge in Medina." Medinat al-Nabi (the prophet's city)

Mohammed was one of the last to leave Mecca and travel to Medina. This journey is called the Hijra, and is the Islamic equivalent of the Exodus. It was done in the year 622, which marks the beginning of the Islamic era. Thus AD 622 became for Muslims AH 1. Mohammed would order his followers to make this "Hajj" as part of their worship.

Hajj is Arabic, meaning "pilgrimage". It is an annual Islamic pilgrimage to Mecca, and a mandatory religious duty for Muslims that must be carried out at least once in their lifetime by all adult Muslims who are physically and financially capable of undertaking the journey, and can support their family during the time it takes to make the journey.

The prophet arrived in Medina to take the position of a holy man and judge or arbitrator to bring peace between the two major tribes of the city, which had been involved in a protracted civil war. The city elders had hoped Mohammed could find a way to settle the arguments between the two sides.

Merriam-Webster's Encyclopedia of World Religions, p.755 reports that Mohammed called for an end to tribal rivalries, preached brotherhood, and formed a united community (umma) out of groups. After establishing himself and taking advantage of the growing numbers of converts in Medina, Mohammed turned his attention to his former tormentors, the Quraysh of Mecca. The Quraysh were an Arab people and merchant tribe, of which Muhammad was a member and which from the 5th century was distinguished by being a religious custodians of the Kaaba at Mecca before Mohammed's invasion. He first began attacking caravans from Mecca, robbing them and killing the riders. The people of Mecca sent around 1000 guards to protect their next caravan. The Muslims attacked with a much smaller force, and they won what came to be known as the Battle of Badr. Mohammed escalated and launched a war. The first military expedition against them was dispatched about seven to nine months after Mohammed's arrival in Medina in what is known as Hamza's Expedition to the Seashore. This is the beginning of the first Jihad.

For the next ten years until Mohammed's death in 632 AD, the Muslims never stopped fighting. Mohammed fought several more key battles against Mecca (the Battle of Uhud and the Battle of the Trench), finally taking the city in 630.

David Wood, in his article, "The Historical Mohammed: The Good, the Bad, and the Downright Ugly" writes:

Mohammed attacked other groups as well. In 629, Muslims attacked a Jewish settlement in the oasis of Khaybar in Northwestern Arabia. Shortly after the conquest of Mecca, Mohammed received Surah 9:29, which ordered Muslims to fight non-Muslims (including Christians and Jews) until they submit to Islam:

"Fight those who do not believe in Allah, nor in the latter day, nor do they prohibit what Allah and His Apostle have prohibited, nor follow the religion of truth, out of those who have been given the Book, until they pay the tax in acknowledgment of superiority and they are in a state of subjection."

Obeying this command to fight, Mohammed marched an army against the Byzantine Empire, though the Byzantines chose not to fight. Mohammed became sick and died shortly thereafter.

When one is following a religious leader one is emotionally invested in them and their lives. In such cases it is easy to see only the good characteristics and to completely ignore less desirable qualities.

Thus far we have seen Mohammed as a robber and as a warlord, waging battles for revenge and retaliation. When Mohammed allowed cities to be sacked and sex slaves to be taken he set up a situation where greed became one of the primary factors for men's rapid conversion to Islam. Mohammed used the spoils of war to entice converts to Islam.

An Islamic source quotes Mohammed defense of this tactic:
"Are you disturbed in mind because of the good things of this life by which I win over a people that they may become Muslims while I entrust you to your Islam?"

Sahih Muslim, Abdul Hamid Siddiqi, tr., Number 2313

Muslims try to compare the violence in the Quran to the violence in the Old Testament. However, verses in the Old Testament command a war or and act of violence against a particular people at a particular time for a particular reason. When the situation is resolved the violence ceases. In the Quran the violence is commanded and is not restrained by the historical situations, times, or context. The command is open-ended. To simply say, "kill all unbelievers" leaves no end to the bloodshed until the world is bathed in blood or converted to Islam. This is a statement unconstrained by time or circumstances. The commands become part of the eternal and unchanging word of Allah and must be obeyed forever. The Old Testament constraint of violence against a particular army or people at a certain time for a certain reason is why we do not see Jewish imperialism and killing word-wide, but Muslim violence does not cease. To strictly follow the Quran, it cannot cease. Islam must kill, destroy, and conquer to grow. This is the command.

Quran (17:16) - "And when We wish to destroy a town, We send Our commandment to the people of it who lead easy lives, but they transgress therein; thus the word proves true against it, so We destroy it with utter destruction." Osama bin Landen used this verse to justify attacking New York.

Quran (47:3-4) - "Those who disbelieve follow falsehood, while those who believe follow the truth from their Lord... So, when you meet (in fight Jihad in Allah's Cause), those who disbelieve smite at their necks till when you have killed and wounded many of them, then bind a bond firmly (on them, take them as captives)... If it had been Allah's Will, He Himself could certainly have punished them (without you). But (He lets you fight), in order to test you, some with others. But those who are killed in the Way of Allah, He will never let their deeds be lost."

Some say Islam is a religion of peace, but peaceful religions strive for peace both among their own followers and the with the rest of the world. Let us compare the above quotes with how the Torah tells Jews to treat strangers.

Leviticus 19:34 33 And if a stranger sojourn with thee in your land, ye shall not vex him. 34 But the stranger that dwelleth with you shall be unto you as one born among you, and thou shalt love him as thyself; for ye were strangers in the land of Egypt.

One may argue that the Jewish sect, now called Christianity, was the evolution of Judaism into the second Axial Age. One may also argue that all of Judaism has evolved into the second Axial Age if one observes that Judaism teaches equal treatment of all people when they are not at war and there is no more ritualized animal sacrifice, stoning, flogging, or other such punishment in Judaism today.

This is not to say that religions do not waver with acts, movements or splinter sects that are pre-Axial Age or post-Axial age, but a religion should be judged by how it generally embraces peace, grace, generosity, and love of mankind. Religions should not be judged on the national political movement that is predominately comprised of a faith. This is difficult, but one should not judge the people by the actions of their government. Nor, if the state and religion are separate, should we judge a religion by a nation. The Islam State is different. The nation, government, and religion are one and must be judged as a single force.

If the world can be divided between people and faiths split between those that are pre-Axial Age and post-Axial Age it can be said without equivocation that Islam is a religion that represents all elements of the pre-Axial Age. It is ritualized, externalizes, and driven by a harsh set of rules and laws, all set in place to please a God who demands the killing of people and animals if one is to attain the carnally based heaven offered by Islam to its loyal followers and martyrs. This is the Islam of terrorism. It is said this is the Islam of up to 20% of all Muslims. It will be up to the greater body of Islam to bring the faith firmly and completely into the Axial Age – an age of enlightenment – an age of peace.

Mohammed's Sexual Views

Mohammed had very liberal views regarding sex and marriage. Most Islamic sources report he married a total of eleven wives, but the maximum number of wives married at one time was nine. This makes the prophet an exception to his own rule of marrying a maximum of four wives. Among Mohammed's wives were a six-year-old child and a thirteen year old girl. In addition to his wives, Mohammed also had concubines and sex-slaves. Between slaves, concubines, and several divorces, numbers of wives have blurred through time. One slave girl was a Christian slave given to Mohammed by the governor of Egypt. Her name was Mariyam. After she gave birth to a son, some sources say Mohammed married her. Other sources disagree. Thus, the number of total wives vary between sources depending if one counts slaves and concubines he may have married, and if one counts divorces. Sources vary so widely on the number of wives he had that a list of women and their status is offered in Appendix "B".

Mohammed married his cousin, Zaynab bint Jahsh, who was one of his father's sisters. They married soon after she divorced Mohammed's adopted son, Zayd ibn Haritha.
Al-Tabari, Vol. 39, p. 180; cf Guillaume/Ishaq 3; Maududi (1967)

Marriage to cousins was common among Arabs at the time and among certain groups it remains so today. Culturally, marriage between first cousins is still regarded as the best choice. In the Middle East, alliances fall along lines of family/tribe, religion, and ethnicity. Marrying cousins keeps these lines strong and clear. Marrying cousins also keeps inheritance, wealth, land and livestock concentrated within the family, adding to the value of the practice. Due to Mohammed's marriage to his cousin, Islam continues to encourage this type of inbreeding, which has led to many issues and has damaged the gene pool greatly.

In her New York Times May 1, 2003 article, Sarah Kershaw reported, "In some parts of Saudi Arabia, particularly in the south, the rate of marriage among blood relatives ranges from 55 to 70 percent, among the highest rates in the world, according to the Saudi government."

The practice of inbreeding has produces a variety of physical and metal defects.

Nikolai Sennels, a Danish psychologist who has written about the problem of inbreeding in the Muslim communities, reports the percent of marriages between cousins is 67% in Saudi Arabia, 64% in Jordan, and Kuwait, 63% in Sudan, 60% in Iraq, and 54% in the United Arab Emirates and 54 % in Qatar. According to Sennels, research shows that children of consanguineous marriages lose 10-16 points off their IQ and social abilities develop much slower in inbred babies. The risk of having an IQ lower than 70, the official demarcation for being classified as "retarded," increases by an astonishing 400 percent among children of first cousin marriages. Spinal and neurological defects, including microcephaly occur. Due to inbreeding, microcephaly is so common in Pakistan they refer to those who suffer the condition as "rat people" due to the way their small heads make them look. (Consanguineous – blood relations)

According to a February 2016 report in Kristeligt Dagblad, a Danish newspaper published in Copenhagen, Denmark, the increased risk of insanity among children of marriages between cousins might explain why immigrant patients are stressing the psychiatric system and are strongly overrepresented among insane criminals. In June of 2007 the same paper reported, "In Sct. Hans Hospital, which has the biggest ward for clinically insane criminals in Denmark, more than 40 percent of the patients have an immigrant background."

If inbreeding among first cousins accounts for lower intelligence and increased criminal and psychiatric problems, it could explain the extreme acts of violence and disregard of logic and law we are now witnessing from the Islamic refugees. When these conditions were fueled and guided by fundamental Islam the result is the terrorism spewing from the Islamic nations and from ISIS.

In addition to encouraging marriage between cousins, Mohammed's choices also promoted pedophilia. Mohammed's third wife, Aishah, was only 6 when the arranged marriage took place. Aishah remained in her parent's house until she was nine, when the marriage was consummated. It is said Aishah was the favored wife of Mohammed and he died in her arms June 8, 632.

The religious scholar, Karen Armstrong writes:
"To the point that Aishah was only nine or ten years of age, it was common for arranged marriages to take place, even in absentia, in order to forge alliances between families. However, it was left up to the husband as to the time and at what age the marriage would be consummated. Sex with a pre-pubescent girl does fly in the face of our modern western senses. "

The scenario is summed up nicely in an article on the website "answering-islam.org", Mohammed, Aisha, Islam, and Child Brides by "Silas":
"A 49 year old man asks his best friend if he could have his permission to marry his 6 year old daughter. His friend agrees. The man then visits his best friend's house and speaks with the 6-year-old daughter. Her parents watch as the he proposes marriage to the child. He is serious; he wants to marry the little girl and is asking for her consent. The little child says nothing; she only stares at him in silence. She does not understand the concept of marriage or sex.

Mohammed proposed marriage to Aisha when she was 6. He assumed her silence constituted her consent. Some 2 to 3 years later, just after he had fled to Medina, he consummated his marriage with her. He was 52 and she was 9. This occurred prior to Aisha's first menses and by Islam's legal definition Aisha was still considered a child. Islam teaches that a child enters adulthood at the beginning of puberty. Sex before then leads to physical, and psychological, damage to the child."

Hadith of Bukhari, volume 5, #234
"As narrated by Aisha: The prophet engaged me when I was a girl of six. We went to Medina and stayed at the home of Harith Kharzraj. Then I got ill and my hair fell down (out). Later on my hair grew (again) and my mother, Um Ruman, came to me while I was playing in a swing with some of my girl friends. She called me,

and I went to her, not knowing what she wanted to do to me. She caught me by the hand and made me stand at the door of the house. I was breathless then, and when my breathing became all right, she took some water and rubbed my face and head with it. Then she took me into the house. There in the house I saw some Ansari women who said, "Best wishes and Allah's blessing and good luck." Then she entrusted me to them and they prepared me (for the marriage). Unexpectedly Allah's messenger came to me in the forenoon and my mother handed me over to him, and at that time I was a girl of nine years of age."

Ibn Kathir born c. 1300, died 1373) was a highly influential Sunni scholar of the Shafil School. He was considered an expert in Quranic exegesis and jurisprudence, as well as a historian. In the Journal of Qur'anic Studies 16 (1): 3. 2014-02-01, Ibn Kathir writes regarding Quran 65:4:

"The `Iddah is the ritual periods based on cleanliness and the menstrual period." The ritual periods are set up so a man cannot divorce his wife until she has had her period and is clean and they have not had sex. This is to make sure she is not pregnant when they divorce. According to scholars there are three types of divorce. There is one that conforms to the Sunnah. Sunnah is the verbally transmitted record of the teachings, deeds and sayings, permissions, or disapprovals of Mohammed. There is another type of divorce called "innovated". The third type of divorce is for the very young or the very old wife, or the wife who refuses to have sex. The divorce that conforms to the Sunnah is one where the husband pronounces he is going to divorce his wife after she has finished her period and they have not had sexual intercourse. The innovated divorce occurs when one divorces his wife when she is having her menses, or after the menses ends, but he has sexual intercourse with her and then divorces her, even though he does not know if she became pregnant or not. There is a third type of divorce, which is neither a Sunnah nor an innovation divorce. This is done when a YOUNG WIFE HAS NOT BEGUN TO HAVE MENSES or the wife is beyond the age of having menses or one divorces his wife before the marriage was consummated.

Gaston Wiet tells us in his book "The Great Medieval Civilizations" that Al-Tabari (839–923 AD) was a prominent and influential

Persian scholar, and historian. Today, Al-Tabari is best known for his expertise in Quranic commentary, law and history, as well as cultural and scientific development.

Al-Tabari said regarding the interpretation of the verse Quran 65:4, "And those of your women as have passed the age of monthly courses, for them the 'Iddah (prescribed period), if you have doubt (about their periods), is three months; and for those who have no courses (i.e. they are still immature) their 'Iddah (prescribed period) is three months likewise". The same applies to the 'idaah for girls who do not menstruate because they are too young if their husbands divorce them after consummating the marriage with them.

Abu-Ala' Maududi states:
"Therefore, making mention of the waiting-period for girls who have not yet menstruated, clearly proves that it is not only permissible to give away the girl at this age but it is permissible for the husband to consummate marriage with her. Now, obviously no Muslim has the right to forbid a thing which the Quran has held as permissible." (Maududi, volume 5, p. 620, note 13)

The only reason this type of marriage does not take place is the constraints of a society and its laws that forbid such imbalanced marriages from happening. The reason it is beginning to take place once again is that states such the Islamic State or ISIS have set up governments under Sharia Law, which permits this kind of act.

Sharia Law is a set of laws drawn up according to Mohammed's actions or words in the Quran and other writings, such as the hdaith. Since Muslims believe Mohammed and the Quran are perfect, no Sharia Law can be altered. (More on Sharia law later.)

There seems to be a reactionary bend to Mohammed. When his first wife died, whom he seemed to love and with whom he maintained a happy marriage, he turned to polygamy and ended his days with nine wives, one of whom he had sex with when she was nine. After Mohammed's first wife died he seemed to lose his compassion and tolerance and declined into a more selfish lifestyle.

Likewise, when things did not go well for him and his new religion in Mecca and he was forced to flee for his life to Medina, his attitude of tolerance changed to that of a despot. He would later return to Mecca and take it over, killing those who had opposed him.

Although Mohammed endured persecution in Mecca, his attitude quickly changed when the number of his followers grew in Medina to the point where he could maintain control and fight those who opposed him. Soon he would tolerate no criticism whatsoever.

According to our earliest biographical source, a man named Abu Afak was more than a hundred years old when he wrote a poem criticizing people for converting to Islam. Mohammed demanded he be killed, and Abu Afak was murdered in his sleep. When a woman named Asma heard that Muslims had killed such an elderly man, she wrote a poem calling for people to take a stand against Islam. Ibn Ishaq relates what happened next:
    "When the apostle heard what she had said he said, "Who will rid me of Marwan's daughter?" Umayr bin Adiy al-Khatmi who was with him heard him, and that very night he went to her house and killed her. In the morning he came to the apostle and told him what he had done and he said, "You have helped God and His apostle, O Umayr!" When he asked if he would have to bear any evil consequences the apostle said, "Two goats won't butt their heads about her," so Umayr went back to his people."
Sirat Rasul Allah (A. Guilaume's translation "The Life of Mohammed") pages 675, 676.

Mohammed's violence was directed towards groups as well. Mohammed once said to his followers, "I will expel the Jews and Christians from the Arabian Peninsula and will not leave any but Muslims." The Jews of Qurayza resisted Mohammed and attempted to form an alliance against him. When the alliance faltered, Mohammed acted quickly. His armies surrounded them and "besieged them for twenty-five nights until they were sore pressed and God cast terror into their hearts."
W. Muir in his Life of Mahomet, vol. III, pp. 276-279

When they surrendered, Mohammed confined them in Medina. Then Mohammed sent his men out to the market to dig trenches in the middle of the market. Then he sent for the captives to be brought to the market. There he placed them in the trenches and struck off their heads. Some sources place the number of deaths between 600 or 700. Other sources put the figure as high as 800 or 900.

Guillaume reports, "Every male who had reached puberty was killed on that day. Mohammed then divided the women, children, and property among his men (taking a fifth of the spoils for himself). "
Guillaume, p. 461-464., Peters, Mohammed and the Origins of Islam, p. 222-224., Stillman, p. 141f.

Mohammed was first and foremost a warlord, a military leader, and a conqueror. Many of his "revelations" came from god at opportune times conveying the correct messages to keep his troupes appeased during battle. As the Muslim armies raided towns and villages, they captured their women. These women were considered slaves and would be used, sold or traded. Since the Muslim army needed to be away from their wives for extended periods they wanted to use the women as sex slaves. Upon inquiring to Mohammed about the practice the prophet reported he had received a message from Allah to guide them. The revelation allowed the soldiers to rape the women as they pleased.

Wikipedia - en.wikipedia.org/wiki/Battle_of_Autas reports,
    "Allah's Messenger sent an army to Autas and encountered the enemy and fought with them. Having overcome them and taken them captives, the Companions of Allah's Messenger seemed to refrain from having intercourse with captive women because of their husbands being polytheists. Then Allah, Most High, sent down regarding that... Quran 4:24 Arberry Translation: and wedded women, save what your right hands own. So God prescribes for you. Lawful for you, beyond all that, is that you may seek, using your wealth, in wedlock and not in license. Such wives as you enjoy thereby, give them their wages portions; it is no fault

in you in your agreeing together, after the due portion. God is All-knowing, All-wise.

Sayyid Maududi (d. 1979), a highly respected traditional commentator and scholar, it lawful for Muslim holy warriors to marry women prisoners of war even when their husbands are still alive. He explains, "Forbidden to you are wedded wives of other people except those who have fallen in your hands [as prisoners of war] .

Thus, it is lawful to have sex with multiple wives, slave girls taken in war, and children. Muslims are to emulate their prophet. Mohammed himself had sex with a prepubescent girl and this makes it not only legal but also something to be sought by Muslim men. Before his courtship of Aisha began Mohammed had a dream about her, which led him to believe that God wanted him to marry the young girl. Muslim sources report that Aisha still hadn't reached puberty. Aisha described her sexual experiences with the prophet. When she was six years old, he could not have intercourse with her due to her young age. As a consolation prize, he placed his penis between her thighs and massaged it softly. Aisha explained that "unlike other believers, the prophet had control over his penis."

Sam Shamoun, in the paper," An Examination of Mohammed's Marriage to a Prepubescent Girl And Its Moral Implications" wrote,
"After the permanent committee for the scientific research and fatwahs (religious decrees) reviewed the question presented to the grand Mufti Abu Abdullah Mohammed Al-Shemary, the question forwarded to the committee by the grand scholar of the committee with reference number 1809 issued on 3/8/1421 (Islamic calendar). The inquirer asked the following:
It has become wide spread these days, and especially during weddings, the habit of mufa'khathat of the children (mufa'khathat literally translated means "placing between the thighs" which means placing the male member between the thighs of a child). What is the opinion of scholars knowing full well that the prophet, the peace and prayer of Allah be upon him, also practiced the "thighing" of Aisha - the mother of believers - may Allah be please with her.

After the committee studied the issue, they gave the following reply:

It has not been the practice of the Muslims throughout the centuries to resort to this unlawful practice that has come to our countries from pornographic movies that the kufar (infidels) and enemies of Islam send. As for the prophet, peace and prayer of Allah be upon him, thighing his fiancée Aisha. She was six years of age and he could not have intercourse with her due to her small age. That is why [the prophet] peace and prayer of Allah be upon him placed his [male] member between her thighs and massaged it softly, as the apostle of Allah had control of his [male] member not like other believers.

Also see:

http://www.sout-al-haqe.com/pal/musical/mofakhaza.ram
http://www.islamic-fatwa.net/viewtopic.php?TopicID=8330

The problem here is not so much that an old man decided to have sex with a nine year old girl, or that a warlord gave his army permission to force themselves on women from cities they conquered and plundered. These things have gone on throughout history. The problem is Mohammed is held up as the example to follow.

If one is a Muslim one attempts to emulate the behavior of Mohammed. If the man held up as God's prophet is cruel then the god he represents will be internalized as cruel and following the prophet of this god demands one become cruel and call it righteous.

It is said that Mohammed had an insatiable sexual appetite.

"The prophet used to visit all his wives in a round, during the day and night and they were eleven in number." I asked Anas, 'had the prophet the strength for it?' Anas replied, 'we used to say that the prophet was given the strength of thirty men." Bukhari (5:268)

Given this, is it easy to see why his heaven, the Islamic heaven, should have a definite sexual orientation. We are told the male believers of Islam will have 72 virgins awaiting their arrival in the after-life. The Quran does not specify the number as 72, it does say that those who fight in the way of Allah and are killed will be given a great reward. It goes on to stipulate that Muslims will be awarded with women with physical attributes of large eyes (Q 56:22) and big, firm, round "swelling breasts" that are not inclined to sagging (Q 78:33). The Quran refers to these virgins as houri, pure and well-matched companions of equal age. These bodily characteristics, including their virginity, gave rise to many hadiths (Hadiths are collections of the reports claiming to quote what the prophet Mohammed said verbatim on any matter. The term comes from the Arabic meaning "report", "account" or "narrative".) and other Islamic writings.

Hadith 2687 is where the number 72 is mentioned. "The smallest reward for the people of Heaven is an abode where there are eighty thousand servants and 72 houri, over which stands a dome decorated with pearls, aquamarine and ruby, as wide as the distance from al-Jabiyyah to San'a."

Quranic commentator Al-Suyuti, 1505 CE and Orthodox Muslim theologians such as al Ghazali , 1100 CE, and Al-Ash'ari, 930 CE, graphically describe the sexual and sensual pleasures provided to Muslims in paradise. One likens it to a slave market where men may choose any woman and have sex with her then and there.

Al-Suyuti wrote, "Each time we sleep with a Houri we find her virgin. Besides, the penis of the Elected never softens. The erection is eternal; the sensation that you feel each time you make love is utterly delicious and out of this world and were you to experience it in this world you would faint. Each chosen one [i.e. Muslim] will marry seventy houris, besides the women he married on earth, and all will have appetizing vaginas."

Ibn Kathir, in his Qur'anic Commentary, the Tafsir ibn Kathir writes:
"Women will have large, firm breasts that do not sag, large black eyes, appetizing vaginas, with resetting hymens (ever virgins) and men with erections that never go flaccid.... "

Abu Umama narrated: "The Messenger of God said,

'Everyone that God admits into paradise will be married to 72 wives; two of them are houris and seventy of his inheritance of the [female] dwellers of hell. All of them will have libidinous sex organs and he will have an ever-erect penis.' " - Sunan Ibn Majah, Zuhd (Book of Abstinence) 39

On the whole, the Quran and the hadiths are filled with sexual fantasies that Muslim men are awarded when they reach Islamic heaven. Anas bin Malik, an Islamic scholar, claimed that "The prophet used to visit all his wives in a round, during the day and night and they were eleven in number... The prophet was given the strength of thirty (men)." Mohammed (hadith 24) apparently claimed that devout Muslims would be given the sexual strength of 100 persons upon their arrival in Heaven. (This is apparently more than what was attributed to the prophet himself).

One must ask what such carnality has to do with a spiritual heaven. The Islamic version of heaven, or Paradise, is nothing more than an extension of life here on earth brought to a place where all aspects of male Islamic life is perfected in such a way that those men of the 7th and 8th centuries would perceive it. This includes living under Sharia Law in a world where male appetite and domination is the cornerstone of the perfect society.

The sexual obsession by Muslim men as conveyed by Islamic writings, takes its cue from the founder of the religion. There is a world of difference, then, between the Mohammed of history and the Mohammed of faith.

Sexuality has become part of the Muslim war strategy. Muslim clerics are encouraging Muslim families in the UK, EU and US to have as many children as possible. "We will breed you out of existence," clerics warn. Some sources report an average birth rate among native EU, UK, and US families to be about 2.1 - 2.3 children per family. Muslims in the same countries are having 5 children per family on average. The activist, Pamela Geller reports :
    "Afghan and Somali women in Britain have four times as many kids as UK born mums," by David Pilditch, Express, August 17, 2015:

The UK is now home to more families containing four or more children than at any time since the early 1970s.
The average Afghan-born woman living in the UK has 4.25 children and the average Somali-born woman has 4.19 children.
The average for Pakistani women is 3.82. UK-born women have an average of 1.79 children, according to the data from European statistics agency Eurostat.
That compares with 2.19 for women living in the UK who were born in one of the 12 eastern European states, and 1.52 for women born in western European countries.
Meanwhile women born in Australia and New Zealand who live in the UK have an average of 1.38 children."
Pamelageller.com/2015/08

We shall see that these numbers vary between research groups. Governments are telling their people not to worry because the birthrates of Muslim families are dropping as they become westernized and discontinue their practices of polygamy and large families. We shall see. So far, this fits in with the warning that clerics have announced.

Pew Research, December 7, 2015 report states:
"There are two major factors behind the rapid projected growth of Islam, and both involve simple demographics. For one, Muslims have more children than members of other religious groups. Around the world, each Muslim woman has an average of 3.1 children, compared with 2.3 for all other groups combined.

Muslims are also the youngest (median age of 23 years old in 2010) of all major religious groups, seven years younger than the median age of non-Muslims. As a result, a larger share of Muslims already are, or will soon be, at the point in their lives when they begin having children. This, combined with high fertility rates, will fuel Muslim population growth.

While it does not change the global population, migration is increasing the Muslim population in some regions. Forty years after Sweden decided to welcome Islamic immigrants, cases of rape increased by 1,472%. Sweden is now number two on the list of rape countries, surpassed only by Lesotho in Southern Africa.

Why is the treatment of women so abhorrent among Muslim men? The religious and cultural views on women are quite negative and they are reinforced over generations.

The Quran says a husband has sex with his wife, as a plow goes into a field, and he can plow her as he wishes.
The Quran in Sura (Chapter) 2:223 Your women are your fields, so go into your fields whichever way you like . . . . (MAS Abdel Haleem, The Qur'an, Oxford UP, 2004)

Hadith back up this position. 'If a man invites his wife to sleep with him and she refuses to come to him, then the angels send their curses on her till morning.' (Bukhari)

Husbands are a degree above their wives. The Quran in Sura 2:228 - Wives have the same rights as the husbands have on them in accordance with the generally known principles. Of course, men are a degree above them in status.

According to Mohammed, hell is full of women.
The Prophet said, 'I looked at Paradise and found poor people forming the majority of its inhabitants; and I looked at Hell and saw that the majority of its inhabitants were women.' (Bukhari)

Men are worth twice as much as a women. A male gets a double share of the inheritance over that of a female.
The Quran in Sura 4:11 - The share of the male shall be twice that of a female.

The word or testimony of a women is worth only half that of a man. The Prophet said, 'Isn't the witness of a woman equal to half of that of a man?' The women said, 'Yes.' He said, 'This is because of the deficiency of a woman's mind.' (Bukhari)

Men may strike their wives if he thinks she is being disrespectful. Quran in 4:34 . . . If you fear highhandedness from your wives, remind them [of the teaching of God], then ignore them when you go to bed, then hit them. If they obey you, you have no right to act against them. God is most high and great.

Islam has turned a blind eye to offenses against women, children, and even animals. When confronted and given the chance to change, Islamic leaders have chosen to cling to ways of life that are as old as the religion itself. Many offenses are actually practices that are cultural but they are not rectified by enforcing the law, thus they continue and grow. Some are permitted and therefore reinforced. Sodomy of young boys and sexual abuse of animals may not be part of the Quran, but the offenses are not discouraged. Islamic men who wish to marriage very young girls are given permission even today.

In December, 2014 Islamic reformists attempted to change the laws of Saudi Arabia on pre-pubescent marriages. The law stated that a mature man may marry a prepubescent girl. Quran 65:1-4, particularly verse 4, assumes, but does not command the practice. Classical law says a father may give away his prepubescent daughter, but she also has a few rights. Officially many Islamic nations have raised the legal marriage age, but pockets in the Islamic world still follow this old custom. The Grand Mufti of Saudi Arabia okayed marriage to ten-year-old girls.

Mary Chastain wrote about this in the December 2014 issue of the publication "Brietbart".
"Saudi Arabia's Grand Mufti Shaikh Abdul Aziz Al Shaikh announced there is "nothing wrong" with girls under the age of 15 getting married. This is a blow to human rights activists who hoped the strict Islamic country would at least set the minimum marriage age at 15.
"There is currently no intention to discuss the issue," he said.

In 2011, Saudi Arabia's Justice Ministry wanted to pass a law that set a minimum age to marry since many young girls are forced to marry much older men. Saudi Justice Minister Mohammed Al Issa said the issue came to light after "a surge in such weddings and growing criticism by local human rights groups."

Al Issa continued, "The Ministry is studying a draft law to regulate the marriage of teenage girls...the marriage of under-age girls in the country is not a phenomenon yet as some claim... those who say this are wrong." he said. "We are considering regulations in line with the Islamic Sharia to govern this kind of marriage."

The ministry submitted a study about the "negative psychological and social effects of underage marriages" to scholars and "requested a fatwa." However, the religious scholars never responded.

There is irony in the fact that the United Nations Commission on the Status of Women concluded its 60th annual session in New York (2016) by condemning only Israel – and no other nation in the world – as an abuser of women's rights. Not Muslim countries where women are killed for not obeying their husbands, stoned for adultery, or burned alive in honor killings. Why? Because the U.N. named Saudi Arabia as the chair on human rights and Iran to the committee on women's rights. Instead of stopping the horrible abuse of women in their own countries, they used their time and position to condemn Israel, simply out of spite. Their hate for Israel and the U.S. will never cease. Israel is one of the most progressive countries in the region. Women of Israel share equally with men in duties and freedoms, including serving in the military. Muslim countries have abused women and allowed marriages to girls so young it can only be termed pedophilia.

Today in Afghanistan the practice of pedophilia is rampant and has spread to the abuse of young boys. Men in power use boys as sex slaves. Owning these children is viewed as a status symbol.

Huffington Post, September 25, 2015 reported that the Pashtu (a large ethic group living in parts of Afghanistan and Pakistan) have a saying that 'women are for (having) children and boys are for pleasure.' Social norms dictate that bacha bazi (boy play), is not un-Islamic or homosexual if the man does not love the boy. The sexual act is not reprehensible, and is far more ethical than defiling a woman. "

In his September 20, 2015 New York Times article, Joseph Goldstein reported: "Rampant sexual abuse of children has long been a problem in Afghanistan, particularly among armed commanders who dominate much of the rural landscape and can bully the population. The practice is called bacha bazi, literally "boy play," and American soldiers and Marines have been instructed not to intervene — in some cases, not even when their Afghan allies have abused boys on military bases, according to interviews and court records." One soldier complained, ""At night we can hear them screaming, but we're not allowed to do anything about it."

At times it is difficult to discern what is permissible culturally as opposed to what is permitted religiously. Bestiality among Muslims in certain areas is accepted as a normal fact of life. This seems to be a cultural phenomenon that has become tolerated religiously. It is much like the Pashtu practice to having sex with young boys because culturally it is better than having illicit sex with a women.

Iran's former "supreme" leader Ayatollah Khomeini wrote over 200 books and interpretations on the teachings of Islam.

"A man can have sex with animals such as sheep, cows, camels and so on. However he should kill the animal after he has his orgasm. He should not sell the meat to the people in his own village, however selling the meat to the next door village should be fine." – From Khomeini's book, Tahrir al-Vasyleh, fourth volume, Darol Elm, Gom, Iran, 1990

Yahya ibn Sharaf al-Nawawi (d. 676/1277) was considered a Sufi and a saint. Imam Yahya ibn Sharaf al-Nawawi was born in the village of Nawa in Southern Syria, Nawawi spent most of his life in Damascus where he lived in a simple manner, devoted to Allah, engaging single-mindedly in worship, study, writing and teaching various Islamic sciences. Imam Nawawi died at the young age of 44 years, leaving behind him numerous works of great importance. Some of these works were commentaries. All are accepted and credible. Below are comments by Al-Nawawi regarding washing after sex, including bestiality.

Commentary of Imam Al-Nawawi on the Hadith -
The saying of the prophet – peace be upon him- 'If one sits between a woman's fours (shu'biha Al-arba) and then fatigues her'

In another narration the word 'Ashu'biha' is used. The scholars have disagreed about the intended meaning of 'shu'biha Al-arba' (the fours) for some said that it means the arms and the legs, while others have said that it refers to the legs and thighs, and other said it means the legs and the edge of the pubic area. Al-Qadi Ayad chose the meaning of the four areas surrounding the vagina. The word (Shu'b) means areas, its singular form being (Shu'bah). As for those who say (Ashba'iha) that is the plural of the word (Shu'b).

The word Aj-hada-ha (fatigue her) means to plow her, which was also stated by Al-Khatabi. Others have said it means to make her reach exhaustion as in the phrase 'she made him toil and labor till he was exhausted'. Al-Qadi Ayad – may Allah rest his soul- said 'Primarily, the word (Jahada'ha) means that the man exerted his effort working in a woman, where the word (Juh'd) means energy and refers to motion by describing the type of work. This is similar to his (the prophet) saying 'he who plowed her' meaning he who penetrated her by his motion. Otherwise, what other fatigue could a man experience because of her, and Allah knows best.

The meaning of the hadith is that the necessity to wash is not limited to when semen is ejaculated, rater it is when the penile head (Hash-fa, lit. "the head of the male member," i.e. head of the penis) penetrates the vagina, then it is necessary for the man and the woman to wash. There is no disagreement on this today, even though there was disagreement on this by some of the early companions and others later. However, an agreement was later reached and this is what we have shown and presented previously.

Our companions have said that if the penile head has penetrated A WOMAN'S ANUS, or A MAN'S ANUS, or AN ANIMAL'S VAGINA or ITS ANUS then it is necessary to wash whether the one being penetrated is alive OR DEAD, YOUNG OR OLD, whether it was done intentionally or absentmindedly, whether it was done willfully or forcefully. This also applies if the woman places the male member inside her while the man is asleep, whether the penis is erect or not, whether the penis is circumcised or uncircumcised. All these situations require that the person committing the act and the one the act is committed on must wash themselves, unless the person committing the act or the person the act is committed on is a young male or female.

In another commentary written by Sayyid Sistani there is a ruling regarding bestiality.

Sayyid Sistani: Towdih al-Masa'il, ruling 2648:

Eating the meat of a horse, mule, or donkey is disliked. If one has intercourse with them their meat will become haram (defiled). Likewise, their milk will become haram – as well as their future generations, per obligatory precaution – and their urine and feces will become najis. They must be exiled from the city and sold to another location. The person who had intercourse with them, if its not their owner, will have to pay the owner their value…if one has intercourse with an animal whose meat is usually consumed, such as a cow, sheep, or camel, then its urine and feces will become najis and its meat will become haram. Likewise, per obligatory precaution, drinking its milk will become haram and its future generations will be the same. This animal must be killed and burned. The person who had intercourse, if he is not the owner, must pay the owner its value.

These commentaries seem to indicate bestiality is permitted in Islam, but this is not necessarily so. These articles rather address what to do if the act occurs and they give instructions regarding ritual purification and washing should bestiality occur. These articles do not discuss prohibition of bestiality. Rather, they only concentrate of the consequences of the animals and what the person should do to be clean afterward. The obvious fact is the act was becoming a problem and had to be addressed. Thus, bestiality is not encouraged under Islam but culturally it had become a common occurrence. Islam has not enforced laws to stop rape of boys or animals, thus silence implies consent.

In the publication "Chronicles a Magazine of American Culture" Eugene Girin writes in a July, 2014 article,

A video, reportedly shot by an Israeli drone over the war-torn Gaza Strip has been circulating on various social networks. The footage shows several Hamas fighters, decked out in kuffiya headscarves, having sexual intercourse with a goat or a sheep.

Stunningly revolting, but hardly surprising. After all, zoophilia was always quite common, if not widespread in Islamic societies from the

Maghreb to Central Asia. Numerous non-Muslims from Uzbekistan told me about the rife practice of bestiality by young Uzbeks in villages and small towns.

Robert Fisk, a journalist known for his pro-Islam sympathies, wrote in his book The Great War for Civilization about seeing an Afghan man, standing on boxes and sodomizing a camel in broad daylight on the side of the road in Kandahar. Also in Afghanistan, a soldier was arrested after having been caught having intercourse with a donkey, explaining that he did not have enough money to get married. Apparently, this was a good enough excuse for the local police who promptly released him without charge.

University of Stockholm professor Ishtiaq Ahmed, a native of Pakistan, wrote in Pakistan's Daily Times:

In southern Punjab, much of NWFP, Sindh and Balochistan sodomy and bestiality are common among rural youths. In fact, he caught two boys trying to rape a goat in the vicinity of the mazar of Hazrat Sultan Bahu. The punishment meted out to them was 10 blows with a chhittar (shoe) each on their butts. They protested however that in many rural areas having sex with an animal was considered a rite of passage on the way to becoming full members of the male society!

The News International newspaper, also in Pakistan, reported a few years ago that a donkey was killed by its owner in an "honor killing" after being raped by another villager who managed to escape the owner's wrath. The poor donkey was declared a kari ("adulterous female") and shot dead. The zoophile was fined 110,000 Pakistani rupees (a little over $1,100).

An entry on Morocco in the International Encyclopedia of Sexuality is authored by four Arab Muslim medical doctors - Nadia Kadiri, Abderrazak Moussaid, Abdelkrim Tirraf, and Abdallah Jadid who can hardly be accused of "Islamophobia" or anti-Arab prejudice. This is what the four Muslim doctors have to say about bestiality in their country:

In the rural world, zoophilia is still very widespread and not blameworthy. With masturbation, it constitutes an obligatory passage in the adolescent male's apprenticeship of sexuality.

Islamic leaders have not punished those who violate young boys and animals. They allow sex with nine year old girls but execute homosexuals by stoning. These are cultural and religious disconnects. In a society where the church and state are one, when the religion is permissive of an act the laws are not applied and cultural habits eclipse religious opinions, no matter how vile the acts. In such cases, it still falls to the religious state to correct the actions of its people. To allow the act is to condone it and encourage its spread.

Sharia Law

The church and state are one. There can be no separation. The church rules the state and all who live therein. Sharia Law is a set of laws based on the Quran and Islamic teachings, including the words and example of Mohammed. Mohammed's life is held up as "a beautiful pattern of conduct for anyone whose hope is in Allah" (Q33:21) and "an exalted standard of character" (Q68:4). Sharia Law is the body of Islamic law. The term means "way" or " path"; it is the legal framework within which the public and some private aspects of life are regulated for those living in a legal system based on Islam. Those laws based on the Quran cannot be altered, although there may be slight latitude given in interpreting the law at times. **Fundamental Muslims will always hold Sharia Law above a nation's civil law.**

Sharia deals with all aspects of day-to-day life, including politics, economics, banking, business law, contract law, sexuality, and social issues.

There is not a strictly codified uniform set of laws that can be called Sharia. It is more like a system of several laws, based on the Quran, Hadith and centuries of debate, interpretation and precedent.

Pure Islamic sharia law is not implemented in any country of the world except where violent fundamentalists are in control, such as in areas controlled by ISIS. Most Muslim countries have their own laws and have chosen laws from Islamic sharia as a foundation to their legal system.

Sharia law is the legal system of Islam. The Sharia (also spelled Shariah or Shari'a) law is derived from the actions, deeds, and words of Mohammed. This means the laws are derived from the Quran and the 'Sunnah'. The Sunnah is the verbally transmitted record of the teachings, deeds and sayings, silent permissions (or disapprovals) of Mohammed, as well as various reports about Mohammed's companions.

Joseph Lumpkin

The Sharia law itself cannot be altered, but the interpretation of the Sharia law, called "fiqh," by imams is given some leeway.

As a legal system, the Sharia law covers a very wide range of topics. While other legal codes deal primarily with public behavior, Sharia law covers public behavior, private behavior and private beliefs.

The article from "simple.wikipedia.org/wiki/Sharia_law" gives us an overview of the laws and applications.

According to the Sharia law and after due process and investigation:
Habitual theft past a specific threshold, and after repeated warnings, is punishable by amputation of a hand.

The punishment for adultery and fornication such that it becomes a public ordeal, according to the Holy Quran is lashing. Before the revelation of these verses, Mohammed followed the Judaic law in implementing the punishment of death by stoning. This was only given if the person admitted to it repeatedly, was not intoxicated and knew the repercussions. Even then, if during the punishment he repented, he was to be released. Although lately what we have been seeing is that once the first stone is thrown the bloodlust of the Islamic crowd deafens them to any cries of repentance by the accused parties and death by stoning occurs.

A woman is allowed to be accompanied by another woman in giving testimony in court for financial affairs.
A female heir inherits half of what a male heir inherits. The concept being that Islam puts the responsibility of earning and spending on the family on the male. Any wealth the female earns is strictly for her own use. The female also inherits from both her immediate family and through agency of her husband, her in-laws as well.

Sharia law is divided into two main sections: Acts of Worship and Human interaction.

The acts of worship, *or al-ibadat, called the 5 pillars of Islam:*
Affirmation (Shahadah): there is no god except Allah and Mohammed is his messenger. However, Allah is the same God of Isaac and Adam. Allah remains the same throughout time

Prayers (Salah): five times a day
Fasts (Sawm during Ramadan)
Charities (Zakat)
Pilgrimage to Mecca (Hajj)

Human interaction, *or al-mu'amalat, which includes:*
Financial transactions
Endowments
Laws of inheritance
Marriage, divorce, and child custody
Foods and drinks (including ritual slaughtering and hunting)
Penal punishments
Warfare and peace
Judicial matters (including witnesses and forms of evidence)

A Muslim can only marry a Muslim or Ahl al-Kitāb. He/She cannot marry an atheist, agnostic or polytheist.
A Muslim minor girl's father or guardian needs her consent when arranging a marriage for her.
A marriage is a contract that requires the man to pay, or promise to pay some of the wedding and provisions the wife needs. This is known as the dowry.
A Muslim man may be married to up to four women at a time, although the Quran has emphasized that this is a permission, and not a rule. The man must be able to house each wife and her children in a different house, he should not give preferential treatment to one wife over another. Marriage is a legal arrangement in Islam, not a sacrament in the Christian sense, and is secured with a contract.
"... marry women of your choice, two or three or four; but if you fear that you shall not be able to deal justly with them, then only one." (Quran 4:3)
Although a man may have a maximum of four wives, he is allowed to have sex slaves, the number of which is not specified.

Sharia recognizes three categories of crime:
Hudud: crimes against God with fixed punishment.
Qisas: crimes against Muslims where equal retaliation is allowed.
Tazir: crimes against Muslims or non-Muslims where a Muslim judge uses his discretion in sentencing.

There are 5 Hudud: theft, highway robbery, illicit sex, sexual slander (accusing someone of illicit sex but failing to produce four witnesses, and drinking alcohol

Sharia requires that there be four adult male Muslim witnesses to a hudud crime or a confession repeated four times, before someone can be punished for a Hudud crime.

Murder, bodily injury and property damage - intentional or unintentional - is considered a civil dispute under sharia law. The victim, victim's heir(s) or guardian is given the option to either forgive the murderer, demand equal retaliation or accept compensation in lieu of the murder, bodily injury or property damage. Under sharia law, the Diyya compensation received by the victim or victim's family is in cash.

The penalty for theft: Theft (stealing) is a hudud crime in sharia, with a fixed punishment. The punishment is cutting off the hand or feet of the thief.

The penalty for illicit sex: Sharia law states that if either an unmarried man or an unmarried woman has pre-marital sex, the punishment should be 100 lashes. There are some requirements that need to be met before this punishment can happen. For example, the punishment cannot happen unless the person confesses, or unless four eyewitnesses each saw, at the same time, the man and the woman in the action of illicit sex. Those who accuse someone of illicit sex but fail to produce four eyewitnesses are guilty of false accusation and their punishment is 80 lashes. Maliki School of sharia considers pregnancy in an unmarried woman as sufficient evidence that she committed the hudud crime of illicit sex and thus would subject the pregnant woman to 100 lashes under the whip. The Hadiths consider homosexuality as illicit sex.

The penalty for apostasy: The punishment for apostasy is thought to be death by several schools of Muslim thought, though the Quran has not advised such a punishment and in fact details that there is absolutely no penal punishment for apostasy. However, if someone does not convert or if a Muslim converts to another religion, or if a Muslim denounces or even criticizes Islam, most schools of thought advise killing the apostate.

An example apostate was Hashem Aghajari, who was sentenced to death for apostasy in Iran (in 2002) after giving a controversial speech on *reforming Islam. His sentence was reduced to 5 years in prison, but only after international and domestic outcry.*

There are two festivals that are considered Sunnah.
Eid ul-Fitr
Eid ul-Adha
During these festivals, specific rituals are used:
Sadaqah (charity) before Eid ul-Fitr prayer.
The Prayer and the Sermon on Eid day.
Takbirs (glorifying God) after every prayer in the days of Tashriq (These are thought to be the days in which pilgrims stay at Mina once they return from Muzdalifah i.e. 10th, 11th, 12th, and 13th of Dhu al-Hijjah.)
Sacrifice of unflawed, four-legged grazing animal of appropriate age after the prayer of Eid ul-Adha in the days of Tashriq. The animal must not be wasted; its meat must be consumed.

Yes, Islam is not the only religion demanding the sacrifice of animals but is it one of the few. Muslims engaged in the Hajj (pilgrimage) are obligated to sacrifice a lamb or a goat or join others in sacrificing a cow or a camel during the celebration of the Eid al-Adha. Other Muslims not on the Hajj to Mecca are also encouraged to participate in this sacrifice to share in the sanctity of the occasion. It is understood as a symbolic re-enactment of Abraham's sacrifice of a ram in place of his son, a narrative present throughout Abrahamism. Meat from this occasion is divided into three parts:
For personal nourishment
For distribution among friends, family, and neighbors, and
as charity for the indigent

Other occasions where the lamb is sacrificed include the celebration of the birth of a child, reaching the final stages of building a house, the acquisition of a valuable commodity, and even the visit of a dear or honourable guest. For Muslims, the sacrifice of lamb was and is associated with celebrations, feasts, generosity, and the seeking of blessings. Most schools of fiqh hold the animal must be killed according to the prohibitions of halal sacrifice.

Dietary laws - *Halal*
Islamic law lists only some specific foods and drinks that are not allowed.

Pork, blood, and scavenged meat are not allowed. People are also not allowed to eat animals that were slaughtered in the name of someone other than God.

Intoxicants (like alcoholic drinks) are not allowed under any circumstances.

While Islamic law prohibits (does not allow) dead meat (meat slaughtered or prepared beyond a period of time after it dies. Animals must be killed in a certain way and prepared directly thereafter. This does not apply to fish and locusts.

Also, hadith literature prohibits beasts having sharp canine teeth, birds having claws, tamed donkeys, and any piece cut from a living animal.

Sacrifice: There are some specific rules regarding the killing of animals in Islam.

The animal must be killed in the most humane way: by swiftly cutting the throat.

The animal must not be diseased.

The animal must not have been exposed to feces, worms, and other impurities.

All blood must drain from the animal before being packaged.

Legal Under Sharia Law:

In his book, "Thirty Sharia Laws That Are Bad For All Societies", James M. Arlandson wrote:

The mosque and state are not separate. To this day, Islamic nations that are deeply rooted in sharia, like Iran and Saudi Arabia, do not adequately separate the two realms, giving a lot of power to courts and councils to ensure that legislation does not contradict the Quran (never mind whose interpretation). Most of the laws listed below come from this confusion. Back-up article: Mosque and State

A woman captive of jihad may be forced to have to sex with her captors (now owners). Quran 4:24 and especially the sacred traditions and classical law allow this. The sacred traditions say that while out on military campaigns under Mohammed's leadership, jihadists used to practice coitus interruptus with their female captives. Women soldiers fighting terrorists today must be forewarned of the danger.

Property can be destroyed or confiscated during jihad. Quran 59:2 and 59:5 discuss those rules. Sacred traditions and classical law expand on the Quranic verses. Modern Islamic law officially improves on the Quran: see Article Three of the 1990 Cairo Declaration of Human Rights, which is nonetheless based on sharia, but it outlaws wanton destruction of property. Would there be any conflict between old Islam and modern Islam in a war today? Back-up articles: Jihad and Qital and The Quran and the Sword

Jihad may be waged to collect spoils. Quran 8:1, 8:7, 8:41, and 48:20 show this clearly. Early Islam followed the old Arab custom of raiding caravans, but as its military grew, the raids were elevated to jihad. The spoils of war were coveted. Which Islam would prevail in a war today – the old one or the modern one?

A second-class submission tax, called the jizyah, must be imposed on Jews and Christians (and other religious minorities) living in Islamic countries. Quran 9:29 offers three options to Jews and Christians: (1) Fight and die; (2) convert to Islam; (3) or keep their religion, but pay a tribute or submission tax, the jizyah, while living under Islam. In Islamic history, vanquished Jews and Christians became known as dhimmis. This word appears in Quran 9:8 and 9:10, meaning a "treaty" or "oath," but it can also mean those who are "condemned" "reviled" or "reproved" (Quran 17:18, 17:22; 68:49). The word "submission" in Quran 9:29 can also be translated as "humiliation," "utterly humbled," "contemptible" or "vile." It can mean "small" as opposed to "great. Islamic nations today still seek to impose this second-class religion tax. Back-up articles: Jihad and Qital and The Quran and the Sword

Slavery is allowed. It is true that freeing slaves was done in original Islam (Quran 5:89 and 24:33), and the Quran says to be kind to slaves (Quran 4:36), but that is not the entire story. In addition to those verses, Quran 4:24, 23:1-7; 33:52 allow the institution. Mohammed owned slaves, even one who was black (so says a sacred tradition). He was militarily and politically powerful during his later life in Medina, but he never abolished slavery as an institution. Officially, Islamic nations have outlawed slavery (Article 11, which is still based on sharia). That proves Islam can reform on at least one matter. Can it reform on the other sharia laws? And we are told that "no other nation or religious group in the world treated slaves better than the Muslims did." The back-up article and next two items in this list contradict that claim. The legacy of slavery still runs deep in Islamic countries even today.

A male owner may have sex with his slave-women, even prepubescent slave-girls. See Quran 4:24 and 23:1-7; but it is classical law that permits sex with prepubescent slave girls and describes them as such. Some Muslim religious leaders and others still advocate this practice, taking the slaves as concubines (though sex with prepubescent slave-girls is another matter).

Slaves may be beaten. That's what sacred traditions and classical laws say. See Islamic Jihad: A Legacy of Forced Conversion, Imperialism, and Slavery

Apostasy laws, including imprisonment or execution, may be imposed on anyone who leaves Islam (an apostate). Normally this is a prescribed punishment, but it is also political, since it is about freedom of religion. Surprisingly the Quran does not cover punishing apostates down here on earth, though in the afterlife they will be punished. Does this modern Islam reform old Islam? Quran 4:88-89, 9:73-74, and 9:123, read in that sequence, might deal with earthly punishments. Mainly, however, the sacred traditions and classical law permit harsh treatment for anyone who leaves Islam. Islamic courts and laws still impose these punishments today, or religious scholars today argue for the law.

Blasphemy laws, including imprisonment or execution, may be imposed on critics of Islam or Mohammed. These verses should be read in historical sequence, for they show that as Islam's military power increased, the harsh treatment of mockers and critics also intensified, as follows: Quran 3:186, 33:57-61, 9:61-66, 9:73 and 9:123. Sacred traditions, classical laws, and historical Islam are unambiguous about the punishments, recording the people, often their names, who were assassinated for mocking Mohammed and the Quran. Islamic nations and pockets of Islam in non-Muslim countries still impose these punishments today.

Homosexuals may be imprisoned, flogged, or executed. Surprisingly, the Quran is not all that clear on this subject, but the traditions and classical laws are. Islamic nations to this day still impose those punishments, and religious leaders still argue for harsh punishments. Back-up article: Homosexuality

Adulterers may be stoned to death. The verse that says to stone adulterers to death went missing from the Quran, so says Umar, a companion of Mohammed and the second caliph (ruled 634-644). But he left no doubt that this penalty was done under Mohammed's direction, and the sacred traditions and classical laws confirm it. But a few rules of evidence must be followed, like confession of the adulterer or four eyewitnesses. In some interpretations of the law, if a woman is raped, but cannot produce four just and pious men who witnessed it, then she is slandering the alleged rapist (or gang rapists) – never mind that the four just and pious eyewitnesses did nothing to stop it, but stood there and watched it. Some modern Islamic nations still do this, and religious and legal scholars argue for it.

A woman inherits half what a man does. Quran 4:11 says it, and the hadith (traditions) and classical law confirm it. Modern Islamic nations still do this, and religious leaders still argue for it. Back-up article: Women's Status and Roles 23. A woman's testimony in a court of law counts half of a man's testimony, since she might "forget." Quran 2:282 says it in the context of business law. But the hadith (traditions) explains that women's minds are deficient; classical law expands this curtailment to other areas than business. Modern Islamic nations still do this, and religious scholars still argue for it.

A man may legally and irrevocably divorce his wife, outside of a court of law, by correctly pronouncing three times "you are divorced." Quran 2:229 says this, and the traditions and classical law explain and confirm it. A judge in a modern Islamic country will ensure that the husband did not speak from a fit of irrational rage (anger is okay) or intoxication, for example. Then the court will validate the divorce, not daring to overturn it, since the Quran says so. Sometimes this homemade and irrevocable divorce produces a lot of regret in the couple and manipulation from the husband in Islam today.

A wife may remarry her ex-husband if and only if she marries another man, has sex with him, and then this second man divorces her. Quran 2:230 says this, and the traditions and classical law confirm it.

Supposedly, this rule is designed to prevent easy divorce (see the previous point), but it produces a lot of pain, in Muslims today.

Husbands may hit their wives. Quran 4:34 says it, and the traditions and classical law confirm it. There is a sequence of steps a husband follows before he can hit her, but not surprisingly this rule creates all sorts of abuse and confusion in Islamic society today.

A man may be polygamous with up to four wives. Quran 4:3 (and 33:50-52) allow this, but only if a man can take care of them. The traditions and classical law confirm it. Modern Muslims still push for this old marital arrangement even in the USA, and many Islamic nations still allow it. But some Muslims are fighting polygamy. The hadith (traditions) paints a picture of Mohammed's household that was full of strife between the wives.

A man may simply get rid of one of his "undesirable" wives. Quran 4:128 says this. The traditions say about the verse that the wife whom Mohammed wanted to get rid of was "huge" and "fat." She gave up her turn to his favorite girl-bride Aisha. He kept the corpulent wife.

There is heartbreak in Islam today.

The Early Community

Mohammed's life as a preacher and leader of a community of believers has two major phases. Mecca set on a major trade road. Its citizens were mostly polytheists who believed there were gods guarding the city and making it successful. Most of the Arab world at the time practiced polytheism. Mohammed's message centered on monotheism. He proclaimed his message in a city in which the majority did not accept his teachings. In the eyes of the ruling people, Mohammed and his message would threaten the profit and success of Mecca and the region. It would have angered the gods protecting the city and causing it to prosper. Why change something that was working so well? The message presented in the "Meccan" period emphasizes the general themes of affirmation of monotheism and warnings of the Day of Judgment. Since the message was in conflict with the established financial and political structure of the city, the message represented a major challenge to the basic power structures of Mecca. The stress between the systems and the new religion demanded Islam become both a religious and political force and therefore, by default, a financial force as well. This would have demanded a redistribution of wealth and commerce in favor of Muslims and the conversion or relinquishing of power by the elite.

The second phase of Mohammed's career and the early life of the Muslim community began when Mohammed went to the city of Yathrib, which became known as Medina.

Although the fact is little publicized, more than one historian has affirmed that the Arab world's second holiest city, Medina, was first settled by Jewish tribes. The roots of Islamic anti-Semitism and the law of taxation of non-believers might be found in the initial plunder of Jewish settlements, and the imposition of a "poll tax" to fund Arab campaigns. Jews that did not convert were killed or taxed.

Bernard Lewis is a British-American historian specializing in oriental studies. He is also known as a public intellectual and political commentator, Professor Emeritus of Near Eastern Studies at Princeton University with expertise is in the history of Islam and the interaction between Islam and the West. Mr. Lewis writes:

"Jizya or jizyah is a religiously required per capita yearly tax historically levied by Islamic states on certain non-Muslim subjects (dhimmis) permanently residing in Muslim lands under Islamic law. The Quran mandates Jizya. However, scholars largely agree that early Muslim rulers adapted existing systems of taxation and tribute that were established under previous rulers of the conquered lands.

"The city of Medina, some 280 miles north of Mecca, had originally been settled by Jewish tribes from the north, especially the Banu Nadir and Banu Quraiza. The comparative richness of the town attracted an infiltration of pagan Arabs who came at first as clients of the Jews and ultimately succeeded in dominating them. Medina, or, as it was known before Islam, Yathrib, had no form of stable government at all. The town was torn by the feuds of the rival Arab tribes of Aus and Khazraj, with the Jews maintaining an uneasy balance of power. The latter, engaged mainly in agriculture and handicrafts, were economically and culturally superior to the Arabs, and were consequently disliked.... as soon as the Arabs had attained unity through the agency of Mohammed they attacked and ultimately eliminated the Jews. Mohammed set up control in Medina and began growing his movement as one would grow a nation. In Medina Mohammed provided leadership in all matters of life."

According to Guillaume,

"At the dawn of Islam the Jews dominated the economic life of the Hijaz [Arabia]. They held all the best land. At Medina they must have formed at least half of the population. The prosperity of the Jews was due to their superior knowledge of agriculture and irrigation and their energy and industry. Jewish prosperity was a challenge to the Arabs, particularly the Quraysh at Mecca and ... [other Arab tribes] at Medina. The prophet Mohammed himself was a member of the Quraysh tribe, which coveted the Jews' bounty, and when the Muslims took up arms they treated the Jews with much greater severity than the Christians, who, until the end of the purely Arab Caliphate, were not badly treated.

Mohammed was changing his outlook with the rapidity of a man who had cast off the mantle of preacher and taken on the helmet of a warrior. He began his message in Mecca by preaching monotheism and a plea of conversion. He taught respect for Jews and Christians, whom he referred to as *"Children of the Book." Yet, he and his followers treated the Jews in Medina with great cruelty.*

It was in 622 Mohammed and his followers moved to Yathrib (Medina), and this emigration, or hijrah, is of such significance that Muslims use this date as the beginning of the Islamic calendar. The oasis became known as the City of the prophet, or simply al-Medina (the city).

In Muslim tradition the sociopolitical community that was created in Medina provides the model for what an Islamic state and society should be. The new community was open to anyone who made the basic affirmation of faith. Loyalty to the Islamic community was to supersede any other loyalty to clan, family or nation. The political structure of the new community evolved toward a sovereign monarchy or theocracy with a religious head. In this way Islam is frequently described as a social and political way of life rather than simply a religion."

Mohammed carried resentment for being thrown out of Mecca and he eventually exacted his revenge in blood. The Muslim army set out for Mecca on Wednesday, 29 November 629 (6 Ramadan, 8 hijra), joined by allied tribes. The Muslim army was swollen to 10,000 men. This was the largest Muslim force ever assembled to date. The army stayed at Marr-uz-Zahran, located ten miles northwest of Mecca. Mohammed ordered every man to light a fire to deceive the Meccans to overestimate the size of the already bloated army.

By the time of Mohammed's death in 632, Islam was established in Mecca, which would become very important to the Muslim world. The Kaaba, a cube shaped shrine in Mecca that had been the center of the polytheistic religious life and the draw of several types of pilgrimages was relabeled as Islamic. Mohammed announced that it was once an altar built by Abraham. Mecca became both the center of the Islamic pilgrimage and the place toward which Muslims faced when they performed their prayers.

Sunni, Shia, Salafis and Sufi

A religion based on behavior, deeds, and rituals, by its nature must become more and more exact in order to insure both its survival and its mission. If the target of this religion is heaven the bull's-eye will become smaller and smaller as rules are added and doctrine becomes more restrictive and specific. In time there will be a faction that splinters away because they will disagree with the main body on points of rule, control, or doctrine. They will see the main body as lacking in commitment or strictness. The main group may not be fundamental enough in the eyes of the emerging group to reach the narrowed goal of heaven. They will break away to gain heaven. Eventually they may even gain influence over the main group.

Suuni and Shia

The schism between the two main branches of Islam is somewhat reminiscent of the split between the Catholic and Orthodox branches of Christianity. Let us not forget it was the attempt to usurp power by the bishop of Rome, who at that time was simply one among many equals that was partially to blame for the great schism. Most schisms begin with a contest of power or control. Most religions containing a fundamental branch will, by its nature, come to a point of division since fundamentalist believe there can be no variation from what they hold as the truth. Anything outside, lacking, or beyond their core doctrine represents error and sin. Firm control over the faith and the faithful is the only way to insure compliance with the religion and the favor of god. So it was with the Sunni and Shia. In its most simple and basic description, the split between the Sunni and Shia was over who should control Islam after the passing of the prophet Mohammed. The point of contention was if control should come through bloodline or through political choice.

Islam had become a set of laws that ruled most aspects of life, including political authority, which was founded upon a monotheistic religion that incorporated some Jewish, Christian, and pagan doctrines. By the time of his death in 632, Mohammed had consolidated power in Arabia. Less than a century after his death Muslims had built an empire that would reach from Central Asia to Spain.

The battles over the control, power and wealth of such an empire would be the downfall to a consolidated Islam. A battle over succession split the followers. Some argued that leadership should be passed to qualified individuals elected by the votes of the leading clerics. Others insisted that the only legitimate ruler must come through Mohammed's bloodline.

One faction turned to their leaders and cleric to elect a Caliph. The group of high level leaders of Islam elected Abu Bakr, a companion of Mohammed. Others favored Ali ibn Abi Talib, Mohammed's cousin and son-in-law as the Caliph because he was a leader who shared a bloodline with Mohammed. The fierce opposition between the two choices eventually evolved into Islam's two main sects, the Shia and the Sunni.

Shias (shia / shi'ite) is a term that stems from shi'atu Ali, Arabic for "partisans of Ali". Shias believe that Ali and his descendants are part of a divine order, descending as a king or emperor should, through inheritance or blood. The party of Ali claimed that Mohammed had designated his son-in-law Ali ibn Abi Talib as his successor, and that the successor of Mohammed had to be a member of the prophet's household.

The Sunnis contended that the prophet of Islam had made no provision for a successor as political, military, and spiritual leader of the Muslim community, and therefore Muslims should choose the best man among them as their leader. Sunnis means "followers of the way" (sunna means way) of Mohammed. Sunnis are opposed to succession based on Mohammed's bloodline and believe succession should come through election.

Shias believe it was expected that the successor would have some of Mohammed's prophetic spirit, as well as infallibility in deciding disputed questions it seemed to some that this ability could follow with the bloodline. Ali was finally chosen as the fourth caliph in

656. In 661 he was assassinated. Hassan, his eldest son and successor, was murdered in 670 on the orders of the Sunni caliph Muawiya. Then the Sunni/Shi'ite split became definitive and permanent when Ali's younger son, Husayn, was killed in the Battle of Karbala in 680.

The Shi'ites (or Shias) were brutalized and their leaders murdered. This feeling of separation, loss and defeat became part of the Shi'ite theology and history. Thus, it affects their worship and behavior.

After the Sunnis beheaded of Husayn, the Shi'ites continued a succession of Imams who were members of Mohammed's household. Each Immam was purported to have been poisoned by order of the Sunni caliph ruling at the time.

In a written report, The Council on Foreign Relations in their article "The Sunni Shia Divide" explains,

"Ali became caliph in 656 and ruled only five years before he was assassinated. The caliphate, which was based in the Arabian Peninsula, passed to the Umayyad dynasty in Damascus and later the Abbasids in Baghdad.

Shias rejected the authority of these rulers. In 680, soldiers of the second Umayyad caliph killed Ali's son, Husayn, and many of his companions in Karbala, located in modern-day Iraq. Fear of continuing reprisal resulted in the further persecution and marginalization of Shias.

Sunnis triumphed politically in the Muslim world and grow in number and thus in control. Shias continued to look to the Imams, who were clerics leading services and prayers in the mosques. These men were the blood descendants of Ali and Husayn and functioned as the legitimate political and religious leaders within the branch of Islam. Even within the Shia community, however, there arose differences over the proper line of succession.

Shia identity is rooted in victimhood over the killing of Husayn, the prophet Mohammed's grandson, in the seventh century, and a long history of marginalization by the Sunni majority. Islam's dominant sect, which roughly 85 percent of the world's 1.6 billion Muslims follow, viewed Shia Islam with suspicion, and extremist Sunnis have portrayed Shias as heretics and apostates.

The Shia sect continued to look to their Imams to guide them. Imams are the blood descendants of Ali and Husayn and the only men that can be their legitimate political and religious leaders."

The Council on Foreign Relations in their article "The Sunni Shia Divide" continues,

"Mainstream Shias believe there were twelve Imams. The majority of Shias, particularly those in Iran and the eastern Arab world, believe that the twelfth Imam entered a state of occultation, or hiddenness, in 939 and that he will return at the end of time. Since then, "Twelvers," or Ithna Ashari Shias, have vested religious authority in their senior clerical leaders, called ayatollahs (Arabic for "sign of God)".

The belief in the return of the twelfth Imam fits into an apocalyptic view, which fuels the terroristic tactics of some Muslims.
According to the traditions of Twelver Shi'ism, the official religion of the Islamic Republic of Iran, the twelfth of these Imams, a boy of five years old, disappeared under mysterious and disputed circumstances in the year 874. However, he remained alive and he communicated to the world through his four chosen agents. The last agent died in 941. At that point the Twelfth Imam went silent, entering the period of "Great Occultation" or a spiritual hiding.

The International Messianic Jewish Alliance wrote in the article, "They Await the Mahdi (ISLAMIC MESSIAH)",
"In his last message to the world in 941 the Twelfth Imam consoled his followers with prophecies regarding his reappearance. The prophecies are now being interpreted in a modern context. This modern view places Iran on center stage and brings fire and destruction to Israel and America. The two powers that the Iranian mullahs have long designated as the "Great Satan" and the "Little Satan" are America and Israel and they would be the first targets in an Iranian attempt to hasten the Twelfth Imam's coming."

Frontpage magazine November, 2013 article reports,
"The Twelfth Imam, in his last message warned, "Hearts will become inaccessible to compassion. The earth will be filled with

tyranny and violence, and the evil that Muslims were suffering was at its absolute apex.

In the Shi'ite tradition Mohammed prophesied (in the hadith) that the Twelfth Imam would be "the Resurrector" and would fill the world with peace and justice as today it is filled with violence and tyranny."

The Shi'ites teach that the Twelfth Imam would return at a time when the Muslims were oppressed as never before, and suffering worse than ever. The Imam, in the company of Jesus, would finally end the horrific persecution of the true believers, taking up arms against their enemies and conquering the world and establishing Islam throughout the earth.

Jesus is held as a prophet in Islam. Jesus will defer to Mohammed and in doing so prove that Muslims had it right all along and Christians would flock to convert."

Today modern, fundamental Muslims attempt to hasten the Twelfth Imam's return by fueling violence around the world. Their agenda is obvious. If they can make the entire world hate and persecute Islam and bring a global war against Muslims they will bring back the Twelfth Imam and with his help Islam would conquer the world.

The true believers of Islam will stop at nothing to bring about a world war against Islam. The world fears they may find a way by launching a nuclear strike against Israel to provoke retaliation that would subject the Muslims in Iran to war and even genocide. They believe this would bring back the Islamic messiah, the Twelfth Imam. Jesus would descend from heaven and order Christians to convert to Islam. Most of the world would convert. Muslims would then destroy those who oppose Islam. At that time they would establish their version of a world religion.

Sunni Shia - Modern Wars

Sects and denominations do not matter if there is no prejudice. In the U.S. one seldom cares if a person is an Orthodox, Catholic, or Protestant Christian because there is no discrimination between the denominations. That was not always the case and the lack of equal consideration fomented wars and fights. This is the tip of the problem when it comes to the Shia-Sunni divide.

Much of the ongoing conflict in the Middle East is fueled by the sectarian wars between the Shia and Sunni. These two sects are fighting proxy wars, where countries, which are either majority Shia or Sunni, are battling for control of large regions. It is not easy to identify these wars as sectarian because there are wars in which countries and not sects are fighting. But, below the surface these countries are simply the extensions of the sects that control them, and thus the wars conducted by the countries and proxy wars between Shia and Sunni.

An article in the Wall Street Journal, "Saudi Arabia vs. Iran: The Sunni-Shiite Proxy Wars" 4/7/2015 states in part,
"In today's Middle East the political and religious divisions are fueling the insurgency in proxy wars. One key driver of this instability is the fourteen hundred year-old sectarian split between Sunni and Shiite Muslim."

Several factors brought the old split back to the forefront. Iran's Islamic Revolution in 1979 deposed the Shah and established a theocratic rule over the country. This was the re-emergence of hard line Shia theology and the Sharia Law that came with it. Saudi Arabia promoted the fundamentalist Salafist strain of Sunni Islam to counter Iran's Shia ideology. Then, when Saddam Hussein was removed from power in Iraq in 2003 Sunni jihadism began and Iran began to influence Iraq. Today of the total Muslim population, 10-13% are Shia Muslims and 87-90% are Sunni Muslims. Most Shias (between 68% and 80%) live in just four countries: Iran, Pakistan, India and Iraq. Saudi Arabia is a driving force in the Sunni world and the largest exporter of terrorism driven by the Sunni sect. Iran is the largest exported of terrorism driven by the Shia sect. Much of the fighting in the Middle East is proxy wars for these two sects.

Now the sects are mixing and fighting within the countries themselves. This is the reason for the internal civil war of Syria.

Syria is a Sunni-majority country but it is ruled by members of a Shiite (Shia) sect. The fighting that began as anti-government has taken on sectarian overtones since the population is predominately one sect and the government and ruling class is of the other sect. That problem has spilled over to Iraq. Iraq's population is mostly Shia with a predominantly Shiite government, Sunni rebels increasingly trouble it. Iraq is caught in the middle between Iran, with its Shiite majority on one side and Saudi Arabia, which has a majority Sunni population.

Iran is exporting fighters to stir up trouble so it can take advantage. The major powers in Saudi Arabia and Iran have long pushed sectarian interests, resulting in civil and international conflicts.

Pew Research explains the conflict like this,
"Iran and Iraq are two of only a handful of countries that have more Shias than Sunnis. While it is widely assumed that Iraq has a Shia majority, there is little reliable data on the exact Sunni-Shia breakdown of the population there, particularly since refugees arriving in Iraq due to the conflict in Syria or leaving Iraq due to its own turmoil may have affected the composition of Iraq's population.

Neighboring Iran is home to the world's largest Shia population: Between 90% and 95% of Iranian Muslims (66-70 million people) were Shias in 2009, according to our estimate from that year.

Their shared demographic makeup may help explain Iran's support for Iraq's Shia-dominated government led by Prime Minister Nouri al-Maliki.

Iran also has supported Bashar al-Assad's government in Syria, where only 15-20% of the Muslim population was Shia as of 2009. But the Syrian leadership is dominated by Alawites (an offshoot of Shia Islam). Under Saddam Hussein's regime in Iraq, which was dominated by Sunnis, the country clashed with Iran."

There are countries where the Sunni and Shia get along and even marry. In these countries the distinctions, which are actually few, are overlooked. It is when people start focusing on the legalistic subtle details that differences are seen and dwelt on. Sunni and Shia are forms of Islam that can be legalistic and external. They tend to interpret the words and deeds of Mohammed literally and in doing so they condemn the religion to be crystallized and entrenched in the era of its creations, about 632 C.E. If there were a polar opposite of the Sunni and Shia, it would be Sufism. The Sunni and Shia are legalistic and religious, Sufism is mystical and spiritual.

Salafis

In one of the best articles on ISIS and Islam, Graeme Wood writes in The Atlantic Magazine 2015/03
What ISIS Really Wants

"The majority of Salafis believe that Muslims should remove themselves from politics. These quietist Salafis, as they are known, agree with the Islamic State that God's law is the only law, and they eschew practices like voting and the creation of political parties. But they interpret the Quran's hatred of discord and chaos as requiring them to fall into line with just about any leader, including some manifestly sinful ones. "The prophet said: as long as the ruler does not enter into clear kufr [disbelief], give him general obedience." The texts warn against causing social upheaval. Quietist Salafis are strictly forbidden from dividing Muslims from one another, for example, by mass excommunication.

Quietist Salafis believe that Muslims should direct their energies toward perfecting their personal life, including prayer, ritual, and hygiene. Much in the same way ultra-Orthodox Jews debate whether it's kosher to tear off squares of toilet paper on the Sabbath (does that count as "rending cloth"?), they spend an inordinate amount of time ensuring that their trousers are not too long, that their beards are trimmed in some areas and shaggy in others. Through this fastidious observance, they believe, God will favor them with strength and numbers, and perhaps a caliphate will arise. At that moment, Muslims will take vengeance and, yes, achieve glorious victory at Dabiq. But Pocius cites a slew of modern Salafi theologians who argue that a caliphate cannot come into being in a righteous way except through the unmistakable will of God.

Joseph Lumpkin

The Islamic State, of course, would agree, and say that God has anointed Baghdadi. Pocius's retort amounts to a call to humility. He cites Abdullah Ibn Abbas, one of the prophet's companions, who sat down with dissenters and asked them how they had the gall, as a minority, to tell the majority that it was wrong. Dissent itself, to the point of bloodshed or splitting the umma, was forbidden. Even the manner of the establishment of Baghdadi's caliphate runs contrary to expectation, he said. "The khilafa is something that Allah is going to establish," he told me, "and it will involve a consensus of scholars from Mecca and Medina. That is not what happened. ISIS came out of nowhere."

The Islamic State mocks the Salafis by calling them "Salafis of menstruation," for their obscure judgments about when women are and aren't clean. ISIS calls this a low-priority and claims the Salafis waste their time in minutia. Salafis are legalists and fundamentalist but not violent. They believe the conquests should be left to Allah. Salafis prepare themselves religiously while they wait for Allah to prepare the world for the end times.

Salafism offers an alternative to Baghdadi-style jihadism. If one seeks a conservative, uncompromising fundamental version of Islam without the jihad, Salafism may be the answer. Most Muslims would consider it an extreme form of Islam but the literal-minded would not find it ideologically hypocritical or blasphemous.

Graeme Wood continues with a warning to Barack Obama by saying it would be best for non-Muslims to refrain from weighing in on matters of Islamic theology, especially if they could be considered as an apostate Muslim themselves. Obama could be considered a Takfiri, which is when one Muslim accuses another of being an apostate, impure, or unbelief. When Obama accused ISIS (the Islamic State) of not representing Islam and of not being Islamic at that point Obama, as the non-Muslim son of a Muslim, may himself be classified as an apostate. The takfir challenge from Obama elicited chuckles from jihadists. Wood reported that one member of ISIS tweeted, Obama is "Like a pig covered in feces giving hygiene advice to others".

Sufi

Sufism is less a sect of Islam than a mystical way of approaching the Islamic faith. It has been defined as "mystical Islam". Sufis believe and practice a way to seek divine love and knowledge through direct personal experience of God. Any religion or sect that seeks direct and personally communion with God is considered mystical.

Suf means wool. Sufi refers to the woolen garment of early Islamic ascetics. The terms evolved in Western languages in the early 19th century and derive from the Arabic term for a mystic.

Sufism has been a prominent movement within Islam throughout most of its history. It grew out of an early ascetic movement within Islam, which, like its Christian monastic counterpart, sought to counteract the worldliness, carnality, and literalism that came with the rapid expansion of the early Muslim community.

ReligionFacts.com in their article, "What is Sufism" reports,
"The earliest form of Sufism arose under the Umayyad Dynasty (661–749) less than a century after the founding of Islam. Mystics of this period meditated on the Doomsday passages in the Quran, thereby earning such nicknames as "those who always weep." Sufi interpretation of the Quran did not follow the rule of abrogation as the other two main branched did. Instead, they focused on the connection between God and humanity.
These early Sufis led an ascetic life of strict obedience to all Islamic scripture and were known for their night prayers. Many of them concentrated their efforts upon an absolute trust in God, which became a central concept of Sufism.
Another century or so later, a new emphasis on love arose in the faith and changed Sufism into a mysticism faith. This development is attributed to Rabi'ah al-'Adawiyah (800 CE), a woman from Basra who formulated the Sufi ideal of a pure love of God. This was a devotion that was beyond and in spite of a fear of hell or greed for paradise. It was a pure and unconditional love not based on the "bribe" of paradise of "threat" of hell. This type of pure love spills over into mankind and changes both practitioner

and those who are astute enough to understand what they are witnessing.

Other important developments soon followed, including strict self-control, psychological insight, "interior knowledge," annihilation of the self, mystical insights about the nature of man and the prophet, as well as hymns and poetry. This period, from about 800-1100 AD, is referred to as classical Sufism or classical mysticism."

God's love for man and man's love for God is central to Sufism, and the subjects of most Islamic mystical poetry. The 13th century is considered the golden age of Sufism. The mystics wrote beautiful and soaring poetry. Figures such as Ibn al'Arabi of Spain, Ibn al-Farid of Egypt, Jalal ad-Din ar-Rumi of Persia, and Najmuddin Kubra of Central Asia emerged, changing the world with their poetry and prose of divine love and insight. Sufism permeated the Islam and began shaping the faith. The Sufi influence would not last as Islam would later give way to legalism and fundamentalism.

Sufis see God in everything and everything as part of God. Even though they testify that God is one and even though they believe in the Quran as the word of God fundamental Muslims sometimes accuse Sufis of being monism or pantheism. The Sufis tend to believe nothing truly exists but God. They also believe nature and God are two aspects of the same reality. Because of these views, other branches of Islam might not consider Sufis orthodox.

Quba-e-siddique.com reports:
"The Path begins with repentance and submission to a guide or teacher. The teacher guides the disciple on a path that usually includes sexual abstinence, fasting and poverty. The ultimate goal of the Sufi path is to fight the true Holy War against the lower self, which is often represented as a black dog."

Mohammed taught that the greatest jihad or holy war is the one fought within, against our own baser nature.

religionfacts.com/sufism says,
"The Sufi will undergo changes in spiritual states. They are listed as:

 Constraint and happy spiritual expansion,
Fear and hope
Longing and intimacy
Abiding in the moment
Interior knowledge, which is the gnosis of love.

This last state is a union of lover and beloved (man and God). In this final stage the ego is lost to the beloved and the person is transformed as the ego boundary is let down in order to allow the complete melding with the beloved. This stage is often accompanied by spiritual ecstasy.

Quba-e-siddique.com continues,
    "After the annihilation of the self and accompanying ecstatic experience, the mystic enters a "second sobriety" in which he re-enters the world and continues the "journey of God."
    Within the Sufi tradition are: Rituals: Prayers, Music and "Whirling." A rosary of 99 or 33 beads has been in use since as early as the 8th century for counting the thousands of repetitions of prayers and the names of God."

The well-known "Whirling Dervishes" are members of the Mevlevi order of Turkish Sufis, based on the teachings of the famous mystic Rumi (d.1273). The practice of spinning around is the group's distinctive form of sama (listening/meditation). The whirlers, called semazens, are practicing a form of meditation in which they seek to abandon the self and contemplate God, sometimes achieving an ecstatic state. The Mevlevi sect was banned in Turkey by Ataturk in 1925, but performances for tourists are still common throughout the country.

Home Grown Terrorists

Sadly, there does not seem to be a clear demographic outlining the terrorists springing from western countries. In the U.S. the average age of the male is around 25 to 30 years of age. For females seeking to join ISIS or become martyrs the age is between late teens and early 30's. Most are married, have children, and are well educated with good jobs. These are not socially disenfranchised people. They would be considered mainstream citizens. Of those successfully joining the cause, 50% of women and 60% of men die within two years.

Why do they join? They simply believe. They believe in the idea of a pure Islamic nation. They believe ISIS has established the Islamic state ruled and ordered in the way Mohammed had established in the beginning. In believing this and the fact that Mohammed was the infallible prophet, they are drawn to the conclusion this state must represent Islamic Paradise.

They believe they should fight to keep and further the caliphate. It is essential that the caliphate continue to hold land and rules as a sovereign state. For the caliphate to be considered legitimate it must control land. For it to be considered sanctioned by Allah it must continue to defeat its enemies and expand. The caliphate is a nation and as such it must be able to protect its borders and supply basic services to its people.

The Faithful also believe Sharia is the law under which they wish to live. Sharia Law, as established by Mohammed and his early followers, must make up the socio-political underpinning of any pure Islamic society and certainly must be how the caliphate is ruled.

Through social media and by direct contract followers are won over to see the pure fundamental meaning of the Quran. When reduced to black and white and asked if these men and women believe in Islam and what the Quran says, according to the rule of Abrogation, they are by their nature fully committed to the truth presented in the Quran and stated in Sharia Law. Islam is the only religion permitted in the caliphate and ultimately in the world. All others must convert or die. Followers become terrorists to fulfill the calling seen in the literal interpretation of the Quran.

Funding and recuiting for Islamic terrorism at home are groups hiding in plain sight. One of the largest is allegedly promoting terrorism and Sharia Law in the U.S. is CAIR. According to some watchdog groups, The Council on American-Islamic Relations, (CAIR), is a clear and present danger. CAIR was founded in June 1994 by three former officers of the Islamic Association of Palestine (IAP)—Omar Ahmad (IAP President; became CAIR President), Nihad Awad (IAP PR Director; became CAIR Secretary & Treasurer), and Rafeeq Jaber (IAP Chicago Chapter President; became CAIR Vice President). CAIR's first office was located in Washington D.C., as is its present-day headquarters on Capitol Hill.

CAIR doubled its efforts to present Islam as a religion of peace in 2003, after Islam came under examination due to attacks inside the U.S. Its function is to attempt to present Islam as peaceful and compatable with the United States, all the while promoting the supremacy of Islam and Sharia Law.

According the FoxNews.com (11/17/2014), *"A U.S.-based pro-Muslim group that enjoys close ties with the Obama administration has landed on one Arab nation's list of terrorist organizations.*

The Council on American-Islamic Relations (CAIR) was one of 82 groups around the world designated terrorist organizations by the United Arab Emirates, placing it in the company of Al Qaeda, Islamic State and others. While CAIR has previously been linked to Hamas, it has held hundreds of meetings with White House officials on a wide range of community issues and has sought to present itself as a mainstream Muslim organization."

Stop and let that sink in. CAIR is in bed with President Obama, who supports them, even though they are connected to Hammas and seek to destroy Israel. The Obama administration conintues to put pressure on the UAE to remove CAIR from their list of terrorist organizations, even though the UAE should know best who the true Islamic terrorists are.

The National Review (11/28/2014) reported, *"We who follow the Islamist movement fell off our collective chair on November 15, when the news came that the United Arab Emirates' ministerial cabinet had listed the Council on American-Islamic Relations (CAIR) as one of 83 proscribed terrorist organizations, up there with the Taliban, al-Qaeda, and ISIS. This came as a surprise because the UAE authorities themselves have a record of promoting Islamism; because CAIR has a history of raising funds in the UAE; and because the UAE embassy in Washington had previously praised CAIR. On reflection, however, the listing makes sense for, in recent years, the Islamist movement has gravely fractured. Sunnis fight Shiites; advocates of violence struggle against those working within the system; modernizers do battle against those trying to return to the seventh century; and monarchists confront republicans. This last divide concerns us here. After decades of working closely with the Muslim Brotherhood (MB) and its related institutions, the Persian Gulf monarchies (with the single, striking exception of Qatar) have come to see the MB complex of institutions as a threat to their existence. The Saudi, Emirati, Kuwaiti, and Bahraini rulers now view politicians like Mohamed Morsi of Egypt as their enemies, as they do Hamas and its progeny — including CAIR.*

Having explained why the UAE listed CAIR on its terror manifest, we must ask a second question: Is the listing warranted? Can a Washington-based organization with ties to the Obama White House, the U.S. Congress, leading media outlets, and prestigious universities truly be an instigator of terrorism? CAIR can rightly be so characterized. True, it does not set off bombs, but, as the UAE's foreign minister explains, "Our threshold is quite low. . . . We cannot accept incitement or funding." Indeed, CAIR incites, funds, and does much more vis-à-vis terrorism: It apologizes for terrorist groups: Challenged repeatedly to denounce Hamas and Hezbollah as terrorist groups, CAIR denounces the acts of violence but not their sponsors. It is connected to Hamas: Hamas, designated a terrorist organization by the U.S. and many other governments, indirectly created CAIR and the two groups remain tight. Examples: In 1994, CAIR head Nihad Awad publicly declared his support for Hamas; the Holy Land Foundation (HLF), a Hamas front group, contributed $5,000 to CAIR; in turn, CAIR exploited the 9/11 attacks to raise money for HLF; and, this past August, demonstrators at a CAIR-sponsored rally in Florida proclaimed "We are Hamas!" It settled a lawsuit: CAIR initiated a libel lawsuit in 2004 over five statements by a group called Anti-CAIR. But two years later, CAIR settled the suit with prejudice (meaning that it cannot be reopened), implicitly acknowledging the accuracy of Anti-CAIR's assertions, which included: "CAIR is a terrorist supporting front *organization that is partially funded by terrorists"; "CAIR . . . is supported by terrorist supporting individuals, groups and countries"; "CAIR has proven links to, and was founded by, Islamic terrorists"; and "CAIR actively supports terrorists and terrorist supporting groups and nations." It includes individuals accused of terrorism: At least seven board members or staff at CAIR have been arrested, denied entry to the U.S., or were indicted on or pled guilty to (or were convicted of) terrorist charges: Siraj Wahhaj, Bassem Khafagi, Randall ("Ismail") Royer, Ghassan Elashi, Rabih Haddad, Muthanna Al-Hanooti, and Nabil Sadoun. It is in trouble with the law: Federal prosecutors in 2007 named CAIR (along with two other Islamic organizations) as "unindicted co-conspirators and/or joint venturers" in a criminal conspiracy to support Hamas financially. In 2008, the FBI ended contacts with CAIR because of concern about its continuing terrorist ties. On learning of the UAE listing, CAIR called it "shocking and bizarre," then got to work to have the Department of State protest and undo the ruling. Nothing loath, department spokesperson Jeff Rathke noted that the U.S. government, which "does not consider these organizations to be terrorist organizations," has asked for more information about the UAE decision. The UAE minister of state for foreign affairs replied that if organizations can show that their "approach has changed," they are eligible to appeal "to have their names eliminated from the list." Pressure from the Obama administration might reverse the UAE listing. Even so, this will not undo its lasting damage. For the first time, an Islamist government has exposed the malign, terroristic quality of CAIR — a stigma CAIR can never escape. "*

Omar Ahmad is the co-Founder of the Council on American-Islamic Relations, CAIR-SFBA Executive Committee Member, President and CEO of Silicon Expert Technologies, and Former Islamic Association for Palestine (IAP) Officer. Ahmad writes,

"Those who stay in America should be open to society without melting, keeping Mosques open so anyone can come and learn about Islam. If you choose to live here, you have a responsibility to deliver the message of Islam ... Islam isn't in America to be equal to any other faiths, but to become dominant. The Koran, the Muslim book of scripture, should be the highest authority in America, and Islam the only accepted religion on Earth."

"Fighting for freedom, fighting for Islam, that is not suicide," ... "They kill themselves for Islam." (Ahmad Praising Suicide Bombers)

"Address people according to their minds. When I speak with the American, I speak with someone who doesn't know anything."

Ibrahim Hooper is CAIR Spokesperson, and Former Employee of Islamic Association for Palestine (IAP). Commenting on CAIR's record of supporting Hamas, Hezbullah and other official terrorist groups He writes, "CAIR does not support these groups publicly."

He goes on to say, "I wouldn't want to create the impression that I wouldn't like the government of the United States to be Islamic sometime in the future...But I'm not going to do anything violent to promote that. I'm going to do it through education."

According to "Middle East Forum",
The Department of Homeland Security refuses to deal with it. Senator Charles Schumer (Democrat, New York) describes it as an organization "which we know has ties to terrorism."[3] Senator Dick Durbin (Democrat, Illinois) observes that CAIR is "unusual in its extreme rhetoric and its associations with groups that are suspect."[4] Steven Pomerantz, the FBI's former chief of counterterrorism, notes that "CAIR, its leaders, and its activities effectively give aid to international terrorist groups."[5] The family of John P. O'Neill, Sr., the former FBI counterterrorism chief who perished at the World Trade Center, named CAIR in a lawsuit as having "been part of the criminal conspiracy of radical Islamic terrorism"[6] responsible for the September 11 atrocities. Counterterrorism expert Steven Emerson calls it "a radical fundamentalist front group for Hamas."[7]

Of particular note are the American Muslims who reject CAIR's claim to speak on their behalf. The late Seifeldin Ashmawy, publisher of the New Jersey-based Voice of Peace, called CAIR the champion of "extremists whose views do not represent Islam."[8] Jamal Hasan of the Council for Democracy and Tolerance explains that CAIR's goal is to spread "Islamic hegemony the world over by hook or by crook."[9] Kamal Nawash, head of Free Muslims Against Terrorism, finds that CAIR and similar groups condemn terrorism on the surface while endorsing an ideology that helps foster extremism, adding that "almost all of their members are theocratic Muslims who reject secularism and want to establish Islamic states."[10] Tashbih Sayyed of the Council for Democracy and Tolerance calls CAIR "the most accomplished fifth column" in the United States.[11] And Stephen Schwartz of the Center on Islamic Pluralism writes that "CAIR should be considered a foreign-based subversive organization, comparable in the Islamist field to the Soviet-controlled Communist Party, USA."[12]

CAIR, for its part, dismisses all criticism, blaming negative comments on "Muslim bashers" who "can never point to something CAIR has done in its 10-year history that is objectionable."[13] Actually, there is much about the organization's history that is objectionable – and it is readily apparent to anyone who bothers to look.

[3] FDCH Political Transcripts, Sept. 10, 2003.

[4] "Bad CAIR Day: Ex-staffer pleads guilty to terror charges, Senate asks questions on 9/11 anniversary," Center for Security Policy, accessed Jan. 9, 2006.

[5] Joseph Farah, "Between the Lines: The Real CAIR," WorldNetDaily, Apr. 25, 2003; Steve Pomerantz, "Counterterrorism in a Free Society," The Journal of Counterterrorism & Security International, Spring 1998.

[6] Estate of John P. O'Neill, Sr. et al. vs. Al Baraka Investment and Development Corporation, DanielPipes.org, accessed Jan. 9, 2006.

[7] Steven Emerson, "Re: Terrorism and the Middle East Peace Process," prepared testimony before the U.S. Senate Foreign Relations Committee, Subcommittee on Near East and South Asia, Mar. 19, 1996.

[8] The Jerusalem Post, Mar. 5, 1999.

[9] Personal communication from Jamal Hasan to Daniel Pipes, July 25, 2003.

[10] The Washington Times, Oct. 1, 2004.

[11] Melissa Radler, "A Different Face of Islam," Jerusalem Post International Edition, July 18, 2003.

[12] Stephen Schwartz, "An Activist's Guide to Arab and Muslim Campus and Community Organizations in North America," FrontPageMagazine.com, May 26, 2003.

[13] Free Muslims Coalition, July 5, 2004.

[14] *Colin Powell, remarks at Iftaar dinner, Benjamin Franklin Room, Washington, D.C., Nov. 18, 2002.*

[15] *"CAIR-St. Louis Meets with Palestinian Journalists," CAIR, July 27, 2004; Nihad Awad biography, CAIR website, accessed Jan. 12, 2006.*

According to the website "religionofpeace.com" alligations against CAIR include:

CAIR was created by the Muslim Brotherhood, an Islamic supremacist organization that pioneered 20th century Islamic terrorism and sanctions violence against civilians.

CAIR only has about 5,000 members, despite a membership fee of just $10.

CAIR represents the opinions of only 12% of Muslim-Americans according to Gallup.

CAIR receives financial support from foreign powers who have also provided direct support to Osama bin Laden, al-Qaeda and Hamas.

CAIR has solicited money from sponsors of terror and received financial support from convicted terrorists.

CAIR founders have praised terrorists to Muslim audiences and said that suicide bombers are acting on behalf of Islam.

CAIR has raised funds for terrorists under the guise of helping 9/11 victims.

CAIR board members have called for the overthrow of the United States and the imposition of Islamic law. CAIR has suggested applying Sharia punishment (ie. the death penalty) to users who criticize Islam on the Internet.

At least 15 high-level CAIR staff members have been under federal investigation for ties to Islamic terror.

CAIR has discouraged Muslim-Americans from cooperating with law enforcement and has spent more time and money advocating on behalf of convicted terrorists than for their victims.

There are other Islamic organizations promoting unrest while putting on a nice face for the media. One of the major problems in America today is the blindness and leftist leanings of the media. The media of the US does not think, believe, or hold the same values as the American people. They see their job as indoctrination and education rather than reporting the facts. As such, they leave themselves open to propaganda by groups like CAIR.

Sufism fights the metaphorical internal jihad and seeks to find God within a purified heart. Their numbers are few and many Muslims do not consider them truly Islamic.

Shia and Suuni fundamentalists are prepared to kill anyone they do not consider true believers, including those of the other sects.

Salafis prepare for war but wait for Allah to bring it about. At any time their leader could proclaim it is Allah's timing for jihad. Young people, who by their nature see things as black and white, seek the purest form of their faith, which propels them into killing, because that was the last thing Mohammed proclaimed and commanded. Each time there is a division, like many other fundamentalist movements before them, the break away group seeks to become more pious, pure, and holy than the last. Each time this leads to more horrific violence as they seek to emulate the life and teachings of Mohammed. What is the common thread? It is the letter of the law and literal interpretation of the Quran.

Think about how many people have been killed because of a literal interpretation of the Bible. Now, project that scenario into a world where fundamentalists have twenty-first century weapons and capabilities.

With the exception of Sufism, the other sects of Islam are so positive of their religious correctness that each developed a position of fundamentalism. Fundamentalism indicates and unwavering attachment to a set of beliefs. It indicates a tendency among certain religious groups that is characterized by a markedly strict literalism as applied to certain specific scriptures, dogmas, or ideologies, and a strong sense of the importance of maintaining purity of ideals and beliefs among members. Fundamentalism rejects diversity of opinion from accepted religious interpretation within the group. Fundamentalism is exclusive and divisive. It does not have to be violent. Take the Christian Amish for example. They exclude other groups. They believe themselves to be pure. They take a literal view of scripture and doctrine. Yet, they live among others in peace and tranquility. It is only when fundamentalism turns from exclusive to intolerant that violence begins. When one turns from being intolerant of other views to being intolerant of the existence of those maintaining other views intolerance turns to violence and murder. Chapter 9 of the Quran is a command from Mohammed to turn Fundamentalism into an excuse for violence and murder.

A Brief History on the Spread of Islam

In the article "The Truth about Islamic Crusades and Imperialism" November 27, 2005 in American Thinker , James Arlandson writes,

In 630, two years before Mohammed's death of a fever, he launches the Tabuk Crusades, in which he led 30,000 jihadists against the Byzantine Christians. He had heard a report that a huge army had amassed to attack Arabia, but the report turned out to be a false rumor. The Byzantine army never materialized. He turned around and went home, but not before extracting "agreements" from northern tribes. They could enjoy the "privilege" of living under Islamic "protection" if they paid a tax."

This is very much like a tax that businesses had to pay to the mafia for their "protection". Of course the protection was from the mafia itself, which would burn down the buildings and assault those who dared not to pay. Likewise, the only protection one received when paying the Islamic tax were from Muslim raiders who would attack, pillage, and rape those who were not on the list of taxed infidels. The tax was political extortion.

Arlandson continues,
"Two classes of residents were established. The native residents paid a tax that their rulers did not have to pay. Non-Muslim residence lived under certain restrictions.
Christians and Jews could not bear arms.
Christians and Jews could not ride horses.
Christians and Jews had to get permission to build houses or shops.
No under faith could proselytize
Christians and Jews had to bow to their Muslim masters when they paid their taxes.
Christians and Jews had to live under the law set forth in the Quran. Other religious or secular laws were forbidden.
This tax sets the stage for Mohammed's and the later Caliphs' policies. If the attacked city or region did not want to convert to Islam, then they paid a jizya tax. If they converted, then they paid a zakat tax. Either way, money flowed back to the Islamic treasury in Arabia or to the local Muslim governor.

Islam's mission is to correct the injustices of the world. What he has in mind is that if Islam does not control a society, then injustice dominates it, ipso facto. But if Islam dominates it, then justice rules it (In the Shade of the Quran, vol. 7, pp. 8-15). Islam is expansionist and must conquer the whole world to express Allah's perfect will on this planet."

Karen Armstrong, a former nun and well-known writer attempted to explain or justify the Muslim Crusades.
"Once [Abu Bakr] crushed the rebellion [against Islamic rule within Arabia], Abu Bakr may well have decided to alleviate internal tensions by employing the unruly energies within the ummah [Muslim community] against external foes."

One could believe that a ruler of a warlike people may direct their energies outward until he could find a way to channel the energies inward toward production and growth, but the wars went on much longer than that scenario would allow.

Under the Caliphate of Abu Bakr, in 633 Muslim armies began a series of campaigns in Persia, Syria and Iraq. The Muslim armies forced conversion at the end of a sword and killed or converted the polytheists and pagans of Arabia.

This is an important distinction between polytheists and monotheistic "Children of the Book" such as Jews and Christians. Polytheists are not offered the choice of conversion or taxation. Polytheists are only offered the choice of conversion or death.
Monotheists, such as Jews and Christians were treated somewhat differently. They must pay a tax to the Islamic state if they wish to continue to worship. Even then, their religious freedom is truncates and they cannot worship openly or convert anyone to their faith. Punishment for such an act is swift and harsh, and is usually death.

The Caliphate and its generals pushed their armies, even though the soldiers may have been tired of war and wanted to go home. They continually urged the troupes to escalate their atrocities in hopes that terror would spread and the surrounding population would surrender and convert without a struggle.

James Arlandson writes,

But improvement of life materially must be included in this not-so-holy call. When Khalid perceived that his Muslim Crusaders desired to return to Arabia, he pointed out how luscious the land of the Persians was: "Do you not regard [your] food like a dusty gulch? By God, if struggle for God's sake and calling [people] to God were not required of us, and there were no consideration except our livelihood, the wise opinion would [still] have been to strike this countryside until we possess it". . . . (Tabari 11:20 / 2031)

633 The Muslim Crusaders, led by Khalid al-Walid, a superior but bloodthirsty military commander, whom Mohammed nicknamed the Sword of Allah for his ferocity in battle (Tabari, 8:158 / 1616-17), conquer the city of Ullays along the Euphrates River in today's Iraq. So many were beheaded that the central city canal was called Blood Canal (Tabari 11:24 / 2034-35).

Khalid al-Walid (d. 642), a bloodthirsty but superior commander of the Muslim armies at the time, also answers the question as to why the Muslims stormed out of Arabia, in his terms of surrender set down to the governor of al-Hirah, a city along the Euphrates River in Iraq. He is sent to call people to Islam or pay a "protection" tax for the "privilege" of living under Islamic rule (read: not to be attacked again) as dhimmis or second-class citizens. Says Khalid:

"I call you to God and to Islam. If you respond to the call, you are Muslims: You obtain the benefits they enjoy and take up the responsibilities they bear. If you refuse, then [you must pay] the jizyah. If you refuse the jizyah, I will bring against you tribes of people who are more eager for death than you are for life. We will fight you until God decides between us and you." (Tabari, The Challenge to the Empires, trans. Khalid Yahya Blankinship, NY: SUNYP, 1993, vol. 11, p. 4; Arabic page 2017)

Thus, according to Khalid, religion is early Islam's primary motive (though not the only one) of conquering people.

In a short sermon, Abu Bakr says:

. . . Indeed, the reward in God's book for jihad in God's path is something for which a Muslim should love to be singled out, by which God saved [people] from humiliation, and through which He has bestowed nobility in this world and the next. (Tabari 11:80 / 2083-84)

Thus, the Caliph repeats the Quran's trade of this life for the next, in an economic bargain and in the context of jihad (cf. Suras 4:74; 9:111 and 61:10-13). This offer of martyrdom, agreeing with Donner's first factor, religious motivation, is enough to get young Muslims to sign up for and to launch their Crusades out of Arabia in the seventh century.

Khalid also says that if some do not convert or pay the tax, then they must fight an army that loves death as other people love life (see 634).

Khalid was from Mecca. At the time of this "motivational" speech, the Empire of Persia included Iraq, and this is where Khalid is warring. Besides his religious goal of Islamizing its inhabitants by warfare, Khalid's goal is to "possess" the land.

Thereafter, Islam would take on the bloodthirsty approach seen today. In a brief timeline one can see how battles spread outward through the Mid-East and beyond, all under the same banner and battle cry as it began.

634 The beginning of the Battle of Yarmuk. Syria the Muslim Crusaders defeat the Byzantines.

635 Muslim Crusaders conquer Damascus.

636- 637 The defeat of the Byzantines at Yarmuk.

637 The Muslim army conquers Iraq at the Battle of al-Qadisiyyah

638 Islamic army conquers and takes control of the Holy Lands and annex Jerusalem.

638-650 Muslim Crusaders conquer Iran.

639-642 Islamic army conquers Egypt.

641 They take control of Syria and Palestine.

644-650 Muslim Crusaders conquer Cyprus and parts of North Africa. They establish Islamic rule in Iran, which includes what is now Afghanistan.

This begins a period of internal conflict between the Shia and Sunni sects as the fight for who would control Islam. In this period there were assassinations and battles between the sects.

673-678 Arabs attack Constantinople

691 In Jerusalem, the main Mosque, the Dome of the Rock is completed.

710-713 Muslims attack and take the lower Indus Valley.

711-713 Muslim Crusaders conquer Spain and impose the kingdom of Andalus. Six years later the Arabs would rule from Cordova, Spain.

James Arlandson reports that modern Muslims still grieve over their expulsion from Spain, when Christian forces took it back. They believe that the land belonged to them in the first place. How they could come to this conclusion shows the depth of imperialism and their belief in some sort of manifest destiny.

732 Muslim armies continued to venture into Europe and fought the Battle of Poitier in France, where they were stopped.

This begins a period where Islamic roots were deepened in the conquered territories. Mosques were built and governments were established.

809 Muslim armies continued to advance into Europe. They attack and conquer Sardinia, Italy.

813 Christians in Palestine are attacked.

831 Muslims advance into Southern Italy, continuing to push into Europe.

837-901 Muslim Crusaders conquer Sicily and Corsica, Italy. They push into France.

909 Parts of Italy are occupied.

928-969 Byzantine armies fight to retake Cyprus and Tarsus.

937–939 Islamic rulers firm up their grip on the conquered Christians by burning and razing churches and demanding conversion or death.

969 Egypt is taken and the city of Cairo is established as an Islamic seat.

1071 Muslim Turks fight the Battle of Manzikert, defeating the Byzantines. They take Anatolia.

1071 Muslim Turks invade Palestine.

1073 Turks conquer Jerusalem

1076 Muslims venture further into Africa and conquer western Ghana.

1085 Toledo is taken back by Christian armies.

For centuries Christians and Muslims have been playing a child's game of, "He hit me first." They argue about whom first encroached and who threw the first punch. The fact is that Pope Urban II began the Medieval Crusades in 1095 as a response to Muslim aggression that had been going on for centuries. Urban II knew if he did not stop them the Muslim army would destroy Christendom in the Middle East and then spread throughout Europe. So it is only after all of the Islamic aggressive invasions that western Christendom launched its first Crusades.

History.com reports,
"The first of the Crusades began in 1095, when armies of Christians from Western Europe responded to Pope Urban II's plea to go to war against Muslim forces in the Holy Land. After the First Crusade achieved its goal with the capture of Jerusalem in 1099, the invading Christians set up several Latin Christian states, even as Muslims in the region vowed to wage holy war (jihad) to regain control over the region. Deteriorating relations between the Crusaders and their Christian allies in the Byzantine Empire culminated in the sack of Constantinople in 1204 during the Third Crusade. Near the end of the 13th century, the rising Mamluk

dynasty in Egypt provided the final reckoning for the Crusaders, toppling the coastal stronghold of Acre and driving the European invaders out of Palestine and Syria in 1291."

Like his Muslim counterpart, Urban II assured the crusaders that they were not only permitted to kill non-Christians, but they would be rewarded in heaven for doing so. As for their reward here in earth, the Pope granted them complete pardon from all sins they had and would commit. It seems that no matter the faith or nationality, leaders seeking power and control tend to sink to the same low standards.

Islamic expansion continues until well into the seventeenth century. Muslims Crusaders conquer Constantinople in 1453 and attempted to overrun Vienna in 1529 and second time in 1683. By the eighteenth centuries, the Islamic raids began to slow, due to western resistance.

During the 15th and 16th centuries Islam spreads through the Malay Peninsula and the islands of Sumatra and Java.

In the mid 16th century North Africa and lands all the way to India were influenced if not infiltrated.

Why did Muslim Crusades continue for so long and reach so far?

Both the blog, "Winds of Islam" and The American Thinker cites Fred M. Donner, the dean of historians specializing in the early Islamic conquests as saying,
"Three large factors for the Islamic Crusades. First, the ideological message of Islam itself triggered the Muslim ruling elite simply to follow Mohammed and his conquests; Islam had a divinely ordained mission to conquer in the name of Allah. (The Early Islamic Conquests, Princeton UP, 1981, p. 270).
The second factor is economic. The ruling elite "wanted to expand the political boundaries of the new state in order to secure even more fully than before the trans-Arab commerce they had plied for a century or more" (p. 270).

The final factor is political control. The rulers wanted to maintain their top place in the new political hierarchy by having aggressive Arab tribes migrate into newly conquered territories (p. 271). Thus, these reasons have nothing to do with just wars of self-defense. Early Islam was merely being aggressive without sufficient provocation from the surrounding Byzantine and Persian Empires."

Muslim polemicists believe that Islam spread militarily by a miracle from Allah.

From this, we can see the pattern of war, killing, and conquest without provocation has been part of Islam from its beginning.

Did the Islamic Crusades force conversions by the sword?
Historical facts demonstrate that most of the conquered cities and regions accepted taxation and "protection" with the ability to continue their own religious practice if they were "people of the book". Meaning Jews and Christians. Muslim Crusaders offer three options by point of the sword: (1) fight and die, (2) convert and pay the zakat tax; (3) keep their Biblical faith and pay the jizya tax. Most preferred to remain in their own religion and pay the higher tax.

The vast majority of conquered people did not read or write, and did not have a deep grasp of doctrine, even if a general amnesty were granted to People of the Book. When they saw a Muslim army outside their gates many converted and continued with their lives. "

In the Muslim community, the holy war is a religious duty to convert everybody. If the people under attack continued to revolt, simple conquest would turn to killing and slaughtering.

Part of the strategy of conquest was to displace the native population and replace them with a Muslim population. Millions were left homeless and starving under this principle.

Fred M. Donner continues:
"Consider the Ottoman invasion of Christian Eastern Europe in which the Ottoman Empire invaded the west and conquered and colonized Greece, all of the Balkans, Romania, Bessarabia, and Hungary, and was stopped only at the outskirts of Vienna in 1529.

Consider also the Muhgal conquest of Northern India in the early 1600s. In the 20th century alone:

1. Muslim Turkey has expelled approximately 1,500,000 Greeks from its empire in the east and replaced them with Turks. They have massacred approximately 2 million Armenians and replaced them with Turks in the west.

2. Muslim Turkey has invaded and occupied northern Cyprus, displacing the Greeks living there.

3. Muslim northern Sudan has conquered much of southern Sudan, enslaving its Christian and pagan population.

4. Indonesian occupied all of non-Islamic western New Guinea and incorporated it into Indonesia.

5. Muslim Indonesia has invaded and conquered Christian East Timor with horrible loss of life.

6. Muslim Indonesia is attempting to destroy Christianity in what used to be called the Celebes.

7. A half-dozen Arab countries have fought multiple wars in an attempt to destroy Israel and occupy its territory with the consent of 55 of the world's 57 Islamic nations.

8. Muslim Libya has blown up western aircraft, killing many.

9. Muslim Iraq invaded and occupied Muslim Kuwait because they were too connected to the west and were the wrong sect.

10. Muslim Iraq invaded Muslim Iran with a resulting death of 2 million people because they were of different sects.

11. Muslim Albania is attempting to enlarge its borders at Christian Macedonia's expense.

12. Muslim Northern Nigeria is fighting against the Christian south.

13. Muslims expelled approximately 800,000 Jews from their homelands between 1947 and 1955.

14. During Jordan's occupation of the West Bank, the kingdom undertook an unsuccessful attempt to make Jerusalem a Muslim city by forcing out approximately 10,000 Christian inhabitants."

The map below shows the relative concentration of Muslims in the populations in 2014. Black areas show 80-100%. Gray areas show 50-80% Muslim population.

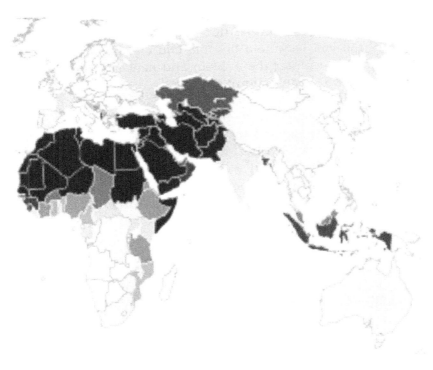

Islam is not just a religion. It is a system, which combines political force with preset laws and structure. It seeks to rule the land as well as the souls of the people. It does this by imposing a strict hierarchy of ruling clerics who have civil and governmental authority. Its aim and focus is to rule over every person on earth and to consolidate a worldwide territory into a single caliphate.

It would be remiss at this point not to briefly mention women in Islam and their recent history. It may not be what one would think. Women had been fighting for their rights and making progress. Afghan women were first eligible to vote in 1919. In the 1950's gender separation, a type of separate but equal division of sexes, was abolished. In the 1960's the constitution of Afghanistan was changed to give women equal rights. By the early 1970's women could be seen in mini skirts walking to see a movie. Then, the Soviets invaded and the Mujahideen rose up and things began to change. By the time the Taliban took over the rights of women had crumbled to nothing. The veil did not appear as a common item until around the tenth century. After that the culture reinforced modesty until the veil became a burqua, Old cultural views were fanned back to flame under the Taliban and hajibs were replaced with burquas as the Taliban's control grew.

Under the Taliban, women and girls were discriminated against. The Taliban enforced their strict version of Sharia law. Women and girls were banned from going to school or studying, from working, from being involved in politics or speaking in public, from leaving the house without a male chaperone, from showing their skin in public, and even from accessing healthcare delivered by men. Later, women would be allowed to serve other women and some basic care would become available.

Cultural pressures returned, as seen in the Pashto phrase: 'A woman belongs in the house or in a grave.' In Kabul, residents were ordered to cover their windows so women inside could not be seen from the street. If a woman left the house, it was to be in a full body burqa. A woman could be flogged for allowing just an inch of skin to show. Women were beaten for attempting to study, stoned if she was found guilty of adultery, and if she wore clear nail polish a woman could get her thumbs cut off.

In 2001 most of the Taliban were ousted and by 2003 schools for girls opened and laws were changed to uphold the rights of women. But the Taliban still rule pockets of the country and where they go, oppression follows. Since ISIS is an ideological extension of the Taliban, under ISIS women have once again returned to being property and slaves.

Islam and Terrorism

Religions usually have a fundamental arm. These individuals see religion from a pre-axial-age viewpoint of external actions pleasing a god who would judge them worthy to inherit a kingdom, either heavenly or earthly. In an attempt to please their god believers will continually eliminate actions and deeds that are not addressed by their books or prophets. They follow the letter of the law more and more fiercely. They will then turn against others who do not follow their strict interpretation. One sect or denomination will split from another, which they view as too lenient or too permissive and will proceed independently in a never-ceasing attempt to purify the faith and please their god, usually by eliminating everyone who is deemed inferior in faith, race, or attitude.

We can see this evolution in small ways even in the modern Christian denominations. If one is Catholic it is permitted to smoke and drink. A Baptist may smoke but not drink. Church of God attendees are told they should neither smoke nor drink. Many "Jesus Only" denominations do not allow smoking, drinking, secular dances, or even playing cards. And so it goes as the more pious the followers become the smaller the target to hit to gain heaven.

In some ways we see this in the ongoing splintering of Islam as it becomes more restrictive and violent. Some splinters were artificially created. These tended to focus on political position and power, since they were created via that pressure. Other splinter groups were not only political but also religious in their goals. Keeping in mind that Islam is a socio-political system in which a religion drives the social order, we see in the following groups various combinations of social, political, and religious concerns. Make no mistake – we, the United States and the western powers, are partially to blame for the spread of radical Islam. We kicked the fire-ant hill without forethought. We supplied arms to groups that in turned fought us with our own weapons. Through our interference we destabilized the Middle East. Power vacuums formed and radical groups took advantage. The wild cat is out of the bag. Now they seek a common enemy to unite them. It is us.

Mujahedeen, Taliban, Al Qaeda, and ISIS

Mujahedeen

Mujahideen is an Arabic word that refers to any person performing Jihad. The modern term refers to a guerrilla group of radical Islamists fighters. The group originated in the 19th century opposition of Afghanistan mountain men who fought against British control. From December 1979 to February 1989 the group fought when Russia invaded Afghanistan. The roots of that war lay in the overthrow of the Afghanistan government in April 1978 by left-wing military officers, who then handed power over to the People's Democratic Party of Afghanistan. The new government forged close ties with the Soviet Union. They began a ruthless purges of all opposition. The killing and reforms were bitterly resented by the devoutly Muslim and largely anti-Communist population. In this climate the Mujahideen fought Russia and the government.

In the Guardian 's article "The 1980s mujahedeen, the Taliban and the Shifting Idea of Jihad" Nushin Arbabzadah wrote:
"The original mujahedeen of the 1980s and today's Taliban may use the same language of holy war, but their understanding of jihad is worlds apart. The key difference between the original mujahedeen and the Taliban is that the former waged a traditional type of jihad. In a traditional jihad, if waged locally, a contest over control of resources takes place between rival strongmen who each run their own private armies. In this scenario, the ultimate legitimacy to rule draws upon military strength, but the contest itself is called jihad simply because Islam is the sole language of political legitimacy. Once there is an aggressor, jihad may be called and the war begins.
Crucially, in a traditional jihad, the victorious party has an unspoken right to pillage, rape and loot the conquered population. This is because militia fighters are not paid soldiers in a regular army. They fight a proxy religious war and hence looting is the material reward they receive for fighting. The original mujahedeen followed this traditional pattern of jihad when it came to power in

1992. Since competition over resources rather than ideology is key to traditional jihad, the mujahedeen's war focused on Kabul where the nation's wealth and the foreign embassies, and other potential sources of funding, could be found.

In the 1920s the Mujahedeen conquered Kabul. At that time the women and girls of the conquered population belonged to the Mujahedeen as a "pillage package" and were offered to militia jihadis. Hence, in the diaries of court chronicler Katib Hazara on the siege of Kabul in 1929, we read that the victorious mujahedeen had demanded to see the list of girls registered at a Kabul school so as to allocate or divide the female students up and give them to the militia fighters."

Recruits to the mujahideen came in large numbers from young Afghan men living in refugee camps in Pakistan. Throughout the 1980s thousands of volunteers joined from across the Muslim world, especially from Arab countries. It was at this time that a young Saudi Arabian, Osama bin Laden began funding the army with his personal wealth.

The Taliban's conquest of Afghanistan in 1996 did not follow traditional paths of raping and pillaging. The Taliban militia did not seek loot. Instead, they searched homes and confiscated weapons and so ensured their power over the people.

The Taliban saw jihad as a means to establish a state. Building a state was of utmost importance to the Taliban because without it the sharia law could not be enforced. If the mujahedeen struggled over resources, the Taliban were concerned with religion and the laws that they believed Islam demanded.

The Taliban's choice of their capital city, Kandahar, was a much poorer city than Kabul. Kabul held the nation's wealth and the foreign embassies were concentrated there but the Taliban seemed not to care about wealth. In contrast, the mujahedeen's vicious fight over the city resulted in thousands of dead and public buildings destroyed in rocket attacks, all for the right to loot the city.

Accounts of meetings with Taliban officials all reveal a lack of interest in material wealth of status. Meetings would be held seated on the floor in a circle. Ironically, such egalitarianism was what the communists had dreamed of in 1978.

This was likely an attempt on the part of the Taliban to force equality with the more educated urban people they had just conquered. When the Taliban took over, rural Afghans came to power, ruling over the more educated urban populations.

Fighting for resources in a traditional fashion complete with looting and pillaging versus fighting for a state that would enforce sharia law even to the point of an obsessive preoccupation with the correct length of young men's pubic hair is what distinguishes the original mujahedeen from their Taliban nemesis."

Taliban

The Taliban emerged as a resistance movement aiming to eject the Soviet troops from Afghanistan. The Soviets had invaded in 1979 and had engaged the Mujahideen. With the United States and Pakistan providing considerable financial and military support, the Afghan Mujahideen were able to push back the Soviet troops. According to The New York Times, the Soviet Union lost about 15,000 soldiers in Afghanistan. In 1989, the Soviet troops withdrew from Afghanistan, leaving a power vacuum. The Afghan government that was backed by the Soviet Union and led by President Sayid Mohammed Najibullah was overthrown. The Afghan Mujahideen, under the leadership of Ahmed Shah Massoud, surrounded the Afghan capital, Kabul, and established rule. This uneasy peace lasted three years as the Mujahideen looted the city. The Mujahideen alliance tried to reach across the country and establish a national government led by Burhanuddin Rabbani. Due to their rough and warlike approach they failed to reach political unity within the party and ended up fighting one another. The Mujahideen fractured into smaller factions. The Taliban was one of these splinter groups that formed during the Soviet occupation and the internal fighting in Afghanistan.

The Taliban emerged as a powerful movement in late 1994 when Pakistan chose the Taliban to guard a convoy trying to open a trade route from Pakistan to Central Asia. Pakistan equipped, trained, and funded the Taliban. Soon, the Taliban gained control over several Afghan cities and in September 1996 they captured Kabul. The Taliban controlled most of Afghan .

Pakistan continues to support the Taliban because of strong religious and ethnic bonds between the Taliban and Pakistan. Tribal areas on and near the North-West borders of Pakistan share common ethnic and religious roots. The Taliban is made up of Sunni Muslim Pashtuns, who make up thirteen percent of the total population of Pakistan but who dominate the Pakistani military.

The people of Afghanistan condemned the Saudi monarchy for allowing U.S. troops to enter and operate in Saudi Arabia. Osama Bin Laden led the outcry. To show his commitment and to retaliate he moved to Afghanistan in 1996, where he was welcomed as a fellow warrior and leader by the Taliban and its leader, Mullah Mohammed Omar. Bin Laden recruited militants and ran training camps for the Taliban. There, Bin Laden staged the attack on the U.S.

Out of approximately 113 documents recovered from Bin Laden, two letters addressed to the American people stand out as an attempt to fully explain his reasons and purpose. Bin Laden wrote letters to the American people in 2002 and 2011. The last letter was seized in the May 2, 2011 raid on Bin Laden's Abbottabad hideout. This letter was recently declassified by the Director of National Intelligence in late March of 2015. A copy of both letters, which severs as al-Qaeda manifestos, are contained in appendix "C".

Five days after September 11, 2001, Pakistan's president, Pervez Musharrafsharraf, pledged support for the U.S. efforts to capture Bin Laden and fight militant groups. Immediately demonstrations by the pro-Taliban groups in Pakistan flooded the streets.

The United States moved to Iraq in 2003 and began hunting the Taliban operating from southern Afghanistan and North-West Pakistan. The Taliban attacked the U.S. and continued to increase until 2006, which was the deadliest year for NATO troops and the Taliban since the 2001 war. NATO launched a large operation against the Taliban militants operating in southern Afghanistan and along the borders with North-West Pakistan, destroying the last Taliban stronghold on Afghan along with most of the Taliban fighters in Afghanistan. The Taliban remains then moved to Pakistan in the Pashtun controlled area.

Between 2003 and 2006 the Pakistani government began to recognize they had lost control of the Taliban and like any such group they had taken on a life and aims of their own. The Pakistani government began to feel threatened. The Taliban had established informants and sympathizers inside the Pakistani military and secret service. The government intervened to contain and counter the Taliban by deploying 80,000 troops in South and North Waziristan. After several confrontations the government had lost eight hundred Pakistani soldiers and the populations, which was pro-Taliban, was becoming more opposed to the government's actions. President Pervez Mushrraf realized that further conflict would destabilize the country.

In September 2006 Pakistan made peace with its demon. President Musharraf signed a peace agreement with seven militant groups in Waziristan, who call themselves Pakistan. Under the terms of the agreement, Pakistan's army agreed to withdraw from the areas controlled by the Taliban, and the Taliban would stop launching attacks against NATO and Afghan troops in Afghanistan and against Pakistani army and government.

It did not take long for the cease-fire to crumble. A Taliban group took over the Red Mosque in Islamabad and attempted to impose Sharia Law in the area. The Pakistani government attacked the mosque and killed over one hundred people. The Taliban responded with a series of suicide- bombings.

Pakistan and the U.S. created the Taliban and they lost control of their creation, causing political venom to be turned on one and religious venom spewed at the other.

On the website of Mount Holyoke College in an article, "Origins of the Taliban" we read:

"The Creation of Taliban goes back to 1979, when the Soviet Union invaded Afghanistan. In 1973, The Soviet Union brought their soldiers into Afghanistan claiming to rebuild the crushing economy. Along with the troops came thousands of weapons. However, the Soviet was resented by the Mujahidin (Mujahideen) (from whom the Taliban evolved). In the 1970's the Soviet Union and United States were engaged in a cold war. Any Soviet venture into another country, whatever the reason, was seen by the U.S. as expansion. The U.S. sought for a counterbalance against the Soviet Union in the area. When the Soviets increased their power and strength in the area the United States decided to intervene.

Because the United States did not want to see the Soviet Union take control over Central Asia, the U.S. decided to fund troops to fight against the Soviet Union. These troops were called the Mujahedeen.

The Mujahedeen were armed and supported by several countries including, the U.S., Pakistan and Saudi Arabia. Under Reagan's presidency, with Congress led by Democrats, the U.S. decided to form a partnership with the ISI (Pakistan's Intelligence Service), which would recruit the Mujahedeen with the support of the Pakistani military. They led the Mujahedeen, with its extreme views of Islam, to fight ferociously against the Soviet Union. The U.S. began dumping arms into the area for use against the Soviet Union. The Soviet Union began to lose their foothold and attempted to increase support and arms into the region. The price of staying in the Middle East took it toll. They could not keep up. The extremist succeeded in driving Soviet militants out in 1989. This unforeseen defeat caused the Soviets to lose billions of dollars, and helped lead to the collapse of the Soviet Union.

After the war, Pakistan was left alone to deal with the problems associated with the post war. Following the 9/11 attacks, the U.S. declared a war against Afghanistan.

At this point the U.S. realized they had created an army of extremists who were now taking on agendas of their own. Taliban was a creation of the Pakistani intelligence agency (the ISI) but was funded by the U.S.

The U.S. gave $3 billion to build this Islamic group in the form of guns and ammunitions, which they forgot to keep track of after the Soviet war.

It should have been no surprise when the millions worth in weapons that they had provided were now being used against them – but sadly, it was.

Since the Taliban was a creation of the Pakistani intelligence agency. Pakistan has been reluctant to fight them. It is said that a lot of Pakistani and other military personal were known to be siding with the Taliban. It has further been said that the U.S. is responsible for providing the Taliban with logistical and military advice, along with military hardware. Therefore the Unites States and Pakistan are accountable for the Creation of the Islamic extremist Group called `Taliban'."

The Taliban has taken a backseat to ISIS only because the Taliban is concerned about local rule and government and is focused on the area in and around Afghanistan. The main objective of the Taliban is to resettle Afghanistan, governed under Sharia Law. They maintain control by implementing a harsh and cruel form of Sharia Law in which there are civilian massacres, random attacks, forced evictions, torture and imprisonment.

Under their version of Sharia Law, Women occupy subservient positions. Their bodies must be completely covered. A man must accompany them if they are outside their home. They can only seek employment in the health care industry and they can attend only to women.
Girls were not allowed to go to school. Men were required to grow untrimmed beards and pray five times a day.

The harsh and unforgiving tactics caused the population to rebel. The more they tried to impose their will, the more the population resented them. They were able to rule about 80% of the territory in their most robust time. But the Taliban was not prepared to govern on a large scale. For that one needs a national infrastructure and an ever-present force.

The United Front, an Islamic group with a less extreme interpretation of Islamic law stepped up to oppose the Taliban. The population began to stand with the United Front against the Taliban.

The Taliban reacted by tightening their grasp and strengthening their enforcement of Sharia Law. Thieves' hands were cut off. Adulterers were stoned to death.

All entertaining activities were banned. Kite flying, listening to music, bird keeping, celebrating, and gambling were forbidden.

All of this alienated the Taliban even more and gained the attention of the United Nations and Amnesty International.

Following the terrorist attacks on the World Trade Center's twin towers in New York City on September 11, 2001, the Taliban actively hid Osama Bin Laden. The Taliban was violently opposed to the United States and its allies. When the Taliban chose to challenge Russia by recognizing the break away government of Chechnya, Russia increased its military support of the United Front.

Taliban's support of Muslim militants in Kashmir turned India against the Taliban. Due to sectarian differences, Iran, Russia, Tajikistan and Uzbekistan missed no opportunity to weaken the Taliban.

With mounting opposition both internally and externally, Taliban and thus Afghanistan became a failed state.

After the attack on the U.S on September 11, President Bush told the American public that the Islamic militant group Al-Qaeda was responsible and the Taliban regime of Afghanistan provided a safe haven for the terrorist organization. The mainstream media and the Bush Administration blended the Taliban and Al-Qaeda together in their rhetoric, but they are not the same. The Taliban played no role in the 9/11 attacks, had no prior knowledge of the attacks. They understood the gravity of the event and know that a response was coming. They quickly publicly condemned the attacks. They offered to try Bin Landen for his crimes, but no western nation believed the trial or sentence would carry any weight. The Taliban refused to turn over Bin Laden. This confirmed the connection between the Taliban and Al-Qaeda in the minds of the American people.

The two organizations are distinct and have very different goals and ideologies. Taliban is plural for talib meaning "student" in Arabic, literally "one who seeks knowledge." They are devoted religious students of Islam who have been in Afghanistan since the creation of madrasas (religious schools), which have been around since the earliest days of Islam. During the Soviet war these Taliban participated in the jihad. The Taliban were known for their skillful fighting capabilities, discipline and determination. They met in the mosque at Sangisar where they officially started the movement to bring order to Afghanistan, believing that education and fighting skills were needed to bring order. They called themselves the Taliban because that is who they were.

The Taliban created the Islamic Emirate of Afghanistan with Mullah Omar as the commander or "ruler of all Muslims." They eliminated warlords and created order. They provided unity, even though it was through a harsh enforcement. Pakistan, Saudi Arabia, and the United Arab Emirates recognized the Taliban as the legitimate government of Afghanistan on May 25, 1997.

Abdulkader Sinno explains the reasons for their success, "The Taliban provided moral clarity, a promise of a just and safe society stemming from a potent vision of Pashtun authenticity, and the satisfaction of being part of a momentous movement that could accomplish what became the stated goal of the jihad started in 1979 – a just Islamic state that would incidentally also terminate non-Pashtun control of the capital" .

The Taliban sought to fix Afghanistan. They restricted their jihad to Afghanistan. Foreign militant groups who declared jihad did not concern Afghanistan and did not involve them. They had a local perspective. The plights of Muslims elsewhere did not concern them. Their goal never went beyond establishing the Taliban's idea of the perfect society within their own borders. Furthermore, the Taliban were not too concerned with the threat of western civilization, instead they were starting to build cozy relationships with the US government and the US oil company UNOCAL. Historically, Afghanistan was different from the Middle East and South Asia in that there was no particular tradition of anti-Western attitudes, excluding the disdain for the British due to a British attempt to invade in years past. If the Taliban could have held on to the government, they would have likely signed agreements with the U.S., transported oil, funded their government, and provided a local Islamic nation, complete with Sharia law, to its people. If the people wish to trade such rule for the chaos and looting of the Mujahideen, what is it to us?

Al-Qaeda

Osama Bin Laden, the founder of Al-Qaeda, first became involved in the jihad in Afghanistan when he established a training facility in Saudi Arabia for jihad recruits travelling to Afghanistan. He provided very basic military training to students and did fundraising for the jihad. Contributors were wealthy individuals, including members of the Saudi royal family. The Saudi government itself pitched in by offering discounts for airlines to Pakistan.

Lawrence Wright explains, "The people who rallied to the Afghan jihad felt that Islam itself was threatened by the advance of communism. Afghanistan meant little to most of them, but the faith of the Afghan people meant a great deal".

This is an important distinction between the Taliban and Al-Qaeda. Al-Qaeda was fighting a global war for Islam, believing it was under attack by western forces and influences. The Taliban fought to free and stabilize Afghanistan.

Osama Bin Laden met Ayman Al-Zawahiri when they both attended a lecture at the hospital where Zawahiri worked as a physician in Saudi Arabia. Al-Zawahiri was the founder of the Egyptian Islamist group Al-Jihad. At first they worked well together. Bin Laden had money and Zawahiri had ideas about recruiting and propaganda.

As the war started to die down in 1988, tension began to rise between Azzam and Zawahiri. Abdullah Yusuf Azzam was the mentor of Bin Laden and is considered the father of global jihad. Bin Laden was caught in the middle and both Azzam and Zawahiri wanted Bin Laden's support and money. Azzam purported to be against the intentional killing of civilians and wanted to focus on the liberation of Palestine, followed by other regions where the U.S. and other nations could not target easily. Zawahiri wanted to start revolutions in Muslim countries in order to destabilize the governments and therefore take control and establish a connected government. Bin Laden wanted to carry the jihad against the Soviet Union. He wanted to go to the Philippines, Kashmir and especially the Central Asian republics. The US was not a target since Bin

Laden and his family were still on the U.S. payroll for the huge construction contracts and other income they had.

On August 11, 1988, at a meeting in Peshawar, the leaders of the Arab legion convened to discuss the future of the jihad. They voted to form a new organization to continue the jihad after the Soviets left Afghanistan. Although some at the meeting were not very familiar with Al-Qaeda, by the end of the meeting they decided to take the name and template of Al-Qaeda as a starting point. The goal was to have 314 men trained within 6 months. The vision of the group was stated, "Al-Qaeda is basically an organized Islamic faction. Its goal is to lift the word of God, to make His religion victorious."

Since Bin Laden had the money and had already established the core group, the council voted him leader. When the Soviets left Afghanistan in 1989, the mujahideen turned their guns on each other. Bin Laden returned to Saudi Arabia to consult with Saudi intelligence and Prince Turki's chief of staff to determine whom to support in the ensuing Afghan civil war. Connections between the Saudi government and Bin Landen were closely connected and jihad flowed accordingly.

Al-Qaeda, sees itself as global, borderless, and committed to stopping western influences by disrupting western society. Al-Qaeda is a diffuse network of individuals, who have no central command. Al-Qaeda leaders do not control or own their operatives, instead they network the operatives through information, contacts, training, and financial support. There is no set of qualities demanded from fighters. Some could drink, smoke, gamble, or enjoy strip clubs. Many are well educated and more secular than religious.

Al-Qaeda's goal is to maintain a globalized, protracted struggle against Israel and the west. Al-Qaeda does not have a prescribed plan for the entire organization but jihad is treated as an individual duty, like any religious ritual, alms, or prayer. Al-Qaeda's holy war transcends politics. It is spiritualized. They do see their jihad as a war against the violation of human rights as informed by their vision of a world dictated by a set of principles. These principles were formed by the study of Islam and Sharia law. The U.S. and other powerful western countries are seen as violators of human rights through their wars and interference with the societies of other countries, which brings about poverty, and injustice, which break with their views of how the world would be under Islam. This is a bit of double-talk since on one side Al-Qaeda claims no "ideology" but justice, and on the other hand the idea of justice is formed in the cauldron of Islam.

According to E-international Relations, *Al-Qaeda's key method of attempting to end US dominance throughout the world is to provide the right circumstances for the US to commit suicide. Because Al-Qaeda is not a conventional force and its operations are coordinated over the internet, quite possibly in an internet café in Atlanta, the US can only confront the terrorist menace by attacking itself, through the shredding of the constitution and the stifling of the technological, demographic, and financial mobility that contributes to the US's economic might.*

In a special hearing to congress on December 08, 2001, J.T. Caruso, the Acting Assistant Director of the FBI's Counterterrorism Division, testified:

"Al-Qaeda" ("The Base") was developed by Usama Bin Laden and others in the early 1980's to support the war effort in Afghanistan against the Soviets. The resulting "victory" in Afghanistan gave rise to the overall "Jihad" (Holy War) movement. Trained Mujahedin fighters from Afghanistan began returning to such countries as Egypt, Algeria, and Saudi Arabia, with extensive "jihad" experience and the desire to continue the "jihad". This antagonism began to be refocused against the U.S. and its allies.

Sometime in 1989, Al-Qaeda dedicated itself to further opposing non-Islamic governments in this region with force and violence. The group grew out of the "mekhtab al khidemat" (the Services Office), also known as the Afghan Services Bureau. Abdullah Azzam and Osama bin Laden to raise funds and recruit foreign mujahidin for the war against the Soviets in Afghanistan founded it in 1984. MAK became the forerunner to al-Qaeda and was instrumental in creating the fundraising and recruitment network that benefited al-Qaeda during the 1990s. The organization maintained offices in various parts of the world, including Afghanistan, Pakistan and the United States.

Al-Qaeda began to provide training camps and guesthouses in various areas for the use of Al-Qaeda and its affiliated groups. They attempted to recruit U.S. citizens to travel throughout the Western world to deliver messages and engage in financial transactions for the benefit of Al-Qaeda and its affiliated groups and to help carry out operations. By 1990 Al-Qaeda was providing military and intelligence training in various areas including Afghanistan, Pakistan and the Sudan, for the use of Al-Qaeda and its affiliated groups, including the Al-Jihad (Islamic Jihad) organization.

One of the principal goals of Al-Qaeda was to drive the United States armed forces out of Saudi Arabia (and elsewhere on the Saudi Arabian peninsula) and Somalia by violence. Members of Al-Qaeda issued fatwahs indicating their attacks were both proper and necessary.

Al-Qaeda opposed the United States for several reasons. First, the United States was regarded as an "infidel" because it was not governed in a manner consistent with the group's extremist interpretation of Islam. Second, the United States was viewed as providing essential support for other "infidel" governments and institutions, particularly the governments of Saudi Arabia and Egypt, the nation of Israel and the United Nations organization, which were regarded as enemies of the group. Third, Al-Qaeda opposed the involvement of the United States armed forces in the Gulf War in 1991 and in Operation Restore Hope in Somalia in 1992 and 1993, which were viewed by Al-Qaeda as pretextual preparations for an American occupation of Islamic countries. In particular, Al-Qaeda opposed the continued presence of American military forces in Saudi Arabia (and elsewhere on the Saudi Arabian peninsula) following the Gulf War. Fourth, Al-Qaeda opposed the United States Government because of the arrest, conviction and imprisonment of persons belonging to Al-Qaeda or its affiliated terrorist groups or with whom it worked, including Sheik Omar Abdel Rahman, who was convicted in the first World Trade Center bombing.

From its inception until approximately 1991, the group was headquartered in Afghanistan and Peshawar, Pakistan. Then in 1991, the group relocated to the Sudan where it was headquartered until approximately 1996, when Bin Laden, Mohammed Atef and other members of Al-Qaeda returned to Afghanistan. During the years Al-Qaeda was headquartered in Sudan the

142

network continued to maintain offices in various parts of the world and established businesses, which were operated to provide income and cover to Al-Qaeda operatives.

Although Al-Qaeda became the umbrella group supporting: the Al-Jihad, the Al-Gamma Al-Islamiyya (Islamic Group - led by Sheik Omar Abdel Rahman and later by Ahmed Refai Taha, a/k/a "Abu Yasser al Masri,"), Egyptian Islamic Jihad, and a number of jihad groups in other countries, including the Sudan, Egypt, Saudi Arabia, Yemen, Somalia, Eritrea, Djibouti, Afghanistan, Pakistan, Bosnia, Croatia, Albania, Algeria, Tunisia, Lebanon, the Philippines, Tajikistan, Azerbaijan, the Kashmiri region of India, and the Chechen region of Russia. Al-Qaeda also maintained cells and personnel in a number of countries to facilitate its activities, including in Kenya, Tanzania, the United Kingdom, Canada and the United States. By banding together, Al-Qaeda proposed to work together against the perceived common enemies in the West - particularly the United States that Al-Qaeda regards as an "infidel" state, which provides essential support for other "infidel" governments. Al-Qaeda responded to the presence of United States armed forces in the Gulf and the arrest, conviction and imprisonment in the United States of persons belonging to Al-Qaeda by issuing fatwahs indicating that attacks against U.S. interests, domestic and foreign, civilian and military, were both proper and necessary. Those fatwahs resulted in attacks against U.S. nationals in locations around the world including Somalia, Kenya, Tanzania, Yemen, and now in the United States. Since 1993, thousands of people have died in those attacks.

At various times from about 1992 until about 1993, Usama Bin Laden, working together with members of the fatwah committee of Al-Qaeda, disseminated fatwahs to other members and associates of Al-Qaeda, which directed that the United States forces stationed in the Horn of Africa, including Somalia, should be attacked. Indeed, Bin Laden has claimed responsibility for the deaths of 18 U.S. servicemen killed in "Operation Restore Hope" in Somalia in 1994.
February, 1998 Fatwah

On February 22, 1998, Bin Laden issued a fatwah stating that it is the duty of all Muslims to kill Americans. This fatwah read, in part, that "in compliance with God's order, we issue the following fatwah to all Muslims: the ruling to kill the Americans and their allies, including civilians and military, is an individual duty for every Muslim who can do it in any country in which it is possible to do it." This fatwah appears to have provided the religious justification for, and marked the start of logistical planning for, the U.S. Embassy bombings in Kenya and Tanzania.

In February 1998, Usama Bin Ladin and one of his top lieutenants and leader of the Al-Jihad organization in Egypt, Ayman Al Zawahiri, endorsed a fatwah under the banner of the "International Islamic Front for Jihad on the Jews and Crusaders." This fatwah, published in the publication Al-Quds al-Arabi on February 23, 1998, stated that Muslims should kill Americans -- including civilians -- anywhere in the world where they can be found. In or about April 1998, one of the defendants in the East Africa trial, Mohamed Sadeek Odeh, discussed the fatwahs issued by Bin Ladin and Al-Qaeda against America with another defendant, Mustafa Mohamed Fadhil. This discussion took place in Kenya.

As was revealed at the trial that took place in New York earlier this year, a former member of Bin Laden's Al-Qaeda network began working with the United States government in 1996. That witness revealed that Bin Laden had a terrorist group, Al-Qaeda, which had privately declared war on America and was operating both on its own and as an umbrella for other terrorist groups. The witness revealed that Al-Qaeda had a close working relationship with the aforementioned Egyptian terrorist group known as Egyptian Islamic Jihad. The witness recounted that Bin Laden and Al-Qaeda were seeking to obtain nuclear and chemical weapons and that the organization engaged in sophisticated training. He also revealed that Al-Qaeda obtained specialized terrorist training from and worked with Iranian government officials and the terrorist group Hezballah. Thereafter, in August 1996, two years prior to the bombings of the embassies in East Africa, Usama Bin Laden issued a public Declaration of Jihad against the United States military. This was followed by a series of other statements including a February 1998 joint declaration, signed by Usama Bin Laden and the leader of Egyptian Islamic Jihad (EIJ), among others, which declared war on the American population, military and civilian. The public statements corroborated the witness information that Bin Laden, Al-Qaeda and EIJ were working to kill Americans. In May 1998, Bin Laden gave a press interview in which he threatened American interests and complained that the United States was using its embassies overseas to track down terrorists.

On August 7, 1998, the bombings of the embassies in Nairobi, Kenya, and Dar es Salaam, Tanzania, occurred roughly simultaneously. The persons who carried out the attacks in Kenya and Tanzania have since been identified publicly: the principal participants were members of Al-

Qaeda and/or the affiliated terrorist group EIJ. Indeed, Mohamed Rashed Daoud al-Owhali, a Saudi who admitted he was in the bomb truck used in Nairobi, confessed that he had been trained in Al-Qaeda camps, fought with the Taliban in Afghanistan (with the permission of Usama Bin Laden), had asked Bin Laden for a mission and was thereafter dispatched by others to East Africa after undergoing extensive specialized training at camps in Afghanistan. Another defendant, Mohamed Sadeek Odeh, in whose residence was found a sketch of the area where the bomb was to be placed, admitted he was a member of Al-Qaeda and identified the other principal participants in the bombing as Al-Qaeda members. Odeh admitted that he was told the night prior to the bombings that Bin Laden and the others he was working with in Afghanistan had relocated from their camps because they expected the American military to retaliate.

There was independent proof of the involvement of Bin Laden, Al-Qaeda and EIJ in the bombings. First, the would-be suicide bomber, al-Owhali, ran away from the bomb truck at the last minute and survived. However, he had no money or passport or plan by which to escape Kenya. Days later, he called a telephone number in Yemen and thus arranged to have money transferred to him in Kenya. That same telephone number in Yemen was contacted by Usama Bin Laden's satellite phone on the same days that al-Owhali was arranging to get money. Moreover, al-Owhali and Odeh both implicated men named "Harun," "Saleh" and "Abdel Rahman," now all fugitives, as organizing the Nairobi bombing. All three have been conclusively shown to be Al-Qaeda and/or EIJ members. Indeed, documents recovered in a 1997 search of a house in Kenya showed Harun to be an Al-Qaeda member in Kenya. The house where the Nairobi bomb was assembled was located and proved to have been rented by that same Al-Qaeda member Harun. Moreover, the records for the telephone located at the bomb factory showed calls to the same number in Yemen which al-Owhali contacted for money after the bombing and which Usama Bin Laden's satellite telephone also contacted before and after the bombings.

The person arrested for the Tanzania bombing, Khalfan Khamis Mohamed, also implicated "Saleh" and "Abdel Rahman" in the Tanzania bombing as did Odeh. Telephone records confirmed that the Kenya and Tanzania cells were in contact shortly before the bombings.

Additional proof of the involvement of Al-Qaeda and EIJ in the East Africa bombings came from a search conducted in London of several residences and business addresses belonging to Al-Qaeda and EIJ members. In those searches, a number of documents were found, including claims of responsibility in the name of a fictitious group. Al-Owhali, the would-be suicide bomber, admitted that he was told to make a videotape of himself using the name of a fictitious group, the same name found on the claims of responsibility. The claims of responsibility were received in London on the morning the bombings occurred, likely before the bombings even occurred. The claim documents could be traced back to a telephone number that was in contact with Bin Laden's satellite telephone. The claims, which were then disseminated to the press, were clearly authored by someone genuinely familiar with the bombing conspirators as they stated that two Saudis in Kenya and one Egyptian in Tanzania carried out the bombings. Investigators did not know the nationality of the bombers until weeks later. Moreover, the plan had been for two Saudis to be killed in the Nairobi bombing but only one was actually killed as al-Owhali ran away at the last minute. Thus the claims were written by someone who knew what the plan was but before they knew the actual results.

In short, the trial record left little doubt that the East Africa embassy bombings were carried out as a joint operation of Al-Qaeda and EIJ. The testimony in the trial confirmed that Al-Qaeda has access to the money, training, and equipment it needs to carry out successful terrorist attacks.

The U.S. doubled efforts to find and take down Bin Laden. On May 2, 2011, Osama bin Laden, the mastermind behind the September 11, 2001, terrorist attacks in the United States, is killed by U.S. forces during a raid on his compound hideout in Pakistan. The notorious, 54-year-old leader of Al Qaeda, the terrorist network of Islamic extremists, had been the target of a nearly decade-long international manhunt. The raid began around 1 a.m. local time, when 23 U.S.

Navy SEALs in two Black Hawk helicopters descended on the compound in Abbottabad, Pakistan.

Ayman al-Zawahiri, al-Qaeda's Deputy Operations Chief prior to bin Laden's death, assumed the role of commander, according to an announcement by al-Qaeda on June 16, 2011. The fight to exterminate al-Qaeda continues.

The manifesto of al-Qaeda is in Appendix "C" of this book.

Laying aside the insane position of some U.S. leader, who proclaims al-Qaeda is diminished or contained, and not being blinded by this miss-information, if we examine the region we see al-Qaeda had grown many arms, and like an octopus, it reaches in all directions to spread its message of terror.

As early as 2012 articles were being written about the increasing number of al-Qaeda affiliate. An article in the Daily Signal in May of 2012 a list of seven arms of affiliates of al-Qaeda were listed.

Al-Qaeda in the Arabian Peninsula (AQAP). Al-Qaeda's Saudi Arabian and Yemeni branches merged in 2009 to form AQAP. It is considered the most dangerous affiliate. The group was linked to the Fort Hood shooting in 2009 perpetrated by a Muslin psychologist in the U.S. Army, Major Nidal Hasan.

Al-Qaeda in the Islamic Maghreb (AQIM). In 2003, the group pledged allegiance to al-Qaeda. It is active in Mali, Afghanistan and Pakistan.

The Haqqani network is thought to have thousands fighters at its command. The group has ties with Pakistan's intelligence agency and the Taliban as well as al-Qaeda.

They provided cover for Al-Qaeda operatives, including Osama bin Laden, after 9/11. The Taliban also has close ties with the Haqqani network. The group is active in the Afghan region but also helps fund groups in Saudi Arabia and Pakistan.

Lashkar-e-Taiba (LET). LET is part of a major Pakistani Islamist organization. The group's goal is to restore India to Islamic rule, with particular focus on Kashmir.

Al-Shabab seeks the overthrow of Somalia's government. They have also attacked Ugandan football fans in Kampala during the 2010 World Cup.

Boko Haram is a Nigerian group. Their name means, "Western education is sinful". They are an Islamist sect that seeks the establishment of an Islamist Nigerian state. They have attacked Christians, and fellow Muslims they believe are too "westernized.

Al-Qaeda is not dead. It is reinventing itself to fit the aims and goals of various Islamic terrorists throughout the world.

In the midst of the Syrian government's attacks on it own people, a new affiliate has stepped up to fill a vacuum. In an interview with the leader of the Syrian al-Qaeda affiliate, Jabhat al-Nusra, he acknowledged that he takes orders from Ayman al-Zawahiri, the new leader of al-Qaeda. In Syria al-Qaeda is known as the al-Nusra Front, or simple, al-Nusra.

As ISIS has established itself as a greater and more violent power than al-Qaeda, affiliates of al-Qaeda are swearing their allegiance to ISIS. One reason for the switch is that al-Qaeda seemed to believe the caliphate would coalesce around the returning Islamic messiah and ISIS seems to believe if they construct and control the caliphate the messiah will return to conquer the rest of the world and unite it all under a single caliphate. This means ISIS has territory and a type of government they can demonstrate now. The trophies of land and power inspire followers.

ISIS – ISIL – Daesh – Caliphate
What do we call this thing?

During the almost nine years from 2003 to 2011 the United States army was stationed in Iraq. Although there were long and repeated attempts, the U.S. failed to establish an effective Iraqi army and security forces to fill the newly-created security vacuum. They encouraged the democratic national Shi'ite regime headed by Nouri al-Maliki. However, against the best advice of the U.S. to remain non-sectarian, the regime alienated the Sunni population, which had traditionally controlled the country, even though they were a minority of about 22% of the Iraqi population.

The branch of al-Qaeda in Iraq, established in 2004, entered the security vacuum and took advantage of the increasing Sunni alienation.

The establishment of the branch of al-Qaeda in Iraq led by Abu Musab al-Zarqawi and called "al-Qaeda in Mesopotamia:" It waged a terrorist-guerilla war against the American and coalition forces and against the Shia (Shi'ite) population. Zarqawi was a street thug when he arrived in Afghanistan as a mujahidee in 1989. The Soviets had retreated and he was left without a target so he went back home to Jordan where he began thinking about international violent jihad. When he returned to Afghanistan he established a training camp for terrorists. There, he met Osama Bin Laden in 1999. At that time he was not part of al-Qaeda.

Although he affiliated with al-Qaeda, Zarqawi wanted to be known for his violence and sought to create his own terror organization. Shortly after the U.S.-led invasion of Iraq in 2003, he set up the forerunner to today's Islamic State. In the beginning it went under several names, including Jama'at al-Tawhid w'al-Jihad (the Party of Monotheism and Jihad).

Unlike Bin Laden, Zarqawi wanted to target everyone he saw as a heretic, including fellow Muslims, especially Iraq's majority Shiite (Shia) population. Bin Laden and al-Qaeda regarded the Shiites as heretics, but rarely targeted them for slaughter.

On June 7, 2006 Zarqawi died. In 2011, when the U.S. troop withdrawal from Iraq was complete, al-Qaeda in Iraq AQI was being run by Abu Bakr al-Baghdadi. Baghdadi and had grown AQI from a largely foreign to a largely Iraqi operation. Baghdadi was a local person. The absence of foreigners made it easier for the Sons of Iraq and their kin to ignore previous resentments against the group. Baghdadi rebranded AQI as the Islamic State of Iraq, or ISI.

Baghdadi took Zarqawi's tactics and enlarged them. All infidels were his targets but the Shiites were near and became his main target. As he escalated the violence he began sending suicide bombers to attack police and military offices, checkpoints, and recruiting stations. ISI's ranks were swelled by former Sons of Iraq, many of whom had previously been commanders and soldiers in Saddam's military. They were already trained and ready.
With thousands of armed men now at his disposal, Baghdadi opened a second front against the Shiites in Syria, where there was a largely secular uprising against President Bashar al-Assad.

Conditions in neighboring Syria facilitated the expansion of ISI. The country was immersed in a bloody civil war that saw various groups openly revolt against Bashar Al Assad's government. One of the groups, the Al Nusra Front, was founded as the Syrian branch of the ISI. Internal disagreements caused a splinter between the Al Nusra Front and ISI. The ISI group would change its name to the Islamic State in Iraq and Greater Syria.

At this point ISIS officially cut ties with al Zawahiri and Al Qaeda and became totally independent.

In 2013 the leader of the Islamic State of Iraq, Abu Bakr al-Baghdadi, renamed it the Islamic State of Iraq and al-Sham, signaling its emergence as a transnational force while sowing the first seeds of confusion over what to call it. Al-Sham is an archaic word for a vaguely defined territory that includes what are now Syria, Lebanon, Israel, the Palestinian territories and Jordan. It is most often translated as the Levant, thus ISIS, the Islamic State of Iraq and Syria or the Islamic State of Iraq and the Levant, ISIL was born. ISIL became the term used by the U.S. government and various U.N. agencies.

Joseph Lumpkin

The term Levant, which appeared in English in 1497, originally meant the East in general or "Mediterranean lands east of Italy". It is borrowed from the French Levant 'rising', referring to the rising of the sun in the east, or the point where the sun rises. The phrase is ultimately from the Latin word levare, meaning 'lift, raise'.

The term became current in English in the 16th century, along with the first English merchant adventurers in the region; English ships appeared in the Mediterranean in the 1570s, and the English merchant company signed its agreement ("capitulations") with the Grand Turk in 1579 (Braudel). The English Levant Company was founded in 1581 to trade with the Ottoman Empire, and in 1670 the French Champagne du Levant was founded for the same purpose. At this time, the Far East was known as the "Upper Levant".

In 19th-century travel writing, the term incorporated eastern regions under then current or recent governance of the Ottoman Empire, such as Greece. In 19th-century archaeology, it referred to overlapping cultures in this region during and after prehistoric times, intending to reference the place instead of any one culture. The French mandate of Syria and Lebanon (1920–1946) was called the Levant states.

Today, "Levant" is the term typically used to designate a region, namely Cyprus, Egypt, Iraq, Israel, Jordan, Lebanon, Palestine, Syria, and Turkey .

DAESH

Occasionally the term DAESH is used, mainly in the Middle East but increasingly beyond. Those opposed to the group turned the Arabic acronym corresponding to ISIS into a single word "Daesh." The word is nonsensical and doesn't mean anything in Arabic but has a mocking tone and is insulting to IS because it diminishes its claim to have revived the Islamic caliphate. It is also close to the words "dahesh" and "da'es," meaning "one who tramples," making it a pun.

CALIPHATE

When the Islamic State or IS group seized vast parts of northern and western Iraq in the summer of 2014, it declared a caliphate in the territories under its control. At that time it dropped Iraq and al-Sham from its name. Today the group refers to itself as the Islamic State or simply The Caliphate. It refers to its affiliates in Libya, Egypt and elsewhere as provinces. For example, the branch in Egypt's Sinai Peninsula is known as "Sinai Province." A caliphate is an Islamic state. It's led by a caliph, who is a political and religious leader who is a successor (caliph) to the Islamic prophet Mohammed. His power and authority is absolute.

Sunni law defines what is needed to be a caliph.
To be the caliph, one must meet conditions outlined in Sunni law. The caliph must be a male and a Muslim adult of Quraysh descent. The Quraysh were a powerful merchant tribe that controlled Mecca and its Ka'aba and that, according to Islamic tradition, descended from Ishmael. The Caliph must be moral and not challenged in any way physically or mentally. He must have authority. The caliph controls a territory as one controls a nation, enforcing Sharia law. When the Caliphate is established a Caliph or ruler must be announced.

Baghdadi's announced the caliphate in his July sermon and was acknowledged as its caliph, at which time jihadists and fighters began to pour in to the new Islamic State with the commitment to expand the caliphate to the ends of the earth.

It is thought that of the Caliphate is real it would be protected by Allah and will continue to grow and expand. Expansion takes place through wars and conquests.

It is interesting to note that Osama bin Laden wrote letters cautioning Taliban leader NOT to announce or form a caliphate. If one announced a caliphate had been formed it is the same as forming a nation. Its borders must be defended. Infrastructures must be built. The population must be supplied with the basic services any legitimate government should give its people. These are difficult and costly projects. When ISIS broke away from the Taliban they did not take this wisdom to heart. The stresses are noticeable.

ISIS

On June 29, 2014, ISIS published a charter claiming an Islamic Caliphate with its leader designated as Abu Bakr al-Baghdadi. According to the document, the Caliphate lies in eastern Syria and western Iraq. ISIS seeks to expand the Caliphate throughout Syria and Iraq and finally take control of them. After that, the states belonging to "greater Syria" will be annexed, that is, Jordan, Lebanon, Israel and the Palestinian Authority, and after them other countries in the Middle East and beyond.

Unlike al-Qaeda, which seeks to right perceived injustice against Islamic countries and rid them of western influences, the goal of ISIS is world domination through the exermination of all non-Muslims at any cost. Part of the manifesto of ISIS is printed in Appendix "D" of this book.

Graeme Wood writes in The Atlantic Magazine 2015/03
What ISIS Really Wants,

"The Islamic State is no mere collection of psychopaths. It is a religious group with carefully considered beliefs, among them that it is a key agent of the coming apocalypse.

President Obama had declared ISIS was not Islamic. He called ISIS

A jayvee (junior varsity) team… all of his views and opinions have been incorrect. This reflects the deeper fact that the president's high-level advisors did not have any idea about what ISIS is and what was driving it.

ISIS sprung onto the scene in 2010. The group seized Mosul, Iraq, and already rules an area larger than the United Kingdom. Abu Bakr al-Baghdadi had been its leader since May 2010. He has actually been in U.S. captivity at Camp Bucca during the occupation of Iraq.

Then he stepped into the pulpit of the Great Mosque of al-Nuri in Mosul, to deliver a Ramadan sermon as the first caliph in generations. There he upgrading his position from hunted guerrilla to commander of all Muslims. The inflow of jihadists that followed, from around the world, was unprecedented in its pace and volume, and is continuing.

His address, and the Islamic State's countless other propaganda videos and encyclicals, are online, and the caliphate's supporters have toiled mightily to make their project knowable. We can gather that their state rejects peace as a matter of principle. It hungers for genocide and the destruction of the west, including all non-Muslims living there. This is a stance driven by religious views, which makes it constitutionally incapable of certain types of change, even if that change might ensure its survival. ISIS considers itself a key player to bring about and fight in the last war bringing about the imminent end of the world."

ISIS stands for the Islamic State of Iraq and al-Sham (ISIS). Al-sham or Bilad al-Sham means "the country of Syria. ISIS has an apocalyptic belief about the last days or Day of Judgment. They believe they will bring it about and this doctrine matters greatly in understanding its strategy

ISIS preaches that there will be a dystopia and apostasy in the world, then the world will turn against Islam and fight to eliminate Islam. This will indicate the coming of the end of days in which God will defend Islam. Thus, the more hate, death and violence ISIS can generate and the more they can bring the world to oppose Islam the more they can point to this doctrine and say the end is coming and they were correct.

ISIS broke away from Al-Qaeda, believing al-Qaeda as too soft and passive. In Philosophy Now Magazine, February/March 2016, Audrey Borowski explains the differences between the two groups.

"Al Qaeda draws the legitimacy for its attacks from the oppression and humiliation it claims the Ummah (the global Islamic community) is subjected to. It conceives its use of violence primarily as reactive and retributive; as a bid to reclaim humanity for the downtrodden and re-make civilization through sacrificial acts. Its thinking is firmly entrenched in the here and now, operating within globalized modernity, whose codes and concepts it has re-appropriated. The Islamist utopia promoted by established Islamic states has been sidelined in favor of a humanitarian narrative that Al Qaeda has reclaimed for itself. Rather than seeking to overthrow this world, it seeks to transform it from within. To do so Al Qaeda has subverted the West's human rights discourse, recasting the Ummah as pure and authentic humanity, oppressed and terrorized by an arrogant and inhumane West.

For example, in his speeches, Osama Bin Laden often denounced the hypocrisy and double standards perceived to be practiced by the West:
"It is not acceptable in such a struggle as this that he [the Crusader] should attack and enter my land and holy sanctuaries, and plunder Muslims' oil, and then when he encounters any resistance from Muslims, to label them terrorists." ('Depose the Tyrants', 16 December 2004, Messages to the World: the Statements of Osama Bin Laden)."

Borowski continues,
"In its co-opting of human rights and humanitarian narratives, Al Qaeda is holding up a mirror to the West's hypocrisy and inscribing on the bodies of its victims the West's failure to live up to its promises. This appears to be more a rallying cry for a counter system than the rebirth of politico-theological aspirations. By claiming to avenge the oppressed and redeem mankind as a whole, Al Qaeda hopes to establish itself as the new global revolutionary vanguard.
While Al Qaeda operates through a geographically diffuse network of autonomous cells, ISIS is dedicated to bringing about

God's government on Earth under the guise of a Caliphate, or Holy Empire.

In this light, ISIS militants view their endeavor as an attempt to resurrect a Golden Age. So with Islamic State, Al Qaeda's rallying cry of global dissent has mutated into a political theology holding out the promise of a return to what is essentially – and ironically – an invented past. The language of intimacy, equivalence and reciprocity of Al Qaeda's narrative has given way to overt aggression.

In his May 2015 sermon, ISIS leader Al Baghdadi left no doubt about his view that **"Islam was never a religion of peace. Islam is the religion of fighting."**; unity to conflict; powerlessness to conquest; transformation to annihilation; revolution to apocalypse. Violence no longer serves a sacrificial, redemptive aim, but a purifying one, bent ultimately on precipitating a cosmic struggle and the End of Times. "

ISIS is prepared to sacrifice the humanity of everyone, both terrorists and victims, in pursuit of an end that law and order could and would not provide. Thus, they fight to the physical death of the victims and the spiritual death of their followers as they murder and rape their way toward a conquered world or a world war. Either way they believe the outcome will bring about the results they seek. The world will be brought under Islamic control or their will be a war against ISIS, which in their eyes is the only true and pure form of Islam, and in the end that war will bring Allah to their defense and Allah will defeat their enemies and convert or destroy all non-Muslims. It is a no-lose situation for them, but it brings pain and death to the world.

Borowshi concludes, "We are misled when we were led to deny the Islamic State's medieval religious. There is a temptation to think jihadists are modern secular people, since they use social media and modern weapons. On the contrary, ISIS has a sincere and carefully considered commitment to returning civilization to a seventh-century legal system. The establishments of which they believe will ultimately bringing about the apocalypse. The most-articulate spokesmen for that position are the Islamic State's officials and supporters themselves. They refer derisively to "moderns." In conversation, they insist that they will not and cannot waver from governing precepts that were establish by the prophet Mohammed and his earliest followers.

In September, Sheikh Abu Mohammed al-Adnani, the Islamic State's chief spokesman, called on Muslims in Western countries such as France and Canada to find an infidel and "smash his head with a rock," poison him, run him over with a car, or "destroy his crops." Smashing, poisoning, destroying crops all sound like a 7th century practice, but the same fever is brought out of the outdated legal system and into modern environment when he also commanded his followers to run over infidels with their cars. Medieval hate mixed with modern weaponry could unleash atomic destruction upon the world by terrorist who may honestly believe Allah will protect them from the plagues they are prepared to unleash."

Graeme Wood writes in The Atlantic Magazine 2015/03
What ISIS Really Wants, Tell us about what motivates ISIS.

"Denying the holiness of the Quran or the prophecies of Mohammed is straightforward apostasy. But Zarqawi and the state he spawned take the position that many other acts can remove a Muslim from Islam. These include, in certain cases, selling alcohol or drugs, wearing Western clothes or shaving one's beard, voting in an election, even for a Muslim candidate, and being lax about calling other people apostates. Here we must stop and think. If one can be excommunicated or punished if they are too lax in calling out the sins of others the result is a self-enforcing "big brother" type nation with ever tightening and restrictive lifestyles. Any deviation from Zarqawi's form of Islam could land one with a death sentence.
The Islamic State claims that common Shiite practices, such as worship at the graves of imams and public self-flagellation, have no basis in the Quran or in the example of the prophet. That means roughly 200 million Shia are marked for death. So too are the heads of state of every Muslim country, who have elevated man-made law above Sharia by running for office or enforcing laws not made by God."

Wood goes on to say that the west has built itself a trap and is caught in it.
"The west is caught in its own trap of political correctness wherein we are reluctant to call Islam outdated, medieval, or vicious. Western leaders do not belief followers of Islam want the destruction of the west and the establishment of Sharia Law, even though the Quran tells us this is their aim. "

We may say that ISIS does not represent Islam, but it thinks it does, and so do 300,000,000 (300 million) common Muslims, who are ready to support if not fight for ISIS, That is the population of the United States. Add to that the estimated 31,500 fighters involved in fighting for ISIS.

To be exactly what Mohammed envisioned it must follow his example and word. They must emulate their prophet. This crystallizes the values and laws in a violent religion from the late 600's C.E. where there was crucifixion, forced slavery, marriage to young girls, divisions of the spoils of wars, which include money and women. Sharia Law has to be followed to the letter.

ISIS (the Islamic State of Iraq and Syria) claim to be following the commands of Allah and Mohammed. Here are the verses ISIS is pulling directly from the Quran and these are what they live by.
Commentary on the verse is provided by David Wood, Front Page Magazine.

Quran 9:5 — (The Verse of the Sword) Then, when the sacred months have passed, slay the idolaters (non-Muslims) wherever ye find them, and take them (captive), and besiege them, and prepare for them each ambush. But if they repent and establish worship and pay the poor-due, then leave their way free. Lo! Allah is Forgiving, Merciful.

Quran 9:29 — Fight those who believe not in Allah nor the Last Day (notice it says, "fight those who do not believe" not - fight people who are attacking you), nor hold that forbidden which hath been forbidden by Allah and His Messenger, nor acknowledge the Religion of Truth, from among the People of the Book
(Jews and Christians), until they pay the Jizyah with willing submission, and feel themselves subdued.

Quran 3:32 — Say: Obey Allah and the Apostle; but if they turn back, then surely Allah does not love the unbelievers.

Quran 48:29 — Mohammed is the Messenger of Allah, and those who are with him are severe against disbelievers, and merciful among themselves. You see them bowing and falling down prostrate (in prayer), seeking Bounty from Allah and (His) Good Pleasure. The mark of them (i.e. of their Faith) is on their faces (foreheads) from the traces of (their) prostration (during prayers). This is their description in the Taurat (Torah). But their description in the Injeel (Gospel) is like a (sown) seed which sends forth its shoot, then makes it strong, it then becomes thick, and it stands straight on its stem, delighting the sowers that He may enrage the disbelievers with them. Allah has promised those among them who believe (i.e. all those who follow Islamic Monotheism, the religion of Prophet Mohammed SAW till the Day of Resurrection), and do righteous good deeds, forgiveness and a mighty reward (i.e. Paradise).

Quran 4:24 — Also (forbidden are) women already married, except those whom your right hand possesses (in other words, married female captives and slaves may be raped). Thus hath Allah ordained (Prohibitions) against you: Except for these, all others are lawful, provided ye seek (them in marriage) with gifts from your property — desiring chastity, not lust, seeing that ye derive benefit from them, give them their dowers (at least) as prescribed; but if, after a dower is prescribed, agree mutually (to vary it), there is no blame on you, and Allah is All-knowing, All-wise.

Quran 5:33 — The punishment of those who wage war against Allah and His apostle and strive to make mischief in the land is only this, that they should be murdered or crucified or their hands and their feet should be cut off on opposite sides or they should be imprisoned; this shall be as a disgrace for them in this world, and in the hereafter they shall have a grievous chastisement.

Quran 9:73 — O Prophet! strive hard against the unbelievers (non-Muslims) and the hypocrites and be unyielding to them; and their abode is hell, and evil is the destination.
The Arabic word translated here as "strive hard" is jahidi, a verb form of the noun jihad and, according to Islamic highest jurisprudence, abrogates (cancels) all the "nice" verses.

Quran 9:111 — Surely Allah has bought of the believers their persons and their property for this, that they shall have the garden; they

fight in Allah's way, so they slay and are slain; a promise which is binding on Him in the Taurat (Torah) and the Injeel (Gospel) and the Quran; and who is more faithful to his covenant than Allah? Rejoice therefore in the pledge, which you have made; and that is the mighty achievement.
(Quran 9:111 very precisely justifies suicide bombing.)

Quran 47:35 — Be not weary and fainthearted, crying for peace, when ye should be uppermost: for Allah is with you, and will never put you in loss for your (good) deeds.

Funding

Kellan Howell wrote in The Washington Times (Wednesday, April 30, 2014)

Afghanistan produces roughly 90 percent of the world's illicit opium, according to the State Department.
The latest data from the U.N. office show that approximately 516,000 acres of land in Afghanistan are under opium poppy cultivation, an all-time high and a 36 percent increase since 2012.

U.S. taxpayers have spent $7.5 billion over the past 12 years on counternarcotics efforts inside Afghanistan, but the withdrawal of troops has prompted a massive surge in the drug trade.

The rise in opium trafficking and production is alarming to U.S. officials, but not for the reasons many might suspect. American heroin use is rising, but that supply comes mostly from South America and not Afghanistan. The real concern for U.S. officials is that the booming Afghan opium trade — mostly with Europe — is enriching warlords, the Taliban and Islamic extremists and helping fund terrorist activity.

The DEA said many high-ranking members of the Taliban are also major opium kingpins and that terrorist attacks often are funded by drug sales.

In July 2005, several suicide bus bombings in central London killed 52 people. DEA spokesman Rusty Payne said these terrorist attacks were funded by the sale of hashish.

"The drugs may never touch the U.S., but the dollars that are raised from the trafficking and the sale of these things are going back to Hezbollah and al Qaeda, people that don't like us very much," Mr. Payne said. "They have operatives all over the world, even here. These are organizations that need money to operate."

Mr. Payne told The Washington Times that the problem is an even bigger issue in West Africa, where cocaine from Central and South America is funneled through trafficking groups in unstable African countries to Europe. Money from sales of the drugs then go back to terrorist groups in Africa and the Middle East.

"We see global drug trafficking as not just a criminal issue, not just a rule-of-law issue, we see it as a national security issue," he said.

Howard J. Shatz of the RAND Coperation (August 2014) wrote, "As part of my research at the RAND Corporation, since late 2006 I have been studying the finances, management and organization of the precursors to the Islamic State—Al Qaeda in Iraq and the Islamic State of Iraq—using their own documents, manuals and ledgers. More recently, RAND has teamed up with scholars from Princeton and Emory universities, as well as analysts from other organizations, to study more than 150 documents produced between 2005 and 2010. Although our work is still not yet done, we can draw a number of conclusions.

The most important thing for U.S. policymakers to remember is that ISIL now possesses the financial means to support a long-term fight—some $2 billion, according to a recent report in the Guardian, citing a British intelligence official. At the same time, ISIL's preferred fundraising methods and many financial commitments create vulnerabilities. The organization was badly damaged by late 2009, thanks to a combination of coalition and Iraqi forces, as well as intervention by the Iraqi government, and it can be badly damaged again. But without the establishment of a widely accepted, legitimate political order in Iraq, ISIL cannot be eradicated—and will continue to seek out and mete out cash.

ISIL raises most of its money domestically in Iraq and Syria. Its income streams include oil smuggled to other countries in the region, extortion, taxes—especially on non-Muslim minorities—and other essentially criminal activities.

Oil is ISIL's biggest source of revenue but also presents the biggest problem. ISIL controls about a dozen fields in Syria and Iraq, in addition to a number of refineries, including mobile refineries. Based on media accounts, RAND has estimated the total production capacity of these fields to be more than 150,000 barrels per day, although actual production is estimated to be much lower: The website Iraq Oil Report has reported that exports for the month of August at about 2.4 million barrels per day, for instance.

ISIL smuggles this oil out in tanker trucks—clearly visible from the sky should any drone pass overhead, so the smuggling is not particularly furtive. The group then sells the oil to whoever will buy it—reported in the media to be buyers in Syria, Turkey, the Kurdistan Region of Iraq and possibly in Iran and even Bashar Assad's regime in Syria, among other countries. Sales take place at rates deeply discounted from world prices. But even so, revenues have been estimated in the media at $1 million, $2 million or even $3 million per day.

We have seen this before. From 2006 to 2009, ISIL's predecessor, the Islamic State of Iraq, raised perhaps $2 billion through smuggled oil originating in the Baiji refinery in northern Iraq. This ended as a result of a concerted effort by U.S. and Iraqi forces to destroy the group and create the conditions in which the Iraqi government could exercise its law-and-order responsibilities, as well as vastly improved management at Baiji, owned by the Iraqi government."

RECENT EVENTS / 2015-2016
Recently, ISIS has been losing some territory in western Iraq and has come under attack by some Russian forces and in the past

162

several days, France, in retaliation for its Paris attacks. Meanwhile, Obama has repeated that simply sending in U.S. troops would not lead to lasting gains once they were withdrawn, and has continued to press a mostly covert war in Syria, using special forces and drone assassinations.

Meanwhile, ISIS' holy war and atrocities continue—mostly in Syria and Iraq, but now it is being exported in the form of refugees.

Refugees are flooding into Turkey, Greece, France, Germany, the EU and the UK. What is most telling is that five of the major Middle Eastern nations have refused to take in any refugees from Syria or Afghanistan. They know better. We should take a lesson from those who are closest to the problem. They understand that whether the Syrians are refugees or soldiers, they carry with them sectarian prejudges, and fundamental Islamic views that bring violence. More importantly, there is no way to tell which ones are soldiers of ISIS, wanting with all that is within them to expand the caliphate into the countries that are attempting to save them. But then, that is a salient point that most governments have missed.

Sweden and Germany, make up Europe's two most generous welfare states. More than a million refugees have flooded into the continent this year from Syria, Afghanistan, Iraq, Pakistan and North Africa. Most refuse to adopt western ways, saying their ways are anti-Islamic and are evil.

The unrest and destabilization in Sweden has turned that country into a high-rape zone. Finland has seen attacks on their women escalate until it spawned a vigilante group called the Soldiers of Odin. As the country struggles to deal with huge influx of migrants criminals the police have lost control. Now the citizens must protect themselves. Turkish and Kurdish immigrants have carried over their ancient rivalry to Sweden causing fighting, killing, and collateral damage.

Germany has seen increasingly violent protests and demonstrations. Paris has seen bombings and attacks. Riots broke out in a refugee camp in Calais France. Clashes erupted as the Dutch demanded that male Muslim migrants be locked up to protect the Dutch women from rape and violence.

The violence is not in the region or the country. It is in the people and it goes wherever they go. Even as they demand asylum and all the welfare they can get, they continue to rape and rampage, at the same time some plan to bring the caliphate to Europe.

When asked what they want, refugees say they want to make Europe and Britain Muslim and install Sharia Law. The culture, the laws, the archaic society, the violence and the oppression of women, all the things that caused the horrible failures in radical Islamic countries, the refugees want to establish here.

The History of the Quran

The majority of our references will be taken directly from Islamic scholars and writings, in order to avoid accusations of Western scholarly bias.

Before we begin to discuss the history of the Quran, it must be stated that knowing the facts will not convince others of a different viewpoint, if their mind is made up. Most Muslims are convinced the Quran was written by Mohammed himself. They believe the book was written over his lifespan and finished before his death. This is not born out by the facts.

In the website of Answering-Islam, Sam Shamoun wrote an article called, "A Muslim Christian Dialogue". The article appears in italicized font below.

The first issue that needs to be addressed is the claim that a complete Quranic Codex existed during the time of Mohammed. This claim finds no support, since the first complete text was compiled during the Caliphate of Abu Bakr, after Mohammed's death:

Narrated Zaid bin Thabit Al-Ansari:
who was one of those who used to write the Divine Revelation: Abu Bakr sent for me after the (heavy) casualties among the warriors (of the battle) of Yamama (where a great number of Qurra' were killed).

'Umar was present with Abu Bakr who said, 'Umar has come to me and said, The people have suffered heavy casualties on the day of (the battle of) Yamama, and I am afraid that there will be more casualties among the Qurra' (those who know the Quran by heart) at other battle-fields, whereby a large part of the Quran MAY BE LOST, unless you collect it. And I am of the opinion that you should collect the Quran." Abu Bakr added, "I said to 'Umar, 'How can I do something WHICH ALLAH'S APOSTLE HAS NOT DONE? ''Umar said (to me), 'By Allah, it is (really) a good thing.'

So 'Umar kept on pressing, trying to persuade me to accept his proposal, till Allah opened my bosom for it and I had the same opinion as 'Umar." (Zaid bin Thabit added:) Umar was sitting with him (Abu Bakr) and was not speaking me. "You are a wise young man and we do not suspect you (of telling lies or of forgetfulness): and you used to write the Divine Inspiration for Allah's Apostle. Therefore, look for the Quran and collect it (in one manuscript)." By Allah, if he (Abu Bakr) had ordered me to shift one of the mountains (from its place) it would not have been harder for me than what he had ordered me concerning the collection of the Quran. I said to both of them, "How dare you do a thing WHICH THE PROPHET HAS NOT DONE?" Abu Bakr said, "By Allah, it is (really) a good thing. So I kept on arguing with him about it till Allah opened my bosom for that which He had opened the bosoms of Abu Bakr and Umar.

So I started locating Quranic material and collecting it from parchments, scapula, leaf-stalks of date palms and from the memories of men (who knew it by heart). I found with Khuzaima two Verses of Surat-at-Tauba WHICH I HAD NOT FOUND WITH ANYONE ELSE, (and they were):--
"Verily there has come to you an Apostle (Mohammed) from amongst yourselves. It grieves him that you should receive any injury or difficulty He (Mohammed) is ardently anxious over you (to be rightly guided)"
(9.128)

The manuscript on which the Quran was collected, remained with Abu Bakr till Allah took him unto Him, and then with 'Umar till Allah took him unto Him, and finally it remained with Hafsa, Umar's daughter. (Sahih al-Bukhari, Volume 6, Book 60, Number 201)

The number of memorizers that died was 450:
"During the battle of Yamama, 450 reciters of the Quran were killed."

According to another source, when these men died they took with them portions of the Quran that they alone had memorized:
Zuhri reports, 'We have heard that many Quran passages were revealed but that those who had memorized them fell in the Yemama fighting. Those passages had not been written down, and following the deaths of those who knew them, were no longer known; nor had Abu Bakr, nor `Umar nor `Uthman as yet collected the texts of the Quran. (Burton: The published text ought here to be amended: for "fa lamma jama`a Abu Bakr", I propose to read: "wa lamma yajma` Abu Bakr", to follow: "lam yuktab".)

Those lost passages were not to be found with anyone after the deaths of those who had memorized them. This, I understand, was one of the considerations which impelled them to pursue the Quran during the reign of Abu Bakr, committing it to sheets for fear that there should perish in further theatres of war men who bore much of the Quran which they would take to the grave with them on their fall, and which, with their passing, would not be found with any other. (John Burton, The Collection of the Quran, pp. 126-127, Abu Bakr `Abdullah b. abi Da'ud, Kitab al-Masahif', ed. A. Jeffery, Cairo, 1936/1355, p. 23)

From these sources we realize that:
No text had been compiled during Mohammed's time. This is further solidified by the following traditions:
[Zaid b. Thabit said:] "The prophet died and the Quran had not been assembled into a single place." (Ahmad b. Ali b. Mohammed al 'Asqalani, ibn Hajar, Fath al Bari [13 vol., Cairo 1939], vol. 9, p. 9)

It is reported... from Ali who said: "May the mercy of Allah be upon Abu Bakr, the foremost of men to be rewarded with the collection of the manuscripts, for he was THE FIRST to collect (the text) between (two) covers". (John Gilchrist, Jam' Al-Quran - The Codification of the Quran Text A Comprehensive Study of the Original Collection of the Quran Text and the Early Surviving Quran Manuscripts, [MERCSA, P.O. Box 342 Mondeor, 2110 Republic of South Africa, 1989], Chapter 1. The Initial Collection of the Quran Text, p. 27 – citing Ibn Abi Dawud, Kitab al-Masahif, p. 5)

However, there are other narrations that contradict this since they claim that Abu Bakr wasn't the first to collect the Quran:
It is reported... from Ibn Buraidah who said: "The first of those to collect the Quran into a mushaf (codex) was Salim, the freed slave of Abu Hudhaifah". (Ibid., citing as-Suyuti, Al-Itqan fii Ulum al-Quran, p. 135)

Interestingly, Salim is one of the four men that Mohammed recommended learning the Quran from:
Narrated Masriq:
Abdullah bin 'Amr mentioned 'Abdullah bin Masud and said, "I shall ever love that man, for I heard the prophet saying, 'Take (learn) the Quran from four: 'Abdullah bin Masud, Salim, Mu'adh and Ubai bin Ka'b.'" (Sahih al-Bukhari, Volume 6, Book 61, Number 521)

He also happened to be one of the Qurra (reciters) killed at the Battle of Yamama. It is evident that Salim's compilation precedes that of Abu Bakr's since the latter only collected the Quran after the death of the Qurra at Yamama.

A great majority of the Quranic reciters had been killed at al-Yamama, forever taking with them portions of the Quran that only they knew.

Zaid Bin Thabit collected the Quran from palm leaves, stones and from the memories of men.

At this point in Quranic history there were several copies of the Quran that had been compiled. Zaid ibn Thabit compiled the Quran into a book form. Ubayy Bin Kab, Muadh Bin Jabal and Abdallah ibn Masud also compiled Qurans. The problem was that none of them agreed. None matched.

When the differences were brought to light Muslims began accusing the men of changing the Quran. The Muslim population began to take sides, which forced the third Caliph Uthman into taking drastic measures. `Uthman who summon Zaid, Sa`id b. al `As, `Abdul Rahman b. al Harith b. Hisham `Abdullah b. al Zubair and commanded them to copy the sheets into several volumes. Addressing the group from Quraish, he added, "Wherever you differ from Zaid, write the word in the dialect of Quraish for it was revealed in that tongue." `Uthman then sent a copy of the newly copied Quran to every major city with the order that all other Qurans and sheets of Quranic material should be burned.

Qurans not only differed between those who were gathering the sheet but there were also major differences between regions and nations.

In the website of Answering-Islam: A Muslim Christian Dialogue, Sam Shamoun writes,
Hudhaifa figures in a second Hadith series that reports textual differences, not only between the Muslims in Iraq and Syria, but also between rival groups of Iraqi Muslims.

We were sitting in the mosque and `Abdullah was reciting the Quran when Hudaifa came in and said, 'The reading of ibn Umm `Abd! [ie. `Abdullah] The reading of Abu Musa! By God! if I am spared to reach the Commander of the Faithful, I will recommend THAT HE IMPOSE A SINGLE QURAN READING!'
'Abdullah became very angry and spoke sharply to Hudaifa who fell silent. (Burton, p. 142, Abu Bakr `Abdullah b. abi Da'ud, "K. al Masahif", ed. A. Jeffery, Cairo, 1936/1355, p. 13)

'Yazid b. Ma`awiya was in the mosque in the time of al Walid b. `Uqba, sitting in a group among them was Hudaifa. An official called out, 'Those who follow the reading of Abu Musa, go to the corner nearest the Kinda door. Those who follow `Abdullah's reading, go the corner nearest `Abdullah's house.' Their reading of Q 2.196 did not agree. One group read, 'Perform the pilgrimage TO GOD' The others read it 'Perform the pilgrimage TO THE KA'BAH.' Hudaifa became very angry, his eyes reddened and he rose, parting his qamis at the waits, although in the mosque. (Burton, p. 143, Abu Bakr `Abdullah b. abi Da'ud, "K. al Masahif", ed. A. Jeffery, Cairo, 1936/1355, p. 11)

Uthman then proceeded to make Zaid's codex the official text, forcing others to accept his decision.

Like Constantine imposing a single doctrine to unite Christians in order to better unite and control the faith, Uthman, being a strong ruler and a mind to continue his rule, did the same in Islam.

Let us not forget that the Quranic tradition began in memorization and men's minds cannot be wiped clean of the versions they had memorized. Error continued as the "reciters" copied down their versions of the Quran.

Shamound reports," Both Ubayy and Ibn Masud were respected for their ability to memorize, with Ubayy being referred to as "the Master of the Quranic Reciters" and Masud reciting 70 surahs without error:
Abdullah (bin Masud) reported that (he said to his companions to conceal their copies of the Quran) and further said: He who conceals anything shall have to bring that which he had concealed on the Day of Judgment, and they said: After whose mode of recitation do

you command me to recite? I in fact recited before Allah's Messenger more than seventy chapters of the Quran and the companions of Allah's Messenger know that I have better understanding of the Book of Allah (than they do), and if I were to know that someone had better understanding than I, I would have gone to him. Shaqiq said: I sat in the company of the companions of Mohammed but I did not hear anyone having rejected that (that is, his recitation) or finding fault with it. (Sahih Muslim, Book 031, Number 6022).

Abu Mu'awiyah al-Darir informed us; (he said): al-A'mash informed us on the authority of Abu Zabyan, he on the authority of Ibn 'Abbas, he asked: Which of the two readings (of the Quran) do you prefer? He (Abu Zabyan) said: We replied: The reading of 'Abd Allah. Thereupon he said: Verily the Quran was recited (by Gabriel) before the Apostle of Allah, may Allah bless him, once in every Ramadan, except the year in which he breathed his last, when it was recited twice. Then 'Abd Allah Ibn Mas'ud came to him (prophet) and he learnt what was abrogated or altered.

At this time there were still adults who actually knew Mohammed and had verified their memory of the verses of the Quran with him directly. Some of these men would not give up their sanctioned renditions in place of versions that were different. One of these men challenged the version being imposed as erroneous.

"I acquired directly from the Messenger of Allah (saw) seventy surahs when Zaid was still a childish youth - must I now forsake what I acquired directly from the Messenger of Allah?" (Ibid., p. 15)

Another of the reciters, Ibn Masud, declared, "The people have been guilty OF DECEIT IN THE READING OF THE QURAN. I like it to read according to the recitation of him (prophet) whom I love more than that of Zayd Ibn Thabit. By Him besides whom there is no god! I learnt more than seventy surahs from the lips of the Apostle of Allah, may Allah bless him, while Zayd Ibn Thabit was a youth, having two locks and playing with the youth. Then he said: By Him besides Whom there is no other god! If I know any one to be more conversant with the Book of Allah than me, and if the camels could carry me to him, I shall surely go to him. Then 'Abd Allah went away. Shaqiq said: Subsequently I sat in the circles of the

Companions of the Apostle of Allah and others BUT NONE contradicted his statement." (Ibn Sa'd'sKitab al-Tabaqat, Volume 2, p. 444)

Some versions differed due to lack of vowels and differing dialects. The Muslim community at Iraq refused to receive Uthman's text, preferring Ibn Masud's version instead.

There is also evidence that verses were missing in some of the copies of the Qurans.
Zaid bin Thabit said: 'I missed an Ayah of Surat Al-Ahzab that I heard the Messenger of Allah reciting: Among the believers are men who have been true to their covenant with Allah, of them, some have fulfilled their obligations, and some of them are still waiting. – so I searched for it and found it with Khuzaimah bin Thabit, or Abu Khuzaimah, so I put it in its Surah.'"

According to Bukhari, there is evidence that even Mohammed forgot certain verses. Bukhari wrote:
'The Messenger of God heard a man recite by night and said, "May God have mercy on that man! He has just reminded me of a verse I had forgotten from a sura (chapter).

Abdul Rahman al Tha`alibi reported, The prophet recited the Quran and omitted an aya. When he had finished the prayer, he asked, 'Is Ubayy in the mosque?' 'Here I am, Messenger of God.'
'Then why didn't you prompt me?'
'I thought the aya had been withdrawn.'
'It hasn't been withdrawn, I forgot it.'
(Ibid., pp. 65-66, ` n", 2 vols., Algiers, 1905, vol. 1, p. 95)

Sam Shamoun writes,
Uthman's text omitted chapters and verses that the other texts included:
According to Ibn Umar and Aisha, Mohammed's wife, one chapter, Surah al-Ahzab [33] had 200 verses in Mohammed's time. Yet, once Uthman was finished only 73 verses remained, eliminating nearly 140 verses. This tradition is also confirmed by Ubay b. Kabb. (True Guidance, p. 61– citing Al-Suyuti's al-Itqan fii ulum al-Quran on nasikh wa mansukh and Darwaza'sal-Quran Al-Majid)

A verse on the stoning of men and women had been expunged from the Uthmanic text. It reads as follows:
"As for old men and women, stone them for the pleasure they have indulged in." Umar al-Khattab stated, "But for people who may say that Umar adds to the Book of Allah, I would have written the verse on stoning." (Ibid., p. 61)

Aisha mentioned an additional clause in her reading of the Quran that is not part of the Muslim scripture we now possess:
(29) 2982.Abu Yunus, the freed slave of Aishah, said: "Aisha ordered me to write a Mushaf for her, and she said: 'When you get to this Ayah then tell me: Guard strictly (the five obligatory) prayers, and the middle Salat [1].' So when I reached it, I told her and she dictated to me: 'Guard strictly (the five obligatory) prayers, and the middle Salat, and Salat Al-Asr. And stand before Allah with obedience.' She said: 'I heard that from the Messenger of Allah.'"

(Sahih)
[1] Al-Baqarah 2:238. (Jami' At-Tirmidhi, Volume 5, Chapter 2. Regarding Surat Al-Baqarah, pp. 302-303)
A tradition in Sahih Muslim indicates that there are at least two surahs that are missing:
Abu Harb b. Abu al-Aswad reported on the authority of his father that Abu Musa al-Ashan sent for the reciters of Basra. They came to him and they were three hundred in number. They recited the Quran and he said: You are the best among the inhabitants of Basra, for you are the reciters among them. So continue to recite it. (But bear in mind) that your reciting for a long time may not harden your hearts as were hardened the hearts of those before you. We used to recite a surah, which resembled in length and severity to (surah) Bara`at. I have, however, forgotten it with the exception of this which I remember out of it: 'If there were two valleys full of riches, for the son of Adam, he would long for a third valley and nothing would fill the stomach of the son of Adam but dust.' And we used to recite a surah which resembled one of the surahs of Musabbihat, and I have forgotten it, but remember (this much) out of it: 'O people who believe, why do you say that which you do not practice' and 'that is recorded in your necks as a witness (against you) and you would be asked about it on the Day of Resurrection.' (Book 005,Number 2286)

172

Confirmation of the legitimacy of the verse on the son of Adam comes from Anas b. Malik:

Anas reported Allah's messenger as saying: If the son of Adam were to possess two valleys of riches, he would long for the third one, and the stomach of the son of Adam is not filled but with dust. And Allah returns to him to repent. (Sahih Muslim, Book 005, Number 2282)

Yet according to al-Aswad it was revealed as part of a surah that no longer exists.

According to Hamida bint Abi Yunus:

"When my father was eighty years of age, he recited the following verse from the codex of Aisha: 'Verily, Allah and His angels pray for the prophet. O ye who believe, pray for him and earnestly desire peace for him and for those who pray in the front rows.'"

She adds:

"This verse had been there before the codices underwent change at the hands of Uthman." (True Guidance, pp. 61-62 – citing al-Suyut's al-Itqan on nasikh wa mansukh [abrogating and the abrogated])

According to Hudhaifa, Muslims read "only a quarter of Sura al-Tawba (9) i.e., meaning a great number of its verses are missing (Ibid., p. 64; citing al-Mustadrak).

According to Shiite scholars, one whole sura titled al-wilaya has been expunged by Mohammed's successors. It reads as follows:

O Apostle! Make known my admonition, so they will know. Truly, those who turn a deaf ear to my verses and judgment are the losers. Those who keep their pledge to you, I shall reward with pleasing paradises. Truly, Allah is forgiving and offers great reward.

Truly, Ali is of the pious, and he shall be granted his merit on the Day of Judgment. In no way are we ignorant of the injustice done to him. We gave him honor over all your household. He and his offspring are the patient. Their adversary is the leader of the criminals.

Say to those who disbelieved after they have believed: "Do you seek the worldly pleasures of life, running after it, forgetting what Allah and His Apostle have promised you, breaking the promises after reaffirming them?" We have given you parables that you may be guided. O Apostle, we have revealed unto you evident verses. In them are those whom Allah may claim as dead, and whoever shall

stand by him will be exposed. Shun away from them as they avoid you. We shall bring them on a day where nothing will help them or grant them mercy.

In hell, they have a status which will befit them. Give praise to your great Lord and be of those who prostrate themselves. We sent Moses and Aaron, yet they wronged Aaron. May it be good patience! We have made monkeys and pigs out of them and cursed them until the day they shall be resurrected. Be patient, for they shall be granted victory. Through you, as it has been for former messengers before you, judgment is fulfilled. From them we have made a legal guardian to you, so that they may repent. Whoever turns his back on My commandment, I shall bring him back, and so let them enjoy their disbelief for a little while.

You shall not be asked about the treacherous. O Apostle! We have made a pledge for you in the necks of those who have believed. Therefore, take hold of it and be of the thankful. Verily, Ali is one of the obedient, lying prostrate at night, warning of the Last Day, and hoping for the reward of his Lord. Say, shall these oppressors be treated equally while knowing of my torture? Feathers will be filled around their necks, and they shall regret their works. We have told you the good news that his offspring was to come. Our order they shall not break. Upon them and for me be prayers and mercy, whether they are alive or dead, until they are resurrected. Upon those who do them wrong after you is My wrath, for they are a losing folk. Upon those who follow their steps be mercy from Me, they shall be safe in the rooms. Praise be to Allah, the Lord of the worlds. (The True Guidance, pt. 4, pp. 65-66 – citing al-Nuri's Fasl al-Khitab, p. 110)

As the reciters came forward and other elderly Muslins reported their memories of the changed verses Uthman came under fire by the people for changing the Quran. They accused him of "obliterated the Book of Allah" because "The Quran was in many books, and you have now discredited them all but one." (Gilchrist, Chapter 2. The Uthmanic Recension of the Quran, pp. 51, 58 – citing Abi Dawud Kitab al-Masahif, p.36, and al-Tabari, Bk.1, chpt. 6, 2952)

The late Egyptian Professor Dr. Taha Hussein summarizes the atrocity of Uthman's actions in his book, The Great Sedition,

The prophet Mohammed said: "The Quran was revealed in seven dialects, all of them are right and perfect." When Uthman banned whichever he banned from the Quran, and burned whichever he burned, he banned passages Allah has revealed and burned parts of the Quran which were given to the Muslims by the Messenger of Allah. He appointed a small group of Sahaba (close friends of Mohammed) to rewrite the Quran and left out those who heard the prophet and memorized what he said. This is why Ibn Massoud was angry, because he was one of the best men who memorized the Quran. He said that he took from the mouth of the prophet seventy suras of the Quran while Zaid Ibn Sabit was yet a young lad. When Ibn Massoud objected to the burning of the other codices of the Quran, Uthman took him out of the mosque with violence, and struck him to the ground, and broke one of his ribs.

Uthman had arbitrarily chosen one reading out of seven, not fully realizing that Mohammed had allowed all seven to exist. He had discredited six of the seven and forced men who had learned verses from Mohammed himself to change complete verses. He had ordered Qurans and sheets of the Quran burned if they differed from the version he chose. That version left out major portions of chapters that Mohammed's young wife remembered hearing directly from him. Things were becoming quite the mess. The Quran was not complete and even the version Uthman was attempting to standardize was not the best copy.

The problem does not end just yet. The traditions record that the governor of Medina, Marwan, confiscated Zaid's text, which had been in Hafsah's possession until her death, and proceeded to destroy it. Marwan said, "I did this because whatever was in it was surely written and preserved in the (official) volume and I was afraid that after a time people will be suspicious of this copy or they will say there is something in it that wasn't written." (Dr. William F. Campbell, The Quran and the Bible in the Light of History & Science

The copy he destroyed was the only official, original copy of Quran written under the authority of Abu Bakr Siddiq, Mohammed's father-in-law and close friend. It was reported that this copy was complete and nothing was missing. Marwan was afraid that the people would see the differences and begin asking which Quran was correct and acceptable. This would have caused divisions, so he destroyed the more perfect version.

The Quran was "modified" by Iraq's governor al-Hajjaj Ibn Yusuf (A.D. 660-714). Gilchrist, in Chapter 5 of Sab'at-I-Ahruf in the Hadith Literature, p.109 noted, "Altogether al-Hajjaj Ibn Yusuf made eleven modifications in the reading of the Uthmanic.
Another issue which the Muslims had to deal with was variant readings. Part of Yusuf's meddling was done in order to more precisely standardize the text by a set of points showing how it was to be read. When the Quran was originally written, there were no vowel marks or diacritical points to differentiate the meaning or meanings of words. This is like old Hebrew. There were no vowels, only consonants. In English this would be comparable to writing
W r fr hr – could be read, "we are from here" or "we are for hair". All the readings should be kept and understood in context and even then one could not be sure of having the reading correct. This is the case even for Yusuf, who took it upon himself to decide which reading was correct and set his decision in stone.

Sam Shamoun writes,

"Other variant readings stem from clauses that were either added or omitted from the text. A comparison of the texts of Uthman and Ibn Masud will illustrate this point:
S. 2:275 in Uthman's copy begins with Allathiina yaq kuluunar - ribaa laa yaquumuuna - "those who devour usury will not stand." Ibn Masud's codex began in the same fashion but added "yawmal qiyamati," The Day of Resurrection - i.e., "those who devour usury will not stand on the Day of Resurrection."
S. 5:91 in Uthman's text reads Fusiyaamu thaalaythati ayyammin - "Fast for three days." Ibn Masud included after the last word the adjective mutataabi'aatin, meaning "successive days."

S. 6:153 begins *Wa anna haatha siraatii* - "Verily this is my path." Yet Ibn Masud's version reads *Wa haatha siraatu rabbakum* - "This is the path of your Lord."

S. 33:6, in regard to Mohammed's wives, states, *Wa azwaajuhu ummahaatuhuu* - "and his wives are their (the believers') mothers." Yet Ibn Masud adds *Wa huwa abuu laahum* - "and he (Mohammed) is their father." (Gilchrist, Chapter 3. The Codices of Ibn Mas'ud and Ubayy Ibn Ka'b, pp. 69-70 – citing Arthur Jeffrey Materials; Abi Dawud's Kitab al-Masahif)

To present a brief summary of our findings we noted that:

1. The Quran was not compiled perfectly.
2. Much of the Quran's contents are missing.
3. More than one Quran was in circulation.
4. Primary eyewitness codices were burned.
5. On the authority of one man an official text of the Quran was approved.
6. Even this official codex was eventually destroyed and eleven revisions were made of it.
7. Thousands of variants existed between these competing texts as documented by Arthur Jeffrey's book, which in turn cites Abi Dawud's own work."

How to Interpret the Quran

Put simply, The Quran is viewed as an unfolding revelation. Thus, the last statement in the Quran regarding a subject supersedes any statement that came before it. This is called ABROGATION.

The abrogation principle basically says that when something from a later chapter (known as a sura) conflicts with something from an earlier chapter, the one written last will stand and the earlier one will be nullified.

Clerics were wrestling with contradictions in the Quran. Either it was not all perfect and complete because it presented statements that could not be reconciled, or it contained errors and could not be fully trusted. To circumvent this dilemma the clerics came upon the theory of abrogation. This solved the problem because it allowed both statement to be true at the time they were spoken and it allowed the last statement to remain pertinent so there was continuity.

Since abrogation uses chronological order, the last chapters written would not contain any abrogated verses. Thus, we look for the last verses written to see what instructions are to be followed by Islam today.

Scholar Farooq Ibrahim writes regarding abrogation, *"Not all Muslim scholars agree on what abrogation covers. Briefly here was my discovery.*

Muslim scholars of old hold to the concept that some ayahs in the Quran abrogate other ayahs in the Quran, but do not all hold to the same set of abrogated and abrogating ayahs.

Other Muslim scholars are of the opinion that the Quran may abrogate the Quran as well as the Sunnah (deed or example of Mohammad) and vice versa.

Some Muslim scholars hold that the Quran abrogates all the previous scriptures, specifically the scriptures sent to Musa and Isa, but not itself.

Some Muslim scholars, especially of recent times do not believe in the concept of abrogation at all."

However, it seems most fundamental Muslins believe in abrogation and use the process to validate their actions. Here are the instructions regarding abrogation from the Quran. These are the actual Quranic verses that reference abrogation. All quotes are from Dawood's English Translation of the Quran.

2:106: "If We abrogate a verse or cause it to be forgotten, We will replace it by a better one or one similar...."

13:39: "God abrogates and confirms what He pleases. His is the Decree Eternal."

17:86: "If We (Allah) pleased We could take away that which We have revealed to you:.."

16:101 "When We change one verse for another (God knows best what He reveals), they say: "You are an impostor...."

22:52: "Never have we sent a single prophet or apostle before you with whose wishes Satan did not tamper. But God abrogates the interjections of Satan and confirms His own revelations."

This last verse is connected to what are known as the "Satanic Verses". In the beginning of Islam Mohammed compromised with the pagans and allowed idol worship. Later he would claim to have been tricked by Satan. The verse allowing idol worship was abrogated in the Quran. This was a time in Mecca that Muslims faced severe persecution. Eighty-three of Mohammed's followers had to flee to Abyssinia (Ethiopia). Mohammed wanted to diffuse the situation as began having "revelations." He declared the possibility of Allah having a wife, Al-Lat and two daughters, Al-Uzza and Mannat, as recorded in Surat an-Najim:

"For truly did he see, the signs of his Lord, the greatest! Have ye seen Lat, and Uzza, and another, the third [goddess] Manat? What! For you the male sex, and for him, the female? Behold, such would be indeed a division most unfair!" (Sura 53:18-22).

The Pagans were appeased and the Muslims who had migrated to Ethiopia returned home. But Mohammed withdrew his Revelation because he realized he got caught up in the pressure and was wrong. He claimed Satan inspired his revelations. The admission of satanic influence is stated in the Sura al-Hajj - Quran 22:52-53

"Never did we send an Apostle or a prophet before thee but when he frame a desire, Satan threw some [vanity] into his desire. But God will cancel anything [vain] that Satan throws in. And God will confirm [and establish] his signs. For God is full of knowledge and wisdom, that he may make the suggestions thrown in by Satan, but a trial. For those in whose hearts is a disease and who are hardened of heart: Verily the wrong doers are in a schism far [from truth]" (Surat al-Hajj - Sura 22:52,53).

The logical consequences of these verses are thunderous. Mohammed was not perfect. The Quran was not without error. Satan could influence the writing of the Quran. Could it happen again without Mohammed realizing it? How many more verses were evil? What if Mohammed's last verses were under satanic influence and there was no time to realize this and abrogate before he died?

One of the last chapters uttered by Mohammed was sura 9. It has a lot to say about how he wanted non-Muslims treated from that point on.

9:5 Slay the idolaters wherever you find them.

9:6 Those who submit and convert to Islam will be treated well. (Those who don't submit will be killed. See previous verse.)

9:7-9 Don't make treaties with non-Muslims. They are all evildoers and should not be trusted.

9:11 Treat converts to Islam well, but kill those who refuse to convert (see 9:5).

9:12-14 Fight the disbelievers! Allah is on your side; he will give you victory.

9:23 Don't make friends with your disbelieving family members. Those who do so are wrong-doers.

9:29 Fight against Christians and Jews "until they pay the tribute readily, being brought low."

9:33 The "Religion of Truth" (Islam) must prevail, by force if necessary, over all other religions.

9:41 Fight for Allah with your wealth and whatever weapons are available to you.

9:42 Those who refuse to fight for Allah (claiming they are unable) are liars who have destroyed their souls.

9:73 Fight the disbelievers and hypocrites. Be harsh with them. They are all going to hell anyway.

9:81-83 Those who refuse to give their wealth and lives to Allah will face the fire of hell.

9:85 Those who refuse to fight for Allah will be treated (along with their children) as unbelievers.

9:111 Believers must fight for Allah. They must kill and be killed. Allah will reward them for it.

9:123 Fight disbelievers who are near you, and let them see the harshness in you.

This is Allah's "last word" on tolerance and peace toward non-Muslims. If nothing else up to this point had abrogated the tolerant verses, the above verses completely wipe out every last positive verse in the Quran for non-Muslims.

Mawdudi's Commentary states that by the time chapter 9 was spoken one third of the entire Arabian Peninsula had bent the knee to Islam:

"Now let us consider the historical background of the Sura. The series of events that have been discussed in this Sura took place after the Peace Treaty of Hudaibiyah. By that time one-third of Arabia had come under the sway of Islam which had established itself as a powerful well organized and civilized Islamic State."

In an article entitled, Peace or Jihad? Abrogation in Islam, David Bukay writes:

"Chapter 9 of the Quran, in English called "Ultimatum," is the most important concerning the issues of abrogation and jihad against unbelievers. It is the only chapter that does not begin "in the name of God, most benevolent, ever-merciful." Commentators agree that Mohammed received this revelation in 631, the year before his death, when he had returned to Mecca and was at his strongest. Mohammed bin Ismail al-Bukhari, compiler of one of the most authoritative collections of the hadith, said that "Ultimatum" was the last chapter revealed to Mohammed although others suggest it might have been penultimate. Regardless, coming at or near the very end of Mohammed's life, "Ultimatum" trumps earlier revelations."

Because this chapter contains violent passages, it abrogates previous peaceful content. Muhsin Khan, the translator of Sahih al-Bukhari, says God revealed "Ultimatum" in order to discard restraint and to command Muslims to fight against all the pagans as well as against the People of the Book if they do not embrace Islam or until they pay religious taxes. So, at first aggressive fighting was forbidden; it later became permissible (2:190) and subsequently obligatory (9:5). This "verse of the sword" abrogated, canceled, and replaced 124 verses that called for tolerance, compassion, and peace.

The Egyptian theologian Abu Suyuti said that everything in the Quran about forgiveness and peace is abrogated by verse 9:5, which orders Muslims to fight the unbelievers and to establish God's kingdom on earth.

The traditional order of the Quran has chapters arranged from the longest to the shortest chapter. This effectively prevents anyone who doesn't know about abrogation from understanding what the Quran really says. Only 43 chapters were not affected by abrogation. This means most of the chapters of the Quran cannot be taken at face value. Appendix "A" contains all verses that were abrogated and gives the verses that superseded or replaced them.

It should be noted that there are some clerics that do not stress the rule of abrogation to their congregation and by allowing the Quran to remain more intact they tend to produce a more moderate congregation. These clerics seem to be in a minority.

In order to establish what verse may abrogate another we must look at the chronological order and then compare what the later verse may supersede in an earlier verse.

To view the traditional order of the Quran, you can sort the table by Traditional Order – "Order in Quran". WikiIslam provides the following chart:

Chronological Order	Name of the Chapter	Verse Number	Revelation Location	Traditional Order
Chronological Order	Surah Name	Number of Verses	Location	Order in Quran
1	Al-Alaq	19	Mecca	96
2	Al-Qalam	52	Mecca	68
3	Al-Muzzammil	20	Mecca	73
4	Al-Muddathir	56	Mecca	74
5	Al-Fatiha	7	Mecca	1
6	Al-Masadd	5	Mecca	111

Chronological Order	Surah Name	Number of Verses	Location	Order in Quran
7	At-Takwir	29	Mecca	81
8	Al-Ala	19	Mecca	87
9	Al-Lail	21	Mecca	92
10	Al-Fajr	30	Mecca	89
11	Ad-Dhuha	11	Mecca	93
12	Al-Inshirah	8	Mecca	94
13	Al-Asr	3	Mecca	103
14	Al-Adiyat	11	Mecca	100
15	Al-Kauther	3	Mecca	108
16	At-Takathur	8	Mecca	102
17	Al-Maun	7	Mecca	107
18	Al-Kafiroon	6	Mecca	109
19	Al-Fil	5	Mecca	105
20	Al-Falaq	5	Mecca	113
21	An-Nas	6	Mecca	114
22	Al-Ikhlas	4	Mecca	112
23	An-Najm	62	Mecca	53
24	Abasa	42	Mecca	80
25	Al-Qadr	5	Mecca	97
26	Ash-Shams	15	Mecca	91
27	Al-Burooj	22	Mecca	85
28	At-Tin	8	Mecca	95
29	Quraish	4	Mecca	106
30	Al-Qaria	11	Mecca	101
31	Al-Qiyama	40	Mecca	75

Chronological Order	Surah Name	Number of Verses	Location	Order in Quran
32	Al-Humaza	9	Mecca	104
33	Al-Mursalat	50	Mecca	77
34	Qaf	45	Mecca	50
35	Al-Balad	20	Mecca	90
36	At-Tariq	17	Mecca	86
37	Al-Qamar	55	Mecca	54
38	Sad	88	Mecca	38
39	Al-Araf	206	Mecca	7
40	Al-Jinn	28	Mecca	72
41	Ya-Sin	83	Mecca	36
42	Al-Furqan	77	Mecca	25
43	Fatir	45	Mecca	35
44	Maryam	98	Mecca	19
45	Taha	135	Mecca	20
46	Al-Waqia	96	Mecca	56
47	Ash-Shuara	227	Mecca	26
48	An-Naml	93	Mecca	27
49	Al-Qasas	88	Mecca	28
50	Al-Isra	111	Mecca	17
51	Yunus	109	Mecca	10
52	Hud	123	Mecca	11
53	Yusuf	111	Mecca	12
54	Al-Hijr	99	Mecca	15
55	Al-Anaam	165	Mecca	6
56	As-Saaffat	182	Mecca	37
57	Luqman	34	Mecca	31

Chronological Order	Surah Name	Number of Verses	Location	Order in Quran
58	Saba	54	Mecca	34
59	Az-Zumar	75	Mecca	39
60	Al-Ghafir	85	Mecca	40
61	Fussilat	54	Mecca	41
62	Ash-Shura	53	Mecca	42
63	Az-Zukhruf	89	Mecca	43
64	Ad-Dukhan	59	Mecca	44
65	Al-Jathiya	37	Mecca	45
66	Al-Ahqaf	35	Mecca	46
67	Adh-Dhariyat	60	Mecca	51
68	Al-Ghashiya	26	Mecca	88
69	Al-Kahf	110	Mecca	18
70	An-Nahl	128	Mecca	16
71	Nooh	28	Mecca	71
72	Ibrahim	52	Mecca	14
73	Al-Ambiya	112	Mecca	21
74	Al-Mumenoon	118	Mecca	23
75	As-Sajda	30	Mecca	32
76	At-Tur	49	Mecca	52
77	Al-Mulk	30	Mecca	67
78	Al-Haaqqa	52	Mecca	69
79	Al-Maarij	44	Mecca	70
80	An-Naba	40	Mecca	78
81	An-Naziat	46	Mecca	79

Chronological Order	Surah Name	Number of Verses	Location	Order in Quran
82	Al-Infitar	19	Mecca	82
83	Al-Inshiqaq	25	Mecca	84
84	Ar-Room	60	Mecca	30
85	Al-Ankaboot	69	Mecca	29
86	Al-Mutaffifin	36	Mecca	83
87	Al-Baqara	286	Medina	2
88	Al-Anfal	75	Medina	8
89	Al-i-Imran	200	Medina	3
90	Al-Ahzab	73	Medina	33
91	Al-Mumtahina	13	Medina	60
92	An-Nisa	176	Medina	4
93	Al-Zalzala	8	Medina	99
94	Al-Hadid	29	Medina	57
95	Mohammed	38	Medina	47
96	Ar-Rad	43	Medina	13
97	Al-Rahman	78	Medina	55
98	Al-Insan	31	Medina	76
99	At-Talaq	12	Medina	65
100	Al-Bayyina	8	Medina	98
101	Al-Hashr	24	Medina	59
102	An-Noor	64	Medina	24
103	Al-Hajj	78	Medina	22
104	Al-Munafiqoon	11	Medina	63

Chronological Order	Surah Name	Number of Verses	Location	Order in Quran
105	Al-Mujadila	22	Medina	58
106	Al-Hujraat	18	Medina	49
107	At-Tahrim	12	Medina	66
108	At-Taghabun	18	Medina	64
109	As-Saff	14	Medina	61
110	Al-Jumua	11	Medina	62
111	Al-Fath	29	Medina	48
112	Al-Maeda	120	Medina	5
113	At-Taubah	129	Medina	9
114	An-Nasr	3	Medina	110

Now that we have a chronological view of the Quran we can now see the verses abrogated.

Abrogations

The verses on the left are the abrogated verses (Mansūkh) of the Quran, while the verses on the right are the abrogating verses (Nāsikh). Thus, will be the verses on the right that Muslims will obey and follow.

The "Verse of the Sword" refers to Quran 9:5, and due to how many verses it abrogates (about 113 in one way or another), we will write "Verse of the Sword" in place of this verse:

But when the forbidden months are past, then fight and slay the Pagans wherever ye find them, and seize them, beleaguer them, and lie in wait for them in every stratagem (of war); but if they repent, and establish regular prayers and practice regular charity, then open the way for them: for Allah is Oft-forgiving, Most Merciful.
Quran 9:5

To drive this verse home we will use another translation to ensure the verse has been interpreted correctly:

SAHIH INTERNATIONAL
And when the sacred months have passed, then kill the polytheists wherever you find them and capture them and besiege them and sit in wait for them at every place of ambush. But if they should repent, establish prayer, and give zakah, let them [go] on their way. Indeed, Allah is Forgiving and Merciful.

An-Nasikh -wal- Mansukh, by Ibn Khuzyamh states 113 verses are abrogated by the Sword verse (9: 5), and 9 verses are abrogated by the Fighting verse (9: 29): "Fight those who believe not in Allah nor the Last Day."

Ibn `Umar said that the Messenger of Allah said, "I have been commanded to fight the people until they testify that there is no deity worthy of worship except Allah and that Mohammed is the Messenger of Allah, establish the prayer and pay the Zakah." This honorable Ayah (verse) (9:5) was called the Ayah (verse) of the Sword, about which Ad-Dahhak bin Muzahim said, "It abrogated every agreement of peace between the prophet and any idolater, every treaty, and every term."

Al-`Awfi said that Ibn `Abbas commented: "No idolater had any more treaty or promise of safety ever since Surah Bara'ah was revealed." - This is the Ayah (verse) of the Sword, (Tafsir al-Jalalayn).

The list and table of Abrogated verses come from the "Resource of Islam" and "WikiIslam".

The list of verses below speak of living peaceful and with mercy and forgiveness, but these verses are now abrogated by verse 9:5. The list is as follows:

Surah (Chapter):

2 | 3 | 4 | 5 | 6 | 7 | 8 | 9 | 10 | 11 | 13 | 15 | 16 | 17 | 19 | 20 | 22 | 23 | 24 | 25 | 26 | 27 | 28 | 29 | 30 | 31 |32 | 33 | 34 | 35 | 36 | 37 | 38 | 40 | 41 | 42 | 43 | 44 | 45 | 46 | 47 | 50 | 51 | 52 | 53 | 54 | 56 | 58 | 60 | 68 |70 | 73 | 74 | 75 | 76 | 80 | 81 | 86 | 88 | 95 | 103 | 109

Please see Appendix "A" for a complete chart of Abrogated verses in the Quran.

Based on the chronological order of the verses, we can now clearly see how Islam morphed from a religion of peace, when Mohammed began preaching, to a religion of hatred, killing, and war at the last of his life. Keeping in mind that the last utterances on a subject abrogates or negates all verses which came before. Beyond a few verses serving as commentary, here is what the Quran offers as commands and instructions today. If one interprets the Quran literally and fundamentally the verses below now represents authentic Muslim teaching.

"Those that make war against Allah and His apostle and spread disorder in the land shall be slain or crucified or have their hands and feet cut off on alternate sides, or be banished from the land. They shall be held up to shame in this world and sternly punished in the hereafter." (Sura 5.33)

"O believers, take not Jews and Christians as friends; they are friends of each other. Whoso of you makes them his friends is one of them. Allah guides not the people of the evildoers." (Sura 5.51)

"Allah revealed His will to the angels, saying: 'I shall be with you. Give courage to the believers. I shall cast terror into the hearts of the infidels. Strike off their heads, strike off the very tips of their fingers!' That was because they defied Allah and His apostle. He that defies Allah and his apostle shall be sternly punished by Allah." (Sura 8.12-13)

"In order that Allah may separate the pure from the impure, put all the impure ones [i.e. non-Muslims] one on top of another in a heap and cast them into hell. They will have been the ones to have lost." (Sura 8.37)

"And fight them until there is no more fitnah (disbelief and polytheism, i.e. worshipping others besides Allah) and the religion (worship) will all be for Allah alone (in the whole world). But if they cease (worshipping others besides Allah) then certainly, Allah is All-Seer of what they do." (Sura 8.39).

"Muster against them [i.e. non-Muslims] all the men and cavalry at your command, so that you may strike terror into the enemy of Allah and your enemy, and others besides them who are unknown to you but known to Allah." (Sura 8.60)

"O Prophet, urge on the believers to fight. If there be twenty of you, patient men, they will overcome two hundred; if there be a hundred of you, they will overcome a thousand unbelievers, for they are a people who understand not." (Sura 8.65)

"It is not for any Prophet to have prisoners until he make wide slaughter in the land." (Sura 8.67).

"Fight those who believe not in Allah and the Last Day and do not forbid what Allah and His Messenger have forbidden -- such men as practice not the religion of truth, being of those who have been given the Book [i.e. Jews and Christians] -- until they pay the tribute out of hand and have been humbled." (Sura 9.29)

"If you do not go to war, He will punish you sternly, and will replace you by other men." (Sura 9.39)

"Prophet, make war on the unbelievers and the hypocrites, and deal harshly with them. Hell shall be their home: an evil fate." (Sura 9.73)

"They [i.e. faithful Muslims] will fight for the cause of Allah, they will slay and be slain." (Sura 9.111)

"O believers, fight the unbelievers who are near to you, and let them find in you a harshness, and know that Allah is with the god-fearing." (Sura 9.123)

"When We resolve to raze a city, We first give warning to those of its people who live in comfort. If they persist in sin, judgment is irrevocably passed, and We destroy it utterly." (Sura 17.16)

"We have destroyed many a sinful nation and replaced them by other men. And when they felt Our Might they took to their heels and fled. They were told: 'Do not run away. Return to your comforts and to your dwellings. You shall be questioned all.' 'Woe betide us, we have done wrong' was their reply. And this they kept repeating until We mowed them down and put out their light." (Sura 21.11-15)

"When you meet the unbelievers in the battlefield strike off their heads and, when you have laid them low, bind your captives firmly. Then grant them their freedom or take a ransom from them, until war shall lay down her burdens." (Sura 47.4)

"Mohammed is Allah's apostle. Those who follow him are ruthless to the unbelievers but merciful to one another." (Sura 48.29)

"May the hands of Abu Lahab [Mohammed's uncle, who had refused to embrace Islam] perish! Nothing shall his wealth and gains avail him. He shall be burnt in a flaming fire, and his wife, laden with firewood, shall have a rope of fiber around her neck!" (Sura 111.1-5)

The Islamic Apocalypse

The Muslim and Christian view of the Apocalypse is remarkably similar, but instead of Jesus returning to establish a Christian kingdom, Mohammed will return along with Jesus to establish an Islamic kingdom. Jesus will be with Mohammed to instruct Christians that Mohammed's interpretation is correct and all must submit to Islamic rule.

Islamic tradition speaks of signs, natural disasters, wars and moral decay that will portend the Last Days, just as laid out in the Book of Revelation. Like Christians, many Muslims believe that Jesus, whom they call Isa, will return to defeat the Antichrist.

As Muslims search for the time and date of the return, some have borrowed from the books of Daniel, Ezekiel and Revelation. The difference is that God's people are Muslims, not Christians.

According to Huffington Post, Muslim Views Of The Apocalypse 02/07/2013 by Daniel Burke:

"The Muslim Jesus destroys the cross and the swine, symbols of Christian innovations, and converts Christians to Islam.

In Islamic tradition, Jesus is joined by a figure named the Mahdi, who helps subdue Satan and rid the world of corruption and injustice."

Jesus' name appears 25 times in the Quran, while the name "Mohammed" shows up only 5 times. Jesus' name in the Quran is actually either "Eesa" or "Īsā". The Quran also refers to Jesus by various titles: Son of Mary, Messenger of Allah, and Messiah.

Mohammed also claimed that he met Jesus when he visited heaven. Belief in Jesus is required in Islam, though in Islamic tradition Jesus is not divine or the son of God.

Some Shiite Muslims don't like the idea of Jesus as the messiah and have assigned a larger role to the Mahdi. The "Twelvers" in Iran, including President Mahmoud Ahmadinejad have spoken of the Mahdi's return.

Twelvers believe that the Mahdi is the 12th imam. This belief is popular in Afghanistan, Iraq, Turkey and Tunisia.

BeliefNet.com, Islamic Apocalypse? Reports:
"The Quran is heavily apocalyptic in the sense that it expects the end of the world to happen imminently. Surah 54:1 talks about the hour approaching when the moon splits apart, stars fall, the heavens roll up. Many of these signs line up with the New Testament scriptures.

A modern interpretation of the Islamic apocalypse says the Byzantine Empire, mentioned on the scripture is actually the United States, and the Muslims of this same apocalyptic scene are those who fought against the Soviet Union in Afghanistan. The tradition goes on to say there will be fallout between the two, and then the Byzantines will attack the Muslims and defeat them. In this odd and modernized interpretation radical Muslims believe the prophecies have been fulfilled because the United States has attacked. Now they await the moment when God will reveal himself and judge the United States."

Each time the Muslims are defeated they point back to the apocalyptic framework of the soon coming of god. In this way of interpreting the Quran defeat solidifies the community, as does any history.

Fundamental Muslims point to those who do not fight or kill and call them apostate Muslims. So from their point of view, the true Muslims will fight and go to war. As in any fundamental belief system, God will not allow true Muslims to be hurt in their holy war, and if they are killed they will be martyrs.

As the clerics look for the end of days they have defined two groups of signs. There are the seventy or so lesser signs pertaining to moral, political, ethical conditions and natural signs that are supposed to happen before the end of the world. According to most present-day Islamic authors, they are said to be fulfilled.

Then there are the "greater signs," which are events that happen before the end. The appearance of the Mahdi, the messianic figure who brings justice to the world and completes the spread of Islam, will appear. Then the antichrist that in Arabic is called the Dajjal will fight.

According to hadith, Mohammed is said to have prophesied that the Masih ad-Dajjal would be the last of a series of thirty Dajjal or "deceivers".
Mohammed is reported to have said:
...Ad-Dajjal is blind in the right eye and his eye looks like a bulging out grape.
Sahih al-Bukhari, 3:30:105

Ali was reported to have said:
His right eye will be punctured, and his left eye would be raised to his forehead and will be sparkling like a star. Only the believers will be able to read the word 'Kafir' [disbeliever], inscribed in bold letters, on his forehead. There will be big mountains of smoke at both front and backsides of his caravan. People will anticipate food within those mountains, during the severe famine. All rivers, falling in his way, will become dry and he will call upon people in a loud voice, "O my friends come to me! I am your lord who has made your limbs and given you sustenance.
Bilgrami, Sayed Tahir (2005). "6". Essence of Life, A translation of Ain al-Hayat by Allama Mohammad Baqir Majlisi. Qum: Ansarian Publications. p. 104.

According to en.wikipedia.org/wiki/Masih_ad-Dajjal
    "Hadith attributed to Mohammed give many signs of the appearance of the Dajjal, and exhorted his followers to recite the first and last ten verses of Sura Al-Kahf (chapter 18 in the Quran), as protection from the trials and mischief of the Dajjal.The following signs are ascribed to Ali in the coming of Dajjal:

People will stop offering the prayers

Dishonesty will be the way of life
Falsehood will become a virtue
People will mortgage their faith for worldly gain
Usury and bribery will become legitimate
There will be acute famine at the time
There will be no shame amongst people
Many people would worship Satan
There would be no respect for elderly people
Signs of emergence
Drying up of Sea of Galilee.
When date-palm trees of Baisan stop bearing fruit (Sahih Muslim
English reference : Book 41, Hadith 7028; Arabic reference : Book 55,
Hadith 7573)
Worship of Satan becomes common."

According to Sunnah.com and Sahih al-Bukhari, 3:30:105:
"Dajjal will emerge in a land in the east called Khorasan, and
will be followed by people with faces like hammered shields and
will travel the whole world preaching his falsehood, but will be
unable to enter Mecca or Medina. Isa (Jesus) will return and the
Dajjal will gather an army of 70,000 from Isfahan, of those he has
deceived and lead them in a war against Jesus who shall be
accompanied by an army of the righteous, along with Imam Mahdi.

en.wikipedia.org/wiki/Masih_ad-Dajjal reports:
"Sunni Muslims believe that Isa (Jesus) will descend on Mount
Afeeq, on the white Eastern Minaret of Damascus. He will descend
from the heavens with his hands resting on the shoulders of two
angels. His cheeks will be flat and his hair straight. When he lowers
his head it will seem as if water is flowing from his hair, when he
raises his head, it will appear as though his hair is beaded with
silvery pearls.

Isa (Jesus) will prepare himself to do battle and shall take up a
sword. An army shall return from a campaign launched before the
arrival of Isa. Isa shall set out in pursuit of Dajjal. All those who
embraced the evil of Dajjal shall perish even as the breath of Isa
touches them. The breath of Isa shall precede him as far as the eye
can see. Dajjal will be captured at the gate of Lod. Dajjal shall begin

to melt, as salt dissolves in water. The spear of Isa shall plunge into Dajjal's chest, ending his dreaded reign."

Shias believe that Dajjal will be killed by Mohammed al-Mahdi.

Some people believe the enemy of the Islamic Messiah is an actual person. Some believe it is a system like the West, like the United States, or a thought process like secularism. Some think it's centered upon a country, usually Israel..

The Quran says God will lift up Jesus and return him back, which is usually interpreted as the Second Coming. This is very similar to the Christian idea of the Rapture, but Islam is winner of the holy conflict and God's mercy.

According to Muslims, Jesus didn't actually die, so there's no issue of Resurrection. As a result, this is viewed more as a completion of his lifespan. In Muslim apocalyptic literature, he lives out a normal life. Then, after Jesus is lifted up, Gog and Magog appear. These are invading people in the vague north, and of course, apocalyptic Christians once believed it was the Russians. Muslims took that approach for a while, but they have now dropped it, just as evangelical Christians have. The standard Muslim interpretation is that God has concealed Gog and Magog, and he will reveal them at the end of the world.

Generally, in war, the faithful Muslim warriors are rewarded richly. They go to the highest levels of heaven because they have been purified. They stand with the martyrs and prophets. Some Muslims believe the martyr and prophet go directly to heaven while the other Muslims will be consigned to the grave until the day of judgment. Apocalyptic Muslims are interested in hundred-year markers because of what is called the Mujaddid tradition, which says that at the beginning of every century, God will send a renewer to the religion.

Based on these interpretations, Iran is leading the push toward the Islamic apocalypse as they move forward with their plan to build a nuclear bomb and bring war. This war will divide the world between Islam and the infidels and set in motion the promised return of the Mahdi.

The National Review article "Islamic Extremists Are Trying to Hasten the Coming of the Mahdi" by Joel Rosenberg reads:

"Just four days after President Obama hailed his nuclear deal with Iran, Khamenei publicly reaffirmed Iran's long-standing policy of destroying the U.S. and Israel. "The slogans of the Iranian nation on Al-Quds [Jerusalem] Day show what its position is," he said in a speech. "The slogans 'Death to Israel' and 'Death to America' have resounded throughout the country, and are not limited to Tehran and the other large cities. The entire country is under the umbrella of this great movement." "Even after this deal, our policy towards the arrogant U.S. will not change," he added. Even Iranian president Hassan Rouhani, widely hailed in the West as a moderate, has urged Iranians to act on that policy. "Saying 'Death to America' is easy," he said when running for office in 2013. "We need to express 'death to America' with action.

We perform jihad here [in Iraq] while our eyes are upon al-Quds," declared Abu Musab Zarqawi, the leader of al-Qaeda in Iraq, the al-Qaeda division that morphed into ISIS. "We fight here, while our goal is Rome with good expectations concerning Allah that He makes us the keys for the prophetic good tidings and godly decrees.

"The Mahdi will come any day," Abu Ayyub al-Masri, the ISIS leader after Zarqawi's death, constantly told his people, recruiting new followers with the promise of being glorious fighters in history's Final Hour.

"Our last message is to the Americans," Abu Bakr al-Baghdadi, another ISIS leader, declared in an audio recording on January 21, 2014. "Soon we will be in direct confrontation, and the sons of Islam have prepared for such a day." In the near term, ISIS is more dangerous because it is on a jihadist rampage now. In the longer term, Iran's leaders are more dangerous. By summer of 2014, Baghdadi, a fervent apostle of Sunni apocalyptic eschatology, had officially declared the caliphate, laying the groundwork for the Mahdi's return. "Rush, O Muslims, to your state," he said in July 2014. "This is my advice to you. If you hold to it you will conquer Rome and own the world, if Allah wills." From his reading of Sunni End Times prophecies, Baghdadi saw Rome not only as the historic center of Christendom but as a symbol of the apostate Western powers, led by the United States, which would soon be vanquished by Muslim forces.

"We will conquer your Rome, break your crosses, and enslave your women," vowed an official ISIS spokesman in Dabiq, the magazine of the Islamic State."

Below is a comparison between the Christian and Muslim apocalyptic figures:

Christianity

Jesus – The Messiah.
Returns on a white horse.
Has name of God on his forehead.
Battles armies of the beast/false prophet.
Destroys the anti-Christ and his army.
Raises the dead.
Establishes a new kingdom.
Will reign on earth for a thousand years.

Signs of Jesus' Return:
People will become: Prideful, Unloving, Boastful, Materialistic, Indifferent to each other. They will Mock Christians. Sin will be rampant. There will be Apostasy & Spiritual Deception.

The Beast– The Antichrist.
World leader who negotiates 7 year peace deal between Israel and a great enemy (some believe it is Islamic nations.)
The Beast suffers a mortal wound but he does not die.(heals or resurrects himself).
Declares himself to be God at the temple in Jerusalem.
The Beast has armies of Gog and Magog at his command. Some believe these are from Eastern nations.
Establishes one world government.
Causes all to receive a mark (Mark of the beast) in their forehead or right hand. Some righteous refuse.
The False prophet: Establishes one world-religion.
Beheads unbelievers.
Works 'miracles in the sight of the beast, which would cause even some of the elect to worship the beast (Antichrist).

Islam

Isa (Jesus) the prophet returns to aid the Mahdi in defeating the Christians and Jews who do not convert.

Isa will be subordinate to the Mahdi. He will direct all attention off of himself and onto the Mahdi. He institutes Islamic Sharia Law. Acts as a Muslim evangelist. Abolishes Christianity. Kills the Dajjal as well as his Jewish followers. Persecutes Christians and Jews and forces them to convert or face death. Remains on earth approximately four years. Marries and eventually dies.

Assists the Imam Mahdi to establish the global caliphate.

The name Al Mahdi, also known as: Imam Mahdi, The 12th Imam, or The Hidden Imam.

Translates into:

The Guided One, The Awaited One, or The Lord of the Age.

Mahdi is seen as being the redeemer of Islam or who some describe as being The Islamic Messiah.

Battles the Dajjal (Muslim Antichrist)

Mahdi, a religious ruler is the commander of the faithful.

He leads the armies of Islam against the Jews, Christians, and Muslim apostates.

Marches with black flags to the temple mount.

Declares a global caliphate and rules from Jerusalem

Brings peace & prosperity.

Causes all to receive a mark in their forehead. Muslims receive "bismillah", in the name of allah – unbelievers receive 'bismilkafir' in the name of unbelievers.

al-masih ad-Dajjal is the Islamic version of Antichrist. (Islam's "the deceiving-messiah") Arrives on a white donkey, has one eye, performs false miracles to lead believers astray. Will be of Jewish decent and will claim to be Jesus.

All rivers he is around will become dry and he will call upon people in a loud voice, "O my friends come to me! I am your lord who has made your limbs and given you sustenance.'

The signs of the coming of Dajjal:

People will stop offering the prayers
Dishonesty will be the way of life
Falsehood will become a virtue
People will mortgage their faith for worldly gain
Usury and bribery will become legitimate
Imbeciles would rule over the wise
Blood of innocents would be shed
Pride will be taken on acts of oppression
The rulers will be corrupt
The scholars will be hypocrites
There will be acute famine at the time
There will be no shame amongst people
Many people would worship Satan
There would be no respect for elderly people

Sahih al-Bukhari, 3:43:656
Allah's Apostle said, "The Hour will not be established until the son of Maryam (Mary) descends amongst you as a just ruler, he will break the cross (Christians), kill the pigs [Jews], and abolish the Jizya tax. Money will be in abundance so that nobody will accept it.

The comment regarding money being so abundant that it is worthless reminds one for the Christian description of heaven where the streets are paved with gold.

Thus far we have seen that Islam began in the mind of a man who believed he had seen demons in a cave where he had a vision. These visions may or may not have been due to epilepsy. His wife convinced him that he did not see a demon but it was the angle Gabriel instead. In one vision Mohammed believed he was called to be a prophet in the same manner of Abraham and Jesus. As the last prophet, his teachings would be the final word. All others that had come before were eclipsed and nullified by his words. We saw that Mohammed began preaching peace and acceptance. He wrote verses stating Allah had a family but later claimed to have been deceived by Satan when he wrote verses saying Allah had a wife and daughters. When he gained enough followers to make a stand Mohammed's approach changed to one of war and conversion by force. As Mohammed aged he seemed to become more and more violent and depraved. In his twenties he married and loved an older, more mature women. By the time he was in his fifties Mohammed had taken a 13 year old girl and had married a 6 year old child.

Mohammed created Islam as a socio-political systems based on a theology he created after he was exposed to Christianity and Judaism. Islam has its own body of law called Sharia Law. Because it is based on the 7th century teachings of Mohammed it is archaic but cannot be changed. Under this law amputation, stoning, slavery, killing non-believers, and other such punishments are enforced.

After Mohammed died, his sayings were collected into a book called the Quran, which is thought to be the last and perfect word of God. In the Quran it is only the last thoughts or ideas about a topic that counts. All prior saying are cancelled by the final utterance. This is called the rule of Abrogation. Before he died Mohammed gave us the "Verse of the Sword", which abrogated all peaceful verses of the Quran and gave Muslims the right to seek out and kill anyone who did not convert to Islam.

Islam is based on the teachings in the Quran and the words, deed, and ideas of Mohammed as passed along by witnesses in a collection called the Hadith. Keeping these things in mind, it is time to look at the Quran in the light of interpretation through abrogation.

Section 2

Prepare and Defend

Solutions That Politicians Will Not Permit

There is a self-enforcing cycle in the Islamic community worldwide. Hate sells. Hate motivates. Preaching hate brings more listeners to the mosques than preaching love. Muslim clerics preach division and hate. They preach anti-American, anti-western, anti-Christian, and anti-Jewish rhetoric, inciting their followers to do violence against all non-believers. Some followers, in turn become clerics who teach as they were taught. To break this cycle the U.S. needs to set up reputable Islamic universities to train moderate cleric, who will then set up mosques and teach their followers a moderate and peaceful version of Islam. The balance must be swung to the side of rational tolerance within Islam, but it will take time. It is time we do not have if we continue down the present path. The flow of Muslim immigrants must be stopped in order to allow time to correct the intolerance and weed out radical Muslims and would be terrorists that are already among us.

Those immigrants coming from Afghanistan, Iraq, Iran, Syria, Pakistan, Yemen, Sudan, and all other nations where radical Islam and terrorism originates or is encouraged should not be allowed in to the United States or any of its territories. If an individual cannot prove their country of origin to be other than these countries they should not be allowed in. This hard line must be drawn in part because the records from the above mentioned countries cannot and do not indentify their citizens, their backgrounds, or their political leanings very well, making it very easy for terrorist to blend in with those we label refugees. This action of restricting immigration is not without precedent.

During the 1979 Islamic Revolution's Iranian hostage crisis in which Islamists took over the country, President Jimmy Carter issued orders to put pressure on Iran. In 1980 Carter declared:
    "...The Secretary of Treasury [State] and the Attorney General will invalidate all visas issued to Iranian citizens for future entry into the United States, effective today. We will not reissue visas, nor will we issue new visas, except for compelling and proven

humanitarian reasons or where the national interest of our own country requires. This directive will be interpreted very strictly."

Even though there was little pushback to Carter's actions, now when it is most important to contain a real and present threat, politicians refuse to act. Do they want internal war and chaos? To prevent terrorist's attacks we must control immigration.

To regulate who enters the country the U.S. must close and control its borders to the south and north. Breaching a country's borders without permission has always been a federal offense and punishable by imprisonment in almost every country in the world. Until very recently all European countries controlled their borders, then they relaxed their stance and went to open borders between certain countries. That has not worked out well for them and they are now attempting to clean up the mess left in Brussels from the terrorists attacks in 2016 where terrorists were able to travel easily between internal borders of the E.U. If one does not have borders one does not have a country. If one cannot or will not protect the borders, the borders are meaningless.

Next, we must neutralize naturalized citizens, preventing them from producing the same results as foreign terrorists. We do this by carefully tracking the movements of citizens into other countries. The framework for this tracking is already in place, but once a person enters the Middle East, it is difficult to follow their movements into more radical areas. If a person enters Turkey they can travel to Syria and possibly avoid detection. Unless we can verify the movements of a person going to the Middle East we must not allow re-entrance into the U.S. Certainly, we must block and refuse re-entrance of anyone who has visited countries connected with terrorism, training terrorists, or funding terrorism.

We must monitor the rhetoric being preached at local mosques. If a cleric preaches sedition or violence he should be deported or arrested. If we wish to protect young men against indoctrination into terrorism we must stop it at the source. Mosques housing radical thoughts of violence against non-believers or western culture should be closed.

ISIS and al-Qaeda websites should be blocked. This has proven to be a difficult project. It may be time to take a blanket approach and seek out all sites preaching Islam and drill down from there. Any website promoting violence or jihad should be blocked or shut down. The western world must cooperate in finding and detaining webmasters who incite terrorism. If the website originates outside the western sphere it should be blocked.

Twitter and Facebooks accounts are a more difficult problem. Soon after one offending account is shut down another account replaces it. Twitter and Facebook must continue to take responsibility for the technology they engineered and produced by assigning departments to track and close accounts encouraging violence or terrorism.

Muslim neighborhoods and gathering placed should be seeded with men and women who are pro-peace. One of the major problems facing police and other authorities is the reluctance of Muslims to report the terrorist activities of jihadists and violent extremists. Until Muslim communities tire of being identified and blamed for the actions of the more radical few, and until they report or stop the assaults by these jihadists, it will fall to others outside the Muslim communities to defeat the terrorists. Once brave, peace-loving Muslims begin watching for and reporting suspicious activities, such as violent rhetoric, weapons purchases and stores of explosive materials, we can begin to trust. Until then all Muslims will be suspected or held accountable. Silence implies consent.

Forced Into Fascism

In a perfect world, without a central government seeking to gain, keep, and exploit power, we would not have to worry about implementing temporary laws that would quickly extinguish ISIS in the U.S., but this is not a perfect world and the U.S. government is no longer a government that can be trusted to relinquish any power once granted. How then can we enact laws to observe, track, and prosecute terrorist without having those same laws turned on all citizen?

The answer is simple but would be objectionable to most liberals and libertarians as well. If we declare the United States of American and Judeo-Christian country, protecting those groups and laws, we would block the passage of Sharia laws, which Muslims are attempting to implement in various states in a number of ways. We would also be able to protect ourselves against groups that seek to do us harm.

How can we claim to be a nation of laws and not men if we support certain groups or target a single group? How can we do these things and not become the next Nazi nation, targeting Muslims instead of Jews? The answer is simple defense of our nation and way of life. There cannot be two sets of laws and Muslims demand to be under Sharia Law. Herman Mustafa Carroll, executive director of the Dallas CAIR branch has said: "If we are practicing Muslims, we are above the law of the land."

Breitbart reports: "Underground sharia courts operate in Muslim communities throughout Europe and also in the United States. Last year, Breitbart Texas reported that a "voluntary" sharia court had already been established in Texas.
Several countries in Europe, including the United Kingdom, France, and Germany, have many underground sharia courts within migrant communities. In the U.K, the government has

formally deputized at least one sharia court to decide non-criminal issues among people who agree to use the court, even as public concerns rise that immigrant women are socially pressured to accept the courts' authority

U.S. opponents of sharia courts point to Europe for evidence that western democracies can gradually cede more de-facto legal authority to self-segregating Muslim communities, so enabling the self-segregation of Muslim communities into no-go zones within cities.

Several states–including Alabama, Arizona, Kansas, Louisiana, North Carolina South Dakota, and Tennessee–have passed "foreign law" bans against sharia. More than a dozen other states are currently considering similar legislation."

Already, Muslim cab drivers are throwing blind passangers and their service dogs to the curb and into traffic because Islam believes dogs are dirty. Muslims have demanded their women be allowed to wear a complete burqa when taking pictures for a driver's license. These acts are so ridiculous as to boggle the mind. The fact they would be permitted in a single instance speaks to the fact we are fighting people who are already convinced they are above the law.

No one should be above our laws. Owing to this growing push toward Sharia Law and the flaccid response of the national government, some states have acted on their own. The state leaders realized the federal government does not have the moral fortitude to pass laws upholding the constitution, nor do they have the moral compass to pass laws to assure our nation continues to be based on Judeo-Christian values, so many states have reacted accordingly. State governments have begun taking it upon themselves to stand in the gap and pass laws restricting or banning Sharia Law.

Since 2013, sixteen U.S. states have introduced legislation to ban or restrict Sharia law.

The list was compiled by the radical, terror-linked CAIR — which meant it to condemn the states.

Alabama became the latest state to ban Sharia law when voters overwhelmingly passed a measure adding an amendment to the state constitution. CAIR said that the motion was "virulently racist" and "outright hostility towards Muslims." Alabamans apparently didn't care what they said.

The list of all 16 states are:

Alabama (two bills)
Arkansas
Florida (two bills)
Indiana (two bills)
Iowa
Kentucky
Mississippi (four bills)
Missouri (two bills)
North Carolina
Oklahoma (seven bills)
South Carolina (two bills)
Texas (six bills)
Virginia
Washington
West Virginia
Wyoming (two bills)

Here we must break with "political correctness" and admit it is a single group that seeks to destroy us. Choosing not to watch and regulate the group that is trying to kill us is a type of denial that borders on insanity and self-destruction. Islamic terrorists or radical Islamists are called these things because they belong to a single group. They are Islamic. It is not reasonable to ignore Muslims as the source of terrorism. Just because all Muslims do not commit terrorism does not mean the group should not be watched since as much as 20% of the group either will be terrorists, will support terrorism, or will approve of the actions and thus aid by their silence.

We permit Muslims to enter the U.S. knowing we cannot discern radical from moderate. Terrorism is becoming a world wide epidemic, but we do not even use the same caution to guard against terrorism as we do to guard against disease. We observe and guard against epidemics coming from certain countries as a matter of national protection and common sense.

Ralph Ellis, CNN, wrote on Friday October 31, 2014:
"Canada will stop processing visa applications from foreign nationals who have visited West African nations with large outbreaks of the Ebola virus, Citizenship and Immigration Minister Chris Alexander said Friday. Applications will be returned to people from Ebola hot spots who have already applied for visas, officials said in a press release."

In the Wall Street Journal, Kristina Peterson wrote on Oct. 21, 2014:
"The Department of Homeland Security on Wednesday will begin limiting flights carrying passengers from three West African countries affected by Ebola to arrival at five U.S. airports.
The move represents only a slight change to flight traffic from Liberia, Sierra Leone and Guinea because most passengers from these countries already arrive in the U.S. at the five designated airports, where extra Ebola screening measures are in place."

Although most Republicans wanted to close the borders to all West African countries with Ebola outbreaks, they were voted down, leading to restrictions instead of a complete halt of traffic. As a result two innocent people lost their lives.

As it stands, too many lawmakers in the U.S. refuse to take the proper precautions against terrorists. Knowing this, the leaders of ISIS and al-Qaeda have stated, "We will use your laws against you."

According to MediaMatters, June 2011, People on terrorist watch lists are not forbidden from purchasing guns and many have done just that. Associated Press reported that more than 200 people with suspected terrorist ties bought guns legally in the United States last year. Following the AP report Representative Mike Quigley introduced an amendment to the Patriot Act that would give the Attorney General the authority to block gun sales to individuals on terror watch lists. The amendment was voted down. Al-Qaeda and ISIS have been instructed to exploit loopholes in laws to obtain support from the U.S. government in the form of housing, welfare, and medical assistance, and while being supported by our nation they are to demonstrate against that same government and acquire weapons to attack The United States and its citizens.

Obviously, the answer is not to restriction gun sales, since terrorists would simply get them via the black market, leaving only terrorists, killers, thieves, and cartels armed. Citizens have a right to protect themselves against robbers, thieves, terrorists, and the government.

Muslims in our country do not want to integrate or to be part of our society or even to be equal with others. They wish to dominate and to be the only privileged group. Muslims achieve this by turning you into a second-class citizen in your own country.

Quran 3:110 Allah said to Muslims: "Thus We have made you the best nation, that you be witnesses over mankind and the Messenger (Muhammad) be a witness over you".

Muslims demand tolerance, but they don't have to tolerate anyone else or any other societies or faiths. They demand accommodation, but they don't have to accommodate other beliefs. They demand respect but they do not respect other people, laws, or ways. They immigrate to western countries and think it is our duty to conform to them and their laws, most of which run contrary to our own laws.

Immigrants should be given no more than six months to find a job, become productive, and begin to assimilate, or be deported. Indeed, we should not allow immigrants into this great country unless they can and will add to the fabric and economy of the nation.

One of the major reasons we permit immigration to proceed as we do is that once immigrants begin to receive welfare they will likely vote for the Democrat party. Thus, the Democrats promote immigration in spite of the risks of depleting government funds, overloading programs or importing violence. Politicains endanger the country in order to strengthen their base. And, if things get bad enough to decalse martial law, it simply means elections will be postponed and the politicians will stay in power.

The only way to combat such arrogence and entrentchment is to vote out all career politicians as soon as possible. One of the first and greatest gifts of protection we can give ourselves as a nation is to remove politicians that value their power and positions more than our safety. If they do not pass laws to protect us we should remove them immediately and permanently. But, for now the U.S. government stands in the way of our best interest and our protection.

In spite of this we must understand radical Islam, its aims, goals, strategies and tactics, and we must prepare and protect ourselves.

How Can We Protect Ourselves?

Who Are The Experts and What Do They Say?

Larry Hartsook is the President of Global Integrated Security Solutions (GISS) and has 35 plus years' combined experience in Counter-Terrorism, Active Army, Army Reserve, National Guard, Special Forces, Special Operations (27 plus years' military service), and International Corporate Security Challenges.
He successfully commanded a Special Forces Company, three Special Forces Operational Detachments-Blue Light (counterterrorist) and served as a Voting Member of the General Officer Steering Committee for Civil Military Cooperation Program. He was the Program Manager for the US Army Reserve Command Civil Military Cooperation Program (CMCP) consisting of 54 individual projects with budgets exceeding $62 million dollars. He served 7 years as the Counterdrug Operations Officer for Second Army, US Army Reserve Command, and JTF-6 Counter-Drug. During his military career, he conducted over 300 operational assessments (CARVER) in security, anti-terrorism, counter-terrorism, and counter-drug "real world" operations. He was a contributing editor to National Guard Mobilization Policy System,

Forces Command Mobilization and Deployment Planning System, and Federal Emergency Management Agency Federal Response Plan (Operations Officer for Joint Task Force Andrew). He is a graduate of the Joint Staff Antiterrorism Training Course, Defense Threat Reduction Agency (DTRA), Strategic Intelligence and Target Analysis Interdiction Course and the Special Weapons Officer Course – Nuclear Surety Program and Counterdrug Manager's Course.

Mr. Hartsook served as the Subject Matter Expert (SME) for Security, Anti-terrorism, Counterterrorism, and Emergency/Crisis Operations Center procedures for the US Army Reserve and Northrop Grumman Corporation. Larry's experience is broad and deep in the following security, risk assessment, emergency management, and counter-terrorism areas:

- Northrop Grumman Corporation Security Subject Matter Expert (SME) for the "New" World Trade Center (Freedom Tower) Master Security Plan development.
- Developed the US Army Reserve Force Protection / Anti-Terrorism Program winning the DA 2005 "Most Innovative Anti-Terrorism Program".
- Developed the Emergency Operations and Military Decision Making Process training module for the US Army Reserve Command.
- Developed the Proactive Threat Analysis (PTA^{2TM}) System to quickly analyze and enhance the Risk Management Process Program.
- Developed the Red Team^{2TM}, a threat based system for designing, managing, exercising, and validating security by objectives which are based on site specific threats.
- Developed Situational Awareness Assessment Training (SAAT^{TM}) (Israeli Predictive Profiling enhanced with the Special Forces Intelligence Gathering Process).
- Developed the Force Protection Validation Guide used in assessing Force Protection Related Programs surpassing the Department of Defense standards in Anti-terrorism.
- Served as Special Liaison Officer for the Secretary of the Army, Reserve Affairs.
- Developed International Proactive Close Combatives/Defense Program^{TM}

He is a member of the American Society for Industrial Security (ASIS), Association of Former Intelligence Officers (AFIO), International Association for Counterterrorism and Security Professionals, American Society of Law Enforcement Trainers, International Association for Counterterrorism and Security Professionals, Security Analysis and Risk Management Association (SARMA), Institute of Terrorism Research and Response Group, Security Analysis and Risk Management Association Group, Counter-Terrorism and Geopolitical Security Group, National Organization of Church Security and Safety Management (NOCSSM), Special Forces Association-Life Member, National Association of Professional Martial Artist, and United States Martial Arts Hall of Fame Inductee.

Colonel Douglas W. Marr, USAR Ret.
Colonel Marr entered active duty Army in 1972 as an Infantry
Officer. During his career he served in the 7th and 9th Infantry
Division, and the 82nd Airborne Infantry Division, Training and
Doctrine Command (TRADOC), Cadet Command, 2nd Support
Command, United Nations Command/USFK/8th Army, and the
United States Army Reserve Command where he served as the
Director of Current Operations, Mobilization, Readiness, Counter-
Drug Operations and Civil-Military Operations until his retirement
in 1996 at Fort McPherson. His assignments included staff and
command positions from Company through Army and Joint
Command levels. He served in Asia, Europe and CONUS.
As a Government Contractor he served as Program/Project
Manager for Omega Training Group, SAIC, Logicon and Northrop
Grumman IT. At Northrop Grumman he served as Program
Manager for establishing the Army Reserve Antiterrorism/Force
Protection Program worldwide, which won the 2005 Department of
the Army Most Innovative Antiterrorism and Force Protection
Program. As on-site manager of the US Army Reserve AT/FP
program he directed, supervised, participated and reviewed over
2,000 vulnerability assessments, 80 force protection programs
validations, 80 DIO vulnerability assessments and engineered a data
base of physical vulnerabilities that was submitted to the

Department of Army and resulted in validating funding justification for $182m in Physical Security upgrades at Reserve Centers in the United States.

Presently, he is Vice President of Global Integrated Security Solutions. In that position he has been involved in performing detailed Security Assessments for Federal Organizations, Commercial Businesses, School and private citizens. He also serves as a key note speaker and consultant.

Training/Education includes:

Bachelors and Masters Degree
Infantry Officer Basic Training
Infantry Officer Advanced Training
Command and General Staff College
Airborne School
Jumpmaster School
Emergency Preparedness Liaison Officer Instructor Course
National Security Emergency Preparedness Officers Course
Command and General Staff Mobilization/Planning Course
Counter-drug Senior Managers Course
Senior Training Managers Course
Certified Protection Professional Training
Physical Security Professional Training
Predictive Profiling & Terrorist Threat Mitigation
Project Management I Course
Force Protection Level I, II, and III
Chemical, Biological, Radiological, Nuclear, High Yield Explosives (CBRNE)

Global Integrated Security Solutions (GISS) is a highly respected provider of world class security solutions. GISS developed the Master Security Management System® to assess and resolve all areas of security challenges and issues. They design and implement integrated processes and training solutions that protect property, information, and most people through the use of the Proactive Threat Analysis Squared (PTA²)® . GISS provides analysis process to mitigate the threats of a terrorist environment. It develops real world strategies and training required to counter actual specific threats. (www.GISS911.com)

According to Hartsook and Marr of GISS, there are ways to prepare and keep us safe. Hartsook and Marr provide the following insights.

If you have read, understand and accept what has been written in the previous chapters about Islam and believe it to be fair and accurate, or at least provide an explanation of why radical Islam is a major threat to the United States as a country, and to Americans as individuals – then what will keep us safe?

Do you accept, as a fact, that the U.S. government, with all of its security layers, agencies and practices, will keep us safe? Combine the federal government's security posture with each state's security posture, and combine that with all the Law Enforcement Agencies (LEA), also referred to as First Responders – are you now comfortable that you and your family are reasonably safe? Might there be actions you, as an individual, can take to further ensure your safety?

The following will let us review some general principles about security, and what components comprise a viable and complete security program. But before delving into that, let's look at the larger picture and ask us some questions.

1.   Does radical Islam present a viable threat to the United States? Yes, unless you don't believe that the attacks on the twin towers (twice) and the Pentagon, the Fort Hood, TX shootings, the Boston Marathon bombing, the San Bernardino shootings all were attacks by radical Islamic terrorists. If you check, you will find there have

been approximately 44 terrorist attacks since 9/11. Many of these were attacks on individuals that didn't make front page news. Since Iran has labeled America as the Great Satan and called for our destruction, one might conclude that is a threat. Add that to the fact that our government is allowing immigrants from primarily Muslim countries into the U.S. without vetting them. Again one can draw the conclusion that our risk has been elevated. So the answer is YES, radical Islam presents a credible threat to the United States.

2.   Is there a regional threat in the United States? Yes, if you consider the attacks cited above and the areas where large concentrations of Muslims (communities) reside in the U.S. (California, Illinois, Minnesota, New York, New Jersey, Indiana, Michigan, Virginia, Ohio, Maryland and Texas) as being indicators of threat, and the possibility for additional threat as communities are establishing near many state universities. Remember the percentage of Muslims that are radical – 15% to 25%. According to the Pew Research Center, the estimated Muslim population in the United States in 2015 was 3.3 million, or 1% of our total population. Do the math – 15% (the low end) of 3.3 million = 495,000 possibly radicalized Muslims, up to 25%, which is 825,000 potentially radicalized Muslims. Is there a credible threat? You know there is!

3.   Do you perceive a threat to yourself or your family? If paragraphs 1 and 2 above are true, then yes, but there are several variables that affect the level of risk. Just as a reminder, review the Verse of the Sword, the Abrogation and specifically what choice the Fundamentalist Islamic terrorist offers those who are not Muslim, particularly Christians and Jews: join or die. That should clear up any confusion you may have as to whether or not there is a credible threat to you and your family.

As a nation, we stay safe by fighting and defeating the radical Islamic terrorist on his own soil, not ours. President Reagan said it best when describing his strategy on the Cold War: "We win; they lose." However, the fact of the matter is that these terrorists are already amongst us thanks to our relaxed immigration policy and posture. So how does our country mitigate the risk we face with the enemy now living, working and practicing their faith within our communities?

Many planned attacks have been foiled thanks to the work of the NSA, CIA, FBI, DIA, ASA, TSA, Border Patrol, Homeland Security, numerous Law Enforcement Agencies (LEA), and private security personnel. Of course a lot of freedoms, civil liberties and tax dollars have disappeared under the guise of keeping the citizens of the United States safe. But, regardless of how many three-letter agencies we have, the fact is that we have been attacked – multiple times. So then what do we do? Frankly, this is a question that all of our citizens ought to contemplate, understand the ramifications of the risks involved, personalize it and then voice their opinion. I strongly suggest you don't let someone else determine what actions are "enough" or "appropriate" when it comes to you and your family's safety. As for me, I'd put political correctness aside and insist action be taken. First let's be clear about who is the threat. Then vet the people who pose a threat, remove them or eliminate the problem until such time that we are certain none poses a threat. If that means interrogation, monitoring communications, exposing the clerics' teachings – so be it. This is far from a social issue; it is a survival issue. Again, what options are you offered by radical Islam? Following are actions you, as an individual, can take.

First, understand that good security is never convenient. Once you start to outsource your security, the level of your security drops. Real security must be human centric and supplemented by technology, not the other way around.

Second, understand that First Responders are exactly that – responders. We aren't saying that the law enforcement officers aren't doing a good job, but they "respond." That means something bad has already happened for them to respond. The idea of good security is to prevent bad things from happening. The Israelis have a great system that is known to the United States – we just don't use it because it violates "our" social sensitivities.

Third, good security should be "proactive not reactive." Identify the event before it is executed and respond accordingly. Too often individuals believe they must call the police – but by the time police arrive, significant damage can occur. There are actions individuals can take to stop or mitigate bad things from happening, and they have to learn what those actions are and practice them.

Fourth, identify what you want to protect, why, and what you are protecting it from.

Fifth, do a threat-based assessment. Not just where you live, but where you travel, what events you attend, vacations, travel overseas, etc. Know what settings make for a soft but lucrative target. It takes some research and some reading, but you can identify your threat, and for the purposes of this book and chapter we are talking about radical Islamic terrorists. Again, remember, good security is never convenient.

After you have done your own research about the level of threat that exists, you can determine your own personal level of risk. We are talking about the potential for an attack of some sort. It could be a personal attack, such as a sexual assault on a female like those committed by Syrian refugees in Germany and Sweden. It could be a mob attack, a bomb attack, verbal intimidation or physical assault.

Once you have determined the level of risk for each of your personal locations (home, school, work, travel to and from work, shopping malls, sporting events, church), you can identify your vulnerabilities in each of these settings, apply assets (typically money, but not always) toward reducing your vulnerability, then develop plans and actions to avoid problems or to mitigate the problems should you be involved in an attack.

What are vulnerabilities and what affects them? You can have all sorts of vulnerabilities, but they don't matter if you have no probable and/or deliverable threat. This is precisely why a good threat assessment is so valuable. Once you identify the threats to what you are trying to protect, then you can identify the vulnerabilities that would allow the threat access to what is to be protected. A vulnerability can be as simple as not being aware of your surroundings: i.e., you are home and don't notice the white van that has gone past your house three times in the last 10 minutes; or each day you drive to work at the same time and use the same route – thus becoming predictable; or you're in a store and don't notice that someone is following you around the store. How about your church? During services, are the doors open and unmonitored? Can anyone looking like they belong simply stroll in? You may have cameras at work to record key spaces with the building and the coming and going of people, but if no one is watching the monitors then all you record is the carnage and those who perpetrated the crime. You know the threat, you know what you are trying to protect, so by identifying the vulnerabilities you can apply your resources to mitigating your vulnerabilities.

Remember we are talking about radical Islamic terrorists. Their intent is to convert or kill you and your family – there is no middle ground.

You know what your vulnerabilities are, so now you apply your resources to eliminate the vulnerabilities. For this book's purpose, we are talking about protecting you and your family from radical Islamic terrorists. As an example, you strengthen your home's security by adding a dog (my preference is a big dog that is protective); you add motion-activated lights outside; you harden your doors with additional or better locks; you cut back or remove shrubs and bushes that could conceal a perpetrator. I do like holly bushes and their prickly leaves against my house as a barrier. Inside the house, you identify safe areas and add weapons to your inventory. (Be sure you know how to use the guns and keep them loaded; otherwise all you have is a rock.) All family members should be familiar with the weapons, where they are located and what their safety measures are. If you have a multi-level house, keep at least one weapon on each floor. Put a peephole in your door if you don't have a locking storm door as the outside door.
You have to apply appropriate measures for activities, travels, vacations, church, school, shopping and all activities of daily living. Awareness of your surroundings is critical, along with changing your routine, altering your route, letting people know where you are going and when you will be back. A good GPS in the car along with a gun carry permit can be invaluable. (Be sure you know your state laws and those of other states you may travel into.) Again,

remember: good security isn't convenient, and as I have told numerous people – I may be paranoid but that doesn't mean I'm not being followed. Your resources are: money, time and effort.

Using Proactive Predictive Profiling, effective security questioning and Threat Based Assessment processes, we have developed and audited hundreds of federal, military, school (college, public, and private) and corporate security programs. You must first identify your "protected and operational" environments. You cannot protect everything!
Once you know your threat, risk, and vulnerabilities, and have applied resources against the vulnerabilities, now you need a plan. What are the components of a proactive comprehensive security program?

- Threat Based Assessment – All Hazards
- Probability Assessment
- Risk Assessment
- Criticalities Assessment
- Consequences Assessment
- Vulnerability Assessment
- Mitigation
- **5P(s)** - *Policy, Plans, Procedures, Protocols, Preparedness* (Training/Exercise)
- Train/Rehearse/Exercise/Test
- Revise – when changes in the "protected or operational" environment occur

It doesn't have to be complex for your home or while traveling, but you do need a set of actions that each family member knows and understands. An example of a home plan would include actions each family takes at the onset of an event, where each member goes in the house, calling 911 while those with weapon(s) react to points of entry. For instance, as a break-in begins, the wife calls 911, and announces it loudly so any perpetrator can hear.

If the intruders depart, a major crisis has been averted; if they don't, you now know exactly what the rules of engagement are: shoot to kill. A side note – this is why you keep a loaded gun available. If the gun is unloaded, do you think the intruders will wait for you to load? If there are children, depending on their age, they either hide at a predesignated location, or if they are older, they can assist with a weapon. This highlights why everyone has to have weapons training and understand the plan. The same process applies for any travel, vacation, school activity, church function, etc. You assess the threat, determine your risk level, consider the vulnerabilities and apply resources to mitigate the vulnerabilities (called hardening the target), and then using the **5P(s)** develop policies, plans, procedures, protocols, and preparedness (training and exercise) to put your security actions in place.

Finally, you want to execute and rehearse your plan to see if all involved understand what the tasks are, and to determine if the plan works. Normally, a reality-based exercise of a plan will highlight shortcomings or details that were overlooked or dysfunctional. You make necessary corrections, and now have an operational plan in case you are the target. What "facts" and/or "constant" is available in your "tool Kit" to assist you in the analysis required for developing a "proactive security program"?

I submit the following information to assist in the analysis:

"WHEN YOU USE PREDICTIVE PROFILING, YOU ARE NEVER UNARMED."

What are "Facts" you must continually address and/or be aware of?

- THREAT IS CONSTANT! ALL SECURITY PROGRAMS MUST BE BASED ON THREAT
- ALL PERCEIVED THREATS "MUST BE" CONFIRMED OR REFUTED!
- "THREAT BASED - ALL HAZARDS" ASSESSMENT MUST BE CONDUCTED FIRST!
- NOT A "POLICE ASSESSMENT"! IT IS NOT SECURITY ORIENTED - OPERATIONAL FOR POLICE ONLY
- PROACTIVE (SECURITY) = PREVENTION!
- REACTIVE (LAW ENFORCEMENT) = RESPONDING TO INCIDENT!

- SCHOOL RESOURCE OFFICERS (SROs) ARE NOT TRAINED IN SECURITY (PREVENTION)
- SCHOOLS ARE SOFT TARGETS THAT AFFORD KILLERS AMPLE TIME!
- PROACTIVE "IS NOT" IMPROVING YOUR "RESPONSE" TIME!
- "LOCK DOWN" IS A 10-YEAR FEDERALLY DOCUMENTED "FAILED SYSTEM"!
- "RUN, HIDE, FIGHT" IS NOT PROACTIVE! SHOOTER IS IN THE BUILDING!
- 5P(s) are POLICY, PLANS, PROCEDURES, PROTOCOLS, PREPAREDNESS WITH INTEGRATION OF FIRST RESPONDERS, ALL IMPORTANT "AFTER" PLANS ARE IN PLACE AND EXERCISED!
- WHEN THE SHOOTING STARTS, IT IS TOO LATE TO CALL 911!
- YES, THESE "FACTS" ARE OVERWHELMING!
- 93 Percent of Corporate Security Officials Say "Human Behavior Presents The Greatest Threat" (Source– ASIS International – January 2016)

ALL PAST, CURRENT, FUTURE INCIDENTS "WERE/ARE" PREDICTABLE AND PREVENTABLE!

Why do you need a thorough understanding of America, regionally and individually? I address the following on a point-by-point basis:

- Society. We all live within a multifaceted society. We must understand what it is and how it works. We must determine what we accept and do not accept. We must develop a process that allows us to co-exist.
- People. Individuals are an enigma to challenge any collective process. We must again determine what we accept and do not accept. We must daily interface and work with many different personalities, cultures, and faiths.
- Culture. Individuals based on environment, faith, and norms become a culture. We must determine how to work and interact with a culture to receive maximum benefit.

- Religion. Faith is not logic. Beliefs abound worldwide and we must find ways to tolerate those beliefs we do not accept. Each person is entitled to a "faith-based" religion, but we are not required to accept the beliefs of others. We must learn to work with consideration and knowledge of other religions.

- Awareness. We must have keen awareness of all aspects of people, cultures, and religions to understand what they represent to others. We need not accept all cultures, religions, people, and/or society outside our own beliefs. However, we must understand them so that we can predict their behavior.
- Assessment. We must continue conducting daily assessments of our protected and operational environments.
- Analysis. We must conduct an analysis of these assessments to determine the impact on the environments that we live in.
- Acceptance. We must determine what we accept and do not accept regardless of the base.
- Preparation. We must develop buffers and reasons for the survival of our protected and operational environments.
- Proactive. Proactive = Prevention. Do you not want to prevent rather than "react"? React = Incident has happened.

Be selective in the company or person you hire for the responsibility of establishing your safety and security. Building an effective proactive security plan/program requires extensive experience and training. A company or individual charged with the responsibility for developing your security footprint must have superior "real world" experience exceeding industry standards. All plans/programs must be coordinated and integrated with local First Responder Programs. You have hired these people to produce a program capable of protecting your life and the lives of your loved ones. Do your research and validate the expertise of the company or person.

What should you take away from this book?
      Verse of the Sword
      Abrogation
      Radical Islam's objectives and goal
      Convert or Die

How to Protect your family?

Learn and use Predictive Profiling components with effective security questioning

Develop home, travel, and business security programs

Use the 5Ps in developing your program

Train to the program and exercise it for revision (yearly or with changes in either environment)

Finally, we refer to people who "wish or hope" for the best outcome as - VICTIMS.

For more information, to arrange speaking engagements, or to acquire services from Global Integrated Security Solutions (GISS), please go to www.giss911.com.

Conclusion

Citizens of the United States of America are constitutionally guaranteed both freedom **of** religion and freedom **from** religion. This means at no time can a person be forced to worship in a particular way, nor can they be forced to practice a religion which they do not believe. They are free to have no religion at all, if they so choose. Citizens cannot be forced to obey religious clerics or laws. We answer only to the laws we, as a nation, state, or municipality have passed.

In Islam, these constitutionally provided freedoms are attacked in most piculiar and harsh ways. Islam is not a religion. Although they seek to use our laws of religious freedoms against us, in no way should these laws be applicable. Islam is a political system of government and laws underwritten by a 7th century document. The religious practices bolstering the underlying political system simply serves to cloud the issue.

Muslims seek to install Sharia Law into all nations. They seek a new world order that establishes a single Islamic nation or caliphate throughout the world. They seek to govern the world through a single ruler called a Caliph. These are political asprirations. Islam must be viewed as a national movement to be understood and controlled. If it is viewed only as a religion the US will make the same mistake the rest of the world has made and we will be infiltrated and destroyed as we see Europe being destroyed even now.

When our politically correct political leaders tell us we have not and will not declare war on Islam, they are being naïve and intentionally missled. We must declare war on a political movement that seeks to conquor us, and kill us. ISIS has already said if they cannot impose Islam on us they will kill us. That is a declaration of war.

What nation, attempting to continue its existence and freedom, would not fight back against those who wish to invade its borders, kill its people, and establish laws which would make its people slaves and second class citizens?

It is not only ISIS that attempts these things. We have read the words of the leaders of CAIR, the orginazation which advises President Obama. The establishment of Sharia Law and the overthrow of our present legal system is the wish of the majority of Muslims.

This is a war, and we should began acting like we are fighting for our freedom.

Appendix "A"
Abrogated Verses

"Abrogate": repeal or do away with (a law, right, or formal agreement). repeal, revoke, rescind, repudiate, overturn, annul.

Abrogation is a concept embraced by Muslim scholars such as Ahmed Bin Ishaq Al-Dinary, Mohammad Bin Bahr Al-Asbahany, Hebat Allah Bin Salamah and Mohammad Bin Mousa Al-Hazmy, whose book about Al-Nasekh and Al-Mansoukh is regarded as one of the leading references in the subject. According to this concept some earlier verses in the Quran are abrogated and invalidated by later verses. These scholars have come up with hundreds of cases of abrogated verses.

Abrogation represents a type of continuing revelation within the Quran. An example of this is the fact that Mohammed first preached peace when in Mecca, then decided that war and conversion by the sword worked better to attain his goals. Thus, he abrogated the verses regarding peace and substituted those about war and conflict. The verse that is the abrogator is call "Al-Nasekh" and the abrogated verse is call "Al-Mansoukh".

Abrogations should not be regarded as contradictions, rather, it is a process of change and what Mohammed thought would work best at the time. The problem is that the last words of Mohammed on any subject dictated the direction of Islam forever and cannot be altered.

Given the fact that the Quran was compiled just after the death of Mohammed and is considered the last word from God through Mohammed, who Muslim's believed to be the last prophet, it is considered without error and must be followed.

Those parts of the Quran that Muslims believed were dictated by the angel Gabriel to Mohammed are usually not abrogated, but Mohammed's thoughts and approaches to spreading Islam and the laws governing the faith evolved over time from peaceful to those of terrorism.

As with any faith, there are differing views and applications to abrogation. The more liberal the Muslim the more likely the verses of peace will be taken into consideration. The more fundamental the Muslim the more likely the rule of abrogation will be applied and the verse of the sword, which was one of the last verses written will be applied.

The Verse of the Sword was used by Osama bin Laden to justify the attack on New York and the Twin Towers. It is also used by the Taliban and ISIS to justify their brand of terrorism and killing.

Since the Verse of the Sword is said to abrogate over a hundred verses and is one of the most important verse used by fundamental Muslims to justify terrorism, it is very important to gain an understanding of the verse. Here are all popular English translations of the verse.

Sahih International: And when the sacred months have passed, then kill the polytheists wherever you find them and capture them and besiege them and sit in wait for them at every place of ambush. But if they should repent, establish prayer, and give zakah, let them [go] on their way. Indeed, Allah is Forgiving and Merciful.

Pickthall: Then, when the sacred months have passed, slay the idolaters wherever ye find them, and take them (captive), and besiege them, and prepare for them each ambush. But if they repent and establish worship and pay the poor-due, then leave their way free. Lo! Allah is Forgiving, Merciful.

Yusuf Ali: But when the forbidden months are past, then fight and slay the Pagans wherever ye find them, an seize them, beleaguer them, and lie in wait for them in every stratagem (of war); but if they repent, and establish regular prayers and practice regular charity, then open the way for them: for Allah is Oft-forgiving, Most Merciful.

Shakir: So when the sacred months have passed away, then slay the idolaters wherever you find them, and take them captives and besiege them and lie in wait for them in every ambush, then if they repent and keep up prayer and pay the poor-rate, leave their way free to them; surely Allah is Forgiving, Merciful.

Mohammed Sarwar: When the sacred months are over, slay the pagans wherever you find them. Capture, besiege, and ambush them. If they repent, perform prayers and pay the religious tax, set them free. God is All-forgiving and All-merciful.

Mohsin Khan: Then when the Sacred Months (the 1st, 7th, 11th, and 12th months of the Islamic calendar) have passed, then kill the Mushrikun (see V.2:105) wherever you find them, and capture them and besiege them, and prepare for them each and every ambush. But if they repent and perform As-Salat (Iqamat-as-Salat), and give Zakat, then leave their way free. Verily, Allah is Oft-Forgiving, Most Merciful.

Arberry: Then, when the sacred months are drawn away, slay the idolaters wherever you find them, and take them, and confine them, and lie in wait for them at every place of ambush. But if they repent, and perform the prayer, and pay the alms, then let them go their way; God is All-forgiving, All-compassionate.

The Verse of the Sword abrogates all verses of regarding peace, since is was spoken last and no other verse was spoken to abrogate it. Many clerics of fundamental Islam includes all religions other that Islam as idolaters. Other verses give Muslims the right to go to war in defense of Islam. By drawing the non-Islamic world into conflict by terrorism they bring about a climate where they declare the civilized world is against Islam and thus they are justified to declare war, kill the innocent, rape women and children, and convert or murder all infidels.

The chart below is lengthy but demonstrates the breadth of abrogation with in the Quran. The layout of the verses were attempted in various ways. All diagrams and layouts seemed lack the clarity of comparison between first verses and those that abrogated them. The default presentation was the simplest. Verses that have been abrogated are presented, then directly below in bold text is the verse that abrogated it. Verses are presented in order of Surah or verses in the Quran. Instead of printing the Verse of the Sword multiple times it will simply be referenced by name.

Surah 2

2:3

Those who believe in the unseen and keep up prayer and spend out of what We have given them.

9:103

Take alms out of their property, you would cleanse them and purify them thereby, and pray for them; surely your prayer is a relief to them; and Allah is Hearing, Knowing.

2:62

Surely those who believe, and those who are Jews, and the Christians, and the Sabians, whoever believes in Allah and the Last day and does good, they shall have their reward from their Lord, and there is no fear for them, nor shall they grieve.

3:85

And whoever desires a religion other than Islam, it shall not be accepted from him, and in the hereafter he shall be one of the losers.

2:83

And when We made a covenant with the children of Israel: You shall not serve any but Allah and (you shall do) good to (your) parents, and to the near of kin and to the orphans and the needy, and you shall speak to men good words and keep up prayer and pay the poor-rate. Then you turned back except a few of you and (now too) you turn aside.

9:5

Verse of the Sword

2:109

Many of the followers of the Book wish that they could turn you back into unbelievers after your faith, out of envy from themselves, (even) after the truth has become manifest to them; but pardon and forgive, so that Allah should bring about His command; surely Allah has power over all things.

9:29
Fight those who do not believe in Allah, nor in the latter day, nor do they prohibit what Allah and His Messenger have prohibited, nor follow the religion of truth, out of those who have been given the Book, until they pay the tax in acknowledgment of superiority and they are in a state of subjection.

2:115
And Allah's is the East and the West, therefore, whither you turn, thither is Allah's purpose; surely Allah is Ample giving, Knowing.

2:144
Indeed We see the turning of your face to heaven, so We shall surely turn you to a qiblah which you shall like; turn then your face towards the Sacred Mosque, and wherever you are, turn your face towards it, and those who have been given the Book most surely know that it is the truth from their Lord; and Allah is not at all heedless of what they do.

2:139
Say: Do you dispute with us about Allah, and He is our Lord and your Lord, and we shall have our deeds and you shall have your deeds, and we are sincere to Him.

9:5
Verse of the Sword

2:158
Surely the Safa and the Marwa are among the signs appointed by Allah; so whoever makes a pilgrimage to the House or pays a visit (to it), there is no blame on him if he goes round them both; and whoever does good spontaneously, then surely Allah is Grateful, Knowing.

2:130
And who forsakes the religion of Ibrahim but he who makes himself a fool, and most certainly We chose him in this world, and in the hereafter he is most surely among the righteous.

2:159
Surely those who conceal the clear proofs and the guidance that We revealed after We made it clear in the Book for men, these it is whom Allah shall curse, and those who curse shall curse them (too)

2:160
Except those who repent and amend and make manifest (the truth), these it is to whom I turn (mercifully); and I am the Oft-returning (to mercy), the Merciful.

2:178
O you who believe! retaliation is prescribed for you in the matter of the slain, the free for the free, and the slave for the slave, and the female for the female, but if any remission is made to any one by his (aggrieved) brother, then prosecution (for the bloodwit) should be made according to usage, and payment should be made to him in a good manner; this is an alleviation from your Lord and a mercy; so whoever exceeds the limit after this he shall have a painful chastisement.
5:45 - 17:33
And We prescribed to them in it that life is for life, and eye for eye, and nose for nose, and ear for ear, and tooth for tooth, and (that there is) reprisal in wounds; but he who foregoes it, it shall be an expiation for him; and whoever did not judge by what Allah revealed, those are they that are the unjust.
And do not kill any one whom Allah has forbidden, except for a just cause, and whoever is slain unjustly, We have indeed given to his heir authority, so let him not exceed the just limits in slaying; surely he is aided.

2:180
Bequest is prescribed for you when death approaches one of you, if he leaves behind wealth for parents and near relatives, according to usage, a duty (incumbent) upon those who guard (against evil).
4:7-4:11
Men shall have a portion of what the parents and the near relatives leave, and women shall have a portion of what the

parents and the near relatives leave, whether there is little or much of it; a stated portion.

Allah enjoins you concerning your children: The male shall have the equal of the portion of two females; then if they are more than two females, they shall have two-thirds of what the deceased has left, and if there is one, she shall have the half; and as for his parents, each of them shall have the sixth of what he has left if he has a child, but if he has no child and (only) his two parents inherit him, then his mother shall have the third; but if he has brothers, then his mother shall have the sixth after (the payment of) a bequest he may have bequeathed or a debt; your parents and your children, you know not which of them is the nearer to you in usefulness; this is an ordinance from Allah: Surely Allah is Knowing, Wise.

2:183-2:184

O ye who believe! Fasting is prescribed to you as it was prescribed to those before you, that ye may (learn) self-restraint,
(Fasting) for a fixed number of days; but if any of you is ill, or on a journey, the prescribed number (Should be made up) from days later. For those who can do it (With hardship), is a ransom, the feeding of one that is indigent. But he that will give more, of his own free will,- it is better for him. And it is better for you that ye fast, if ye only knew.

2:185

The month of Ramadan is that in which the Quran was revealed, a guidance to men and clear proofs of the guidance and the distinction; therefore whoever of you is present in the month, he shall fast therein, and whoever is sick or upon a journey, then (he shall fast) a (like) number of other days; Allah desires ease for you, and He does not desire for you difficulty, and (He desires) that you should complete the number and that you should exalt the greatness of Allah for His having guided you and that you may give thanks.

2:190

And fight in the way of Allah with those who fight with you, and do not exceed the limits, surely Allah does not love those who exceed the limits.

9:5- 9:36
Verse of the Sword
Surely the number of months with Allah is twelve months in Allah's ordinance since the day when He created the heavens and the earth, of these four being sacred; that is the right reckoning; therefore be not unjust to yourselves regarding them, and fight the polytheists all together as they fight you all together; and know that Allah is with those who guard (against evil).

2:191-2:192
And kill them wherever you find them, and drive them out from whence they drove you out, and persecution is severer than slaughter, and do not fight with them at the Sacred Mosque until they fight with you in it, but if they do fight you, then slay them; such is the recompense of the unbelievers.
But if they desist, then surely Allah is Forgiving, Merciful.
9:5
Verse of the Sword

2:215
They ask you as to what they should spend. Say: Whatever wealth you spend, it is for the parents and the near of kin and the orphans and the needy and the wayfarer, and whatever good you do, Allah surely knows it.
9:60
Alms are for the poor and the needy, and those employed to administer the (funds); for those whose hearts have been (recently) reconciled (to Truth); for those in bondage and in debt; in the cause of Allah; and for the wayfarer: (thus is it) ordained by Allah, and Allah is full of knowledge and wisdom.

2:217
They ask you concerning the sacred month about fighting in it. Say: Fighting in it is a grave matter, and hindering (men) from Allah's way and denying Him, and (hindering men from) the Sacred Mosque and turning its people out of it, are still graver with Allah, and persecution is graver than slaughter; and they will not cease fighting with you until they turn you back from your religion, if they can; and whoever of you turns back from his religion, then he

dies while an unbeliever-- these it is whose works shall go for nothing in this world and the hereafter, and they are the inmates of the fire; therein they shall abide.

9:5
Verse of the Sword

2:219

They ask you about intoxicants and games of chance. Say: In both of them there is a great sin and means of profit for men, and their sin is greater than their profit. And they ask you as to what they should spend. Say: What you can spare. Thus does Allah make clear to you the communications, that you may ponder.

4:43 - 5:90 - 9:103
O you who believe! do not go near prayer when you are Intoxicated until you know (well) what you say, nor when you are under an obligation to perform a bath-- unless (you are) travelling on the road-- until you have washed yourselves; and if you are sick, or on a journey, or one of you come from the privy or you have touched the women, and you cannot find water, betake yourselves to pure earth, then wipe your faces and your hands; surely Allah is Pardoning, Forgiving.
O you who believe! intoxicants and games of chance and (sacrificing to) stones set up and (dividing by) arrows are only an uncleanness, the Shaitan's (Satan's) work; shun it therefore that you may be successful.

Take alms out of their property, you would cleanse them and purify them thereby, and pray for them; surely your prayer is a relief to them; and Allah is Hearing, Knowing.

2:221

And do not marry the idolatresses until they believe, and certainly a believing maid is better than an idolatress woman, even though she should please you; and do not give (believing women) in marriage to idolaters until they believe, and certainly a believing servant is better than an idolater, even though he should please you; these invite to the fire, and Allah invites to the garden and to forgiveness by His will, and makes clear His communications to men, that they may be mindful.

5:5
This day (all) the good things are allowed to you; and the food of those who have been given the Book is lawful for you and your food is lawful for them; and the chaste from among the believing women and the chaste from among those who have been given the Book before you (are lawful for you); when you have given them their dowries, taking (them) in marriage, not fornicating nor taking them for paramours in secret; and whoever denies faith, his work indeed is of no account, and in the hereafter he shall be one of the losers.

2:228
And the divorced women should keep themselves in waiting for three courses; and it is not lawful for them that they should conceal what Allah has created in their wombs, if they believe in Allah and the last day; and their husbands have a better right to take them back in the meanwhile if they wish for reconciliation; and they have rights similar to those against them in a just manner, and the men are a degree above them, and Allah is Mighty, Wise.

2:229 - 2:230
Divorce may be (pronounced) twice, then keep (them) in good fellowship or let (them) go with kindness; and it is not lawful for you to take any part of what you have given them, unless both fear that they cannot keep within the limits of Allah; then if you fear that they cannot keep within the limits of Allah, there is no blame on them for what she gives up to become free thereby. These are the limits of Allah, so do not exceed them and whoever exceeds the limits of Allah these it is that are the unjust. So if he divorces her she shall not be lawful to him afterwards until she marries another husband; then if he divorces her there is no blame on them both if they return to each other (by marriage), if they think that they can keep within the limits of Allah, and these are the limits of Allah which He makes clear for a people who know.

2:234

And (as for) those of you who die and leave wives behind, they should keep themselves in waiting for four months and ten days; then when they have fully attained their term, there is no blame on you for what they do for themselves in a lawful manner; and Allah is aware of what you do.

2:240

And those of you who die and leave wives behind, (make) a bequest in favor of their wives of maintenance for a year without turning (them) out, then if they themselves go away, there is no blame on you for what they do of lawful deeds by themselves, and Allah is Mighty, Wise.

2:256

There is no compulsion in religion; truly the right way has become clearly distinct from error; therefore, whoever disbelieves in the Shaitan (Satan) and believes in Allah he indeed has laid hold on the firmest handle, which shall not break off, and Allah is Hearing, Knowing.

9:5

Verse of the Sword

2:284

Whatever is in the heavens and whatever is in the earth is Allah's; and whether you manifest what is in your minds or hide it, Allah will call you to account according to it; then He will forgive whom He pleases and chastise whom He pleases, and Allah has power over all things.

2:286

Allah does not impose upon any soul a duty but to the extent of its ability; for it is (the benefit of) what it has earned and upon it (the evil of) what it has wrought: Our Lord! do not punish us if we forget or make a mistake; Our Lord! do not lay on us a burden as Thou didst lay on those before us, Our Lord do not impose upon us that which we have not the strength to bear; and pardon us and grant us protection and have mercy on us, Thou art our Patron, so help us against the unbelieving people.

2:285
The messenger believes in what has been revealed to him from his Lord, and (so do) the believers; they all believe in Allah and His angels and His books and His messengers; We make no difference between any of His messengers; and they say: We hear and obey, our Lord! Thy forgiveness (do we crave), and to Thee is the eventual course.

2:286
Allah does not impose upon any soul a duty but to the extent of its ability; for it is (the benefit of) what it has earned and upon it (the evil of) what it has wrought: Our Lord! do not punish us if we forget or make a mistake; Our Lord! do not lay on us a burden as Thou didst lay on those before us, Our Lord do not impose upon us that which we have not the strength to bear; and pardon us and grant us protection and have mercy on us, Thou art our Patron, so help us against the unbelieving people.

Surah 3

3:20
But if they dispute with you, say: I have submitted myself entirely to Allah and (so) every one who follows me; and say to those who have been given the Book and the unlearned people: Do you submit yourselves? So if they submit then indeed they follow the right way; and if they turn back, then upon you is only the delivery of the message and Allah sees the servants.
9:5 - 33:50
Verse of the Sword

O prophet! surely We have made lawful to you your wives whom you have given their dowries, and those whom your right hand possesses out of those whom Allah has given to you as prisoners of war, and the daughters of your paternal uncles and the daughters of your paternal aunts, and the daughters of your maternal uncles and the daughters of your maternal aunts who fled with you; and a believing woman if she gave herself to the prophet, if the prophet desired to marry her-- specially for you,

not for the (rest of) believers; We know what We have ordained for them concerning their wives and those whom their right hands possess in order that no blame may attach to you; and Allah is Forgiving, Merciful.

3:28
Let not the believers take the unbelievers for friends rather than believers; and whoever does this, he shall have nothing of (the guardianship of) Allah, but you should guard yourselves against them, guarding carefully; and Allah makes you cautious of (retribution from) Himself; and to Allah is the eventual coming.
8:57 - 9:5 - 51:55
Therefore if you overtake them in fighting, then scatter by (making an example of) them those who are in their rear, that they may be mindful.

- Verse of the Sword -

And continue to remind, for surely the reminder profits the believers.

3:102
O you who believe! be careful of (your duty to) Allah with the care which is due to Him, and do not die unless you are Muslims.
64:16
Therefore be careful of (your duty to) Allah as much as you can, and hear and obey and spend, it is better for your souls; and whoever is saved from the greediness of his soul, these it is that are the successful.

3:111
They shall by no means harm you but with a slight evil; and if they fight with you they shall turn (their) backs to you, then shall they not be helped.
9:29

Fight those who do not believe in Allah, nor in the latter day, nor do they prohibit what Allah and His Messenger have prohibited, nor follow the religion of truth, out of those who have been given the Book, until they pay the tax in acknowledgment of superiority and they are in a state of subjection.

3:145

And a soul will not die but with the permission of Allah the term is fixed; and whoever desires the reward of this world, I shall give him of it, and whoever desires the reward of the hereafter I shall give him of it, and I will reward the grateful.

17:18

Whoever desires this present life, We hasten to him therein what We please for whomsoever We desire, then We assign to him the hell; he shall enter it despised, driven away.

3:186

You shall certainly be tried respecting your wealth and your souls, and you shall certainly hear from those who have been given the Book before you and from those who are polytheists much annoying talk; and if you are patient and guard (against evil), surely this is one of the affairs (which should be) determined upon.

9:29

Fight those who do not believe in Allah, nor in the latter day, nor do they prohibit what Allah and His Messenger have prohibited, nor follow the religion of truth, out of those who have been given the Book, until they pay the tax in acknowledgment of superiority and they are in a state of subjection.

Surah 4

4:43

O you who believe! do not go near prayer when you are Intoxicated until you know (well) what you say, nor when you are under an obligation to perform a bath-- unless (you are) travelling on the road-- until you have washed yourselves; and if you are sick, or on a journey, or one of you come from the privy or you have touched the women, and you cannot find water, betake yourselves to pure earth, then wipe your faces and your hands; surely Allah is Pardoning, Forgiving.

5:90
O you who believe! intoxicants and games of chance and (sacrificing to) stones set up and (dividing by) arrows are only an uncleanness, the Shaitan's work; shun it therefore that you may be successful.

4:63

These are they of whom Allah knows what is in their hearts; therefore turn aside from them and admonish them, and speak to them effectual words concerning themselves.

9:5
Verse of the Sword

4:64

And We did not send any messenger but that he should be obeyed by Allah's permission; and had they, when they were unjust to themselves, come to you and asked forgiveness of Allah and the Messenger had (also) asked forgiveness for them, they would have found Allah Oft-returning (to mercy), Merciful.

9:80
Ask forgiveness for them or do not ask forgiveness for them; even if you ask forgiveness for them seventy times, Allah will not forgive them; this is because they disbelieve in Allah and His Messenger, and Allah does not guide the transgressing people.

4:71

O you who believe! take your precaution, then go forth in detachments or go forth in a body.

9:122

And it does not beseem the believers that they should go forth all together; why should not then a company from every party from among them go forth that they may apply themselves to obtain understanding in religion, and that they may warn their people when they come back to them that they may be cautious?

4:80 - 4:81

Whoever obeys the Messenger, he indeed obeys Allah, and whoever turns back, so We have not sent you as a keeper over them. And they say: Obedience. But when they go out from your presence, a party of them decide by night upon doing otherwise than what you say; and Allah writes down what they decide by night, therefore turn aside from them and trust in Allah, and Allah is sufficient as a protector.

9:5

Verse of the Sword

4:84

Fight then in Allah's way; this is not imposed on you except In relation to yourself, and rouse the believers to ardor maybe Allah will restrain the fighting of those who disbelieve and Allah is strongest in prowess and strongest to give an exemplary punishment.

9:5

Verse of the Sword

4:90 - 4:91

Except those who reach a people between whom and you there is an alliance, or who come to you, their hearts shrinking from fighting you or fighting their own people; and if Allah had pleased, He would have given them power over you, so that they should have certainly fought you; therefore if they withdraw from you and do not fight you and offer you peace, then Allah has not given you a way against them.

You will find others who desire that they should be safe from you and secure from their own people; as often as they are sent back to the mischief they get thrown into it headlong; therefore if they do not withdraw from you, and (do not) offer you peace and restrain their hands, then seize them and kill them wherever you find them; and against these We have given you a clear authority.
9:5
Verse of the Sword

4:92
And it does not behoove a believer to kill a believer except by mistake, and whoever kills a believer by mistake, he should free a believing slave, and blood-money should be paid to his people unless they remit it as alms; but if he be from a tribe hostile to you and he is a believer, the freeing of a believing slave (suffices), and if he is from a tribe between whom and you there is a convenant, the blood-money should be paid to his people along with the freeing of a believing slave; but he who cannot find (a slave) should fast for two months successively: a penance from Allah, and Allah is Knowing, Wise.
9:1
(This is a declaration of) immunity by Allah and His Messenger towards those of the idolaters with whom you made an agreement. (You do not have to honor any agreement made with an infidel. Allah gives you immunity.)

4:140
And indeed He has revealed to you in the Book that when you hear Allah's communications disbelieved in and mocked at do not sit with them until they enter into some other discourse; surely then you would be like them; surely Allah will gather together the hypocrites and the unbelievers all in hell.
9:5
Verse of the Sword

Surah 5

5:2
O you who believe! do not violate the signs appointed by Allah nor the sacred month, nor (interfere with) the offerings, nor the sacrificial animals with garlands, nor those going to the sacred house seeking the grace and pleasure of their Lord; and when you are free from the obligations of the pilgrimage, then hunt, and let not hatred of a people-- because they hindered you from the Sacred Masjid-- incite you to exceed the limits, and help one another in goodness and piety, and do not help one another in sin and aggression; and be careful of (your duty to) Allah; surely Allah is severe in requiting (evil).
9:5
Verse of the Sword

5:13
But on account of their breaking their covenant We cursed them and made their hearts hard; they altered the words from their places and they neglected a portion of what they were reminded of; and you shall always discover treachery in them excepting a few of them; so pardon them and turn away; surely Allah loves those who do good (to others).
9:5 - 9:29
Verse of the Sword

Fight those who do not believe in Allah, nor in the latter day, nor do they prohibit what Allah and His Messenger have prohibited, nor follow the religion of truth, out of those who have been given the Book, until they pay the tax in acknowledgment of superiority and they are in a state of subjection.

5:99

Nothing is (incumbent) on the Messenger but to deliver (the message), and Allah knows what you do openly and what you hide.

9:5
Verse of the Sword

Surah 6

6:66
And your people call it a lie and it is the very truth. Say: I am not placed in charge of you.
9:5
Verse of the Sword

6:68
And when you see those who enter into false discourses about Our communications, withdraw from them until they enter into some other discourse, and if the Shaitan causes you to forget, then do not sit after recollection with the unjust people.
9:5
Verse of the Sword

6:70
And leave those who have taken their religion for a play and an idle sport, and whom this world's life has deceived, and remind (them) thereby lest a soul should be given up to destruction for what it has earned; it shall not have besides Allah any guardian nor an intercessor, and if it should seek to give every compensation, it shall not be accepted from it; these are they who shall be given up to destruction for what they earned; they shall have a drink of boiling water and a painful chastisement because they disbelieved.
9:5 - 9:29
Verse of the Sword

Fight those who do not believe in Allah, nor in the latter day, nor do they prohibit what Allah and His Messenger have prohibited, nor follow the religion of truth, out of those who have been given the Book, until they pay the tax in acknowledgment of superiority and they are in a state of subjection.

6:91

And they do not assign to Allah the attributes due to Him when they say: Allah has not revealed anything to a mortal. Say: Who revealed the Book which Musa brought, a light and a guidance to men, which you make into scattered writings which you show while you conceal much? And you were taught what you did not know, (neither) you nor your fathers. Say: Allah then leave them sporting in their vain discourses.

9:5
Verse of the Sword

6:104

Indeed there have come to you clear proofs from your Lord; whoever will therefore see, it is for his own soul and whoever will be blind, it shall be against himself and I am not a keeper over you.

9:5
Verse of the Sword

6:106 - 6:107 - 6:108

Follow what is revealed to you from your Lord; there is no god but He; and withdraw from the polytheists.

And if Allah had pleased, they would not have set up others (with Him) and We have not appointed you a keeper over them, and you are not placed in charge of them.

And do not abuse those whom they call upon besides Allah, lest exceeding the limits they should abuse Allah out of ignorance. Thus have We made fair seeming to every people their deeds; then to

their Lord shall be their return, so He will inform them of what they
did.
9:5
Verse of the Sword

6:112
And thus did We make for every prophet an enemy, the Shaitans
from among men and jinn, some of them suggesting to others
varnished falsehood to deceive (them), and had your Lord pleased
they would not have done it, therefore leave them and that which
they forget.
9:5
Verse of the Sword

6:121
And do not eat of that on which Allah's name has not been
mentioned, and that is most surely a transgression; and most surely
the Shaitans suggest to their friends that they should contend with
you; and if you obey them, you shall most surely be polytheists.
5:5
**This day (all) the good things are allowed to you; and the food of
those who have been given the Book is lawful for you and your
food is lawful for them; and the chaste from among the believing
women and the chaste from among those who have been given
the Book before you (are lawful for you); when you have given
them their dowries, taking (them) in marriage, not fornicating nor
taking them for paramours in secret; and whoever denies faith,
his work indeed is of no account, and in the hereafter he shall be
one of the losers.**

6:137
And thus their associates have made fair seeming to most of the
polytheists the killing of their children, that they may cause them to
perish and obscure for them their religion; and if Allah had pleased,
they would not have done it, therefore leave them and that which
they forge.
9:5

Verse of the Sword

6:159
Surely they who divided their religion into parts and became sects,
you have no concern with them; their affair is only with Allah, then
He will inform them of what they did.
9:5
Verse of the Sword

Surah 7

7:183
And I grant them respite; surely My scheme is effective.
9:5
Verse of the Sword

7:199
Take to forgiveness and enjoin good and turn aside from the
ignorant.
9:5
Verse of the Sword

Surah 8

8:61
And if they incline to peace, then incline to it and trust in Allah;
surely He is the Hearing, the Knowing.
9:5 - 9:29

Joseph Lumpkin

Verse of the Sword

Fight those who do not believe in Allah, nor in the latter day, nor do they prohibit what Allah and His Messenger have prohibited, nor follow the religion of truth, out of those who have been given the Book, until they pay the tax in acknowledgment of superiority and they are in a state of subjection.

8:65
O prophet! urge the believers to war; if there are twenty patient ones of you they shall overcome two hundred, and if there are a hundred of you they shall overcome a thousand of those who disbelieve, because they are a people who do not understand.
**8:66
For the present Allah has made light your burden, and He knows that there is weakness in you; so if there are a hundred patient ones of you they shall overcome two hundred, and if there are a thousand they shall overcome two thousand by Allah's permission, and Allah is with the patient.**

8:72
Surely those who believed and fled (their homes) and struggled hard in Allah's way with their property and their souls, and those who gave shelter and helped-- these are guardians of each other; and (as for) those who believed and did not fly, not yours is their guardianship until they fly; and if they seek aid from you in the matter of religion, aid is incumbent on you except against a people between whom and you there is a treaty, and Allah sees what you do.
**9:5
Verse of the Sword**

8:73
And (as for) those who disbelieve, some of them are the guardians of others; if you will not do it, there will be in the land persecution and great mischief.

9:5
Verse of the Sword

Surah 9

9:2

So go about in the land for four months and know that you cannot weaken Allah and that Allah will bring disgrace to the unbelievers.

9:5
Verse of the Sword

9:7

How can there be an agreement for the idolaters with Allah and with His Messenger; except those with whom you made an agreement at the Sacred Mosque? So as long as they are true to you, be true to them; surely Allah loves those who are careful (of their duty).
9:5
Verse of the Sword

9:97 - 9:98

The dwellers of the desert are very hard in unbelief and hypocrisy, and more disposed not to know the limits of what Allah has revealed to His Messenger; and Allah is Knowing, Wise.
And of the dwellers of the desert are those who take what they spend to be a fine, and they wait (the befalling of) calamities to you; on them (will be) the evil calamity; and Allah is Hearing, Knowing.

9:99

And of the dwellers of the desert are those who believe in Allah and the latter day and take what they spend to be (means of) the nearness of Allah and the Messenger's prayers; surely it shall be means of nearness for them; Allah will make them enter into His mercy; surely Allah is Forgiving, Merciful.

Surah 10

10:41
And if they call you a liar, say: My work is for me and your work for you; you are clear of what I do and I am clear of what you do.
9:5
Verse of the Sword

10:99
And if your Lord had pleased, surely all those who are in the earth would have believed, all of them; will you then force men till they become believers?
9:5
Verse of the Sword

10:108
Say: O people! indeed there has come to you the truth from your Lord, therefore whoever goes aright, he goes aright only for the good of his own soul, and whoever goes astray, he goes astray only to the detriment of it, and I am not a custodian over you.
9:5
Verse of the Sword

Surah 11

11:12
Then, it may be that you will give up part of what is revealed to you and your breast will become straitened by it because they say: Why has not a treasure been sent down upon him or an angel come with him? You are only a person sounding a warning; and Allah is custodian over all things.
9:5
Verse of the Sword

11:121 - 11:122
And say to those who do not believe: Act according to your state; surely we too are acting.
And wait; surely we are waiting also.
9:5
Verse of the Sword

Surah 13

13:40
And We will either let you see part of what We threaten them with or cause you to die, for only the delivery of the message is (incumbent) on you, while calling (them) to account is Our (business).
9:5
Verse of the Sword

Surah 15

15:3
Leave them that they may eat and enjoy themselves and (that) hope
may beguile them, for they will soon know.
9:5
Verse of the Sword

15:85
And We did not create the heavens and the earth and what is
between them two but in truth; and the hour is most surely coming,
so turn away with kindly forgiveness.
9:5
Verse of the Sword

15:88 - 15:89
Do not strain your eyes after what We have given certain classes of
them to enjoy, and do not grieve for them, and make yourself gentle
to the believers.
And say: Surely I am the plain person sounding a warning.
9:5
Verse of the Sword

15:94
Therefore declare openly what you are bidden and turn aside from
the polytheists.
9:5
Verse of the Sword

Surah 16

16:67

And of the fruits of the palms and the grapes-- you obtain from them intoxication and goodly provision; most surely there is a sign in this for a people who ponder.
5:90
O you who believe! intoxicants and games of chance and (sacrificing to) stones set up and (dividing by) arrows are only an uncleanness, the Shaitan's work; shun it therefore that you may be successful.

16:82
But if they turn back, then on you devolves only the clear deliverance (of the message).
9:5
Verse of the Sword

16:125
Call to the way of your Lord with wisdom and goodly exhortation, and have disputations with them in the best manner; surely your Lord best knows those who go astray from His path, and He knows best those who follow the right way.
9:5
Verse of the Sword

16:127
And be patient and your patience is not but by (the assistance of) Allah, and grieve not for them, and do not distress yourself at what they plan.
9:5
Verse of the Sword

Surah 17

17:23

And your Lord has commanded that you shall not serve (any) but Him, and goodness to your parents. If either or both of them reach old age with you, say not to them (so much as) "Ugh" nor chide them, and speak to them a generous word.

9:113

It is not (fit) for the prophet and those who believe that they should ask forgiveness for the polytheists, even though they should be near relatives, after it has become clear to them that they are inmates of the flaming fire.

17:24

And make yourself submissively gentle to them with compassion, and say: O my Lord! have compassion on them, as they brought me up (when I was) little.

9:113

It is not (fit) for the prophet and those who believe that they should ask forgiveness for the polytheists, even though they should be near relatives, after it has become clear to them that they are inmates of the flaming fire.

17:54

Your Lord knows you best; He will have mercy on you if He pleases, or He will chastise you if He pleases; and We have not sent you as being in charge of them.

9:5

Verse of the Sword

Surah 19

19:39
And warn them of the day of intense regret, when the matter shall have been decided; and they are (now) in negligence and they do not believe.
9:5
Verse of the Sword

19:75
Say: As for him who remains in error, the Beneficent Allah will surely prolong his length of days, until they see what they were threatened with, either the punishment or the hour; then they shall know who is in more evil plight and weaker in forces
9:5
Verse of the Sword

19:84
Therefore be not in haste against them, We only number out to them a number (of days).
9:5
Verse of the Sword

Surah 20

20:130
Bear then patiently what they say, and glorify your Lord by the praising of Him before the rising of the sun and before its setting, and during hours of the night do also glorify (Him) and during parts of the day, that you may be well pleased
9:5
Verse of the Sword

20:135
Every one (of us) is awaiting, therefore do await: So you will come to know who is the follower of the even path and who goes aright.

9:5
Verse of the Sword

Surah 22

22:68
And if they contend with you, say: Allah best knows what you do.
9:5
Verse of the Sword

Surah 23

23:54
Therefore leave them in their overwhelming ignorance till
9:5
Verse of the Sword

Surah 24

24:3
Let no man guilty of adultery or fornication marry and but a woman similarly guilty, or an Unbeliever: nor let any but such a man or an Unbeliever marry such a woman: to the Believers such a thing is forbidden.
24:32
Marry those among you who are single, or the virtuous ones among yourselves, male or female: if they are in poverty, Allah will give them means out of His grace:...

24:4
And those who launch a charge against chaste women, and produce not four witnesses (to support their allegations),- flog them with eighty stripes; and reject their evidence ever after: for such men are wicked transgressors;-
24:5
Unless they repent thereafter and mend (their conduct); for Allah is Oft-Forgiving, Most Merciful.

24:6
And for those who launch a charge against their spouses, and have (in support) no evidence but their own,...
24:6 - 24:7 - 24:9
...their solitary evidence (can be received) if they bear witness four times (with an oath) by Allah that they are solemnly telling the truth;...
And the fifth (oath) (should be) that they solemnly invoke the curse of Allah on themselves if they tell a lie. ...
And the fifth (oath) should be that she solemnly invokes the wrath of Allah on herself if (her accuser) is telling the truth.

24:27
O ye who believe! enter not houses other than your own, until ye have asked permission and saluted those in them:...
24:29
It is no fault on your part to enter houses not used for living in, which serve some (other) use for you: And Allah has knowledge of what ye reveal and what ye conceal.

24:31
And say to the believing women that they should lower their gaze and guard their modesty; that they should not display their beauty and ornaments except what (must ordinarily) appear thereof; that they should draw their veils over their bosoms and not display their beauty except to their husbands,...
24:60

Such elderly women as are past the prospect of marriage,- there is no blame on them if they lay aside their (outer) garments, provided they make not a wanton display of their beauty:...

24:54
Say: "Obey Allah, and obey the Messenger: but if ye turn away, he is only responsible for the duty placed on him and ye for that placed on you....
9:5
Verse of the Sword

24:58
O ye who believe! let those whom your right hands possess, and the (children) among you who have not come of age ask your permission (before they come to your presence), on three occasions: before morning prayer;...
24:59
But when the children among you come of age, let them (also) ask for permission, as do those senior to them (in age): Thus does Allah make clear His Signs to you: for Allah is full of knowledge and wisdom.

Surah 25

25:63
... when the ignorant address them, they say, "Peace!";
9:5
Verse of the Sword

25:68 - 25:69
Those who invoke not, with Allah, any other god, nor slay such life as Allah has made sacred except for just cause, nor commit fornication; - and any that does this (not only) meets punishment.

(But) the Penalty on the Day of Judgment will be doubled to him, and he will dwell therein in ignominy,-**25:70**
Unless he repents, believes, and works righteous deeds, for Allah will change the evil of such persons into good, ...

25:68
... nor kill such life as Allah has forbidden, except for just cause...";
4:93
And whoever kills a believer intentionally, his recompense is Hell to abide therein

Surah 26

26:224 - 26:225 - 26:226
And the Poets,- It is those straying in Evil, who follow them:
Seest thou not that they wander distracted in every valley?-
And that they say what they practise not?-
26:227
Except those who believe, work righteousness, engage much in the remembrance of Allah, and defend themselves only after they are unjustly attacked. ...

Surah 27

Joseph Lumpkin

27:92
And to rehearse the Quran: and if any accept guidance, they do it
for the good of their own souls, and if any stray, say: "I am only a
Person sounding a warning".
9:5
Verse of the Sword

Surah 28

28:55
... "To us our deeds, and to you yours; peace be to you: we seek not
the ignorant."
9:5
Verse of the Sword

Surah 29

29:46
And dispute ye not with the People of the Book, except with means
better (than mere disputation), unless it be with those of them who
inflict wrong (and injury): but say, "We believe in the revelation
which has come down to us and in that which came down to you;
Our Allah and your Allah is one; ...
9:29
**Fight those who believe not in Allah nor the Last Day, nor hold
that forbidden which hath been forbidden by Allah and His
Messenger, nor acknowledge the religion of Truth, (even if they
are) of the People of the Book, until they pay the Jizya (tax on
non-believers) with willing submission, and feel themselves
subdued.**

29:50
Ye they say: "Why are not Signs sent down to him from his Lord?" Say: "The signs are indeed with Allah: and I am indeed a clear Person sounding a warning."
9:5
Verse of the Sword

Surah 30

30:60
So patiently persevere: for verily the promise of Allah is true: nor let those shake thy firmness, who have (themselves) no certainty of faith.
9:5
Verse of the Sword

Surah 31

31:23
But if any reject Faith, let not his rejection grieve thee: to Us is their return, ...
9:5
Verse of the Sword

Surah 32

32:30
So turn away from them, and wait: they too are waiting.
9:5
Verse of the Sword

Surah 33

33:48
And obey not (the behests) of the Unbelievers and the Hypocrites, and heed not their annoyances, ...
9:5
Verse of the Sword

33:52
It is not lawful for thee (to marry more) women after this, nor to change them for (other) wives, even though their beauty attract thee, except any thy right hand should possess (as handmaidens): ...

33:50
O prophet! We have made lawful to thee thy wives to whom thou hast paid their dowers; and those whom thy right hand possesses out of the prisoners of war whom Allah has assigned to thee; and daughters of thy paternal uncles and aunts, and daughters of thy maternal uncles and aunts, who migrated (from Makka / Mecca) with thee; and any believing woman who dedicates her soul to the prophet if the prophet wishes to wed her;- this only for thee, and not for the Believers (at large); ...

Surah 34

34:25
Say: "Ye shall not be questioned as to our sins, nor shall we be questioned as to what ye do."
9:5
Verse of the Sword

Surah 35

35:23
Thou art no other than a person sounding a warning.
9:5
Verse of the Sword

Surah 36

36:76
Let not their speech, then, grieve thee. Verily We know what they hide as well as what they disclose.
9:5
Verse of the Sword

Joseph Lumpkin

Surah 37

37:174 - 37:175
So turn thou away from them for a little while,
And watch them (how they fare), and they soon shall see (how thou farest)!
9:5
Verse of the Sword

37:178 - 37:179
And turn away from them till a time
And (then) see, for they too shall see.
9:5
Verse of the Sword

Surah 38

38:70
'Only this has been revealed to me: that I am to give warning plainly and publicly."
9:5
Verse of the Sword

38:88
"And ye shall certainly know the truth of it (all) after a while.
9:5
Verse of the Sword

Surah 39

39:3
... Truly Allah will judge between them in that wherein they differ.
...
9:5
Verse of the Sword

39:13
Say: "I would, if I disobeyed my Lord, indeed have fear of the Penalty of a Mighty Day."
48:2
That Allah may forgive thee thy faults of the past and those to follow;

39:14 - 39:15
Say: "It is Allah I serve, with my sincere (and exclusive) devotion: "Serve ye what ye will besides him."
9:5
Verse of the Sword

39:36
... for such as Allah leaves to stray, there can be no guide.
9:5
Verse of the Sword

39:39
Say: "O my People! Do whatever ye can: I will do (my part): but soon will ye know-
9:5
Verse of the Sword

Joseph Lumpkin

39:40
"Who it is to whom comes a Penalty of ignominy, and on whom descends a Penalty that abides."
9:5
Verse of the Sword

39:41
He, then, that receives guidance benefits his own soul: but he that strays injures his own soul. Nor art thou set over them to dispose of their affairs.
9:5
Verse of the Sword

39:46
Say: "O Allah! Creator of the heavens and the earth! Knower of all that is hidden and open! it is Thou that wilt judge between Thy Servants in those matters about which they have differed."
9:5
Verse of the Sword

Surah 40

40:12
... the Command is with Allah, Most High, Most Great!"
9:5
Verse of the Sword

40:55
Patiently, then, persevere: for the Promise of Allah is true: and ask forgiveness for thy fault, and celebrate the Praises of thy Lord in the evening and in the morning.
9:5
Verse of the Sword

271

40:77

So persevere in patience; for the Promise of Allah is true: and whether We show thee (in this life) some part of what We promise them,- or We take thy soul (to Our Mercy) (before that),-(in any case) it is to Us that they shall (all) return.

9:5

Verse of the Sword

Surah 41

41:34

Nor can goodness and Evil be equal. Repel (Evil) with what is better: Then will he between whom and thee was hatred become as it were thy friend and intimate!

9:5

Verse of the Sword

Surah 42

42:5

and the angels celebrate the Praises of their Lord, and pray for forgiveness for (all) beings on earth: Behold! Verily Allah is He, the Oft-Forgiving, Most Merciful.

40:7

Those who sustain the Throne (of Allah) and those around it Sing Glory and Praise to their Lord; believe in Him; and implore

Forgiveness for those who believe: "Our Lord! Thy Reach is over all things, in Mercy and Knowledge. Forgive, then, those who turn in Repentance, and follow Thy Path; and preserve them from the Penalty of the Blazing Fire!

42:6
Allah doth watch over them; and thou art not the disposer of their affairs.
9:5
Verse of the Sword

42:15
Now then, for that (reason), call (them to the Faith), and stand steadfast as thou art commanded, nor follow thou their vain desires; but say: "I believe in the Book which Allah has sent down; and I am commanded to judge justly between you. Allah is our Lord and your Lord: for us (is the responsibility for) our deeds, and for you for your deeds. There is no contention between us and you. Allah will bring us together, and to Him is (our) Final Goal.
9:5 - 9:29
Verse of the Sword

Fight those who believe not in Allah nor the Last Day, nor hold that forbidden which hath been forbidden by Allah and His Messenger, nor acknowledge the religion of Truth, (even if they are) of the People of the Book, until they pay the Jizya with willing submission, and feel themselves subdued.

42:20
To any that desires the tilth of the Hereafter, We give increase in his tilth, and to any that desires the tilth of this world, We grant somewhat thereof, but he has no share or lot in the Hereafter.
17:18
If any do wish for the transitory things (of this life), We readily grant them - such things as We will, to such person as We will: in the end have We provided Hell for them: they will burn therein, disgraced and rejected.

42:23
... Say: "No reward do I ask of you for this except the love of those near of kin." ...
34:47
Say: "No reward do I ask of you: it is (all) in your interest: my reward is only due from Allah:...

42:39
And those who, when an oppressive wrong is inflicted on them, (are not cowed but) help and defend themselves.
42:43
But indeed if any show patience and forgive, that would truly be an exercise of courageous will and resolution in the conduct of affairs.

42:41
But indeed if any do help and defend themselves after a wrong (done) to them, against such there is no cause of blame.
42:43
But indeed if any show patience and forgive, that would truly be an exercise of courageous will and resolution in the conduct of affairs.

42:48
If then they run away, We have not sent thee as a guard over them. Thy duty is but to convey (the Message). ...
9:5
Verse of the Sword

Surah 43

43:83
So leave them to babble and play (with vanities) until they meet that Day of theirs, which they have been promised.
9:5
Verse of the Sword

43:89
But turn away from them, and say "Peace!" But soon shall they know!
9:5
Verse of the Sword

Surah 44

44:59
So wait thou and watch; for they (too) are waiting.
9:5
Verse of the Sword

Surah 45

45:14

Tell those who believe, to forgive those who do not look forward to the Days of Allah: It is for Him to recompense (for good or ill) each People according to what they have earned.
9:5
Verse of the Sword

Surah 46

46:9
Say: "I am no bringer of new-fangled doctrine among the messengers, nor do I know what will be done with me or with you. I follow but that which is revealed to me by inspiration; I am but a Person sounding a warning open and clear."
48:1 - 48:2 - 48:3 - 48:4 - 48:5 -48:6
Verily We have granted thee a manifest Victory:
That Allah may forgive thee thy faults of the past and those to follow; fulfill His favor to thee; and guide thee on the Straight Way;
And that Allah may help thee with powerful help.
It is He Who sent down tranquility into the hearts of the Believers, that they may add faith to their faith;- for to Allah belong the Forces of the heavens and the earth; and Allah is Full of Knowledge and Wisdom;-
That He may admit the men and women who believe, to Gardens beneath which rivers flow, to dwell therein for aye, and remove their ills from them;- and that is, in the sight of Allah, the highest achievement (for man),-
And that He may punish the Hypocrites, men and women, and the Polytheists men and women, who imagine an evil opinion of Allah. On them is a round of Evil: the Wrath of Allah is on them: He has cursed them and got Hell ready for them: and evil is it for a destination.

46:35

Therefore patiently persevere, as did (all) messengers of inflexible purpose; and be in no haste about the (Unbelievers). ...
9:5
Verse of the Sword

Surah 47

47:4
... thereafter (is the time for) either generosity or ransom: Until the war lays down its burdens ...
9:5
Verse of the Sword;

Note: The Verse of the Sword abrogates both "generosity or ransom" and "grace" is a more accurate translation than "generosity".

47:36
... and will not ask you (to give up) your possessions.
47:38
Behold, ye are those invited to spend (of your substance) in the Way of Allah: ...

Surah 50

50:39
Bear, then, with patience, all that they say, and celebrate the praises of thy Lord, ...
9:5

Verse of the Sword

50:45
... and thou art not one to overawe them by force. So admonish with the Quran such as fear My Warning!
9:5
Verse of the Sword

Surah 51

51:19
And in their wealth and possessions (was remembered) the right of the (needy,) him who asked, and him who (for some reason) was prevented (from asking).
9:60
Alms are for the poor and the needy, and those employed to administer the (funds); for those whose hearts have been (recently) reconciled (to Truth); for those in bondage and in debt; in the cause of Allah; and for the wayfarer: (thus is it) ordained by Allah, and Allah is full of knowledge and wisdom.

51:54
So turn away from them: not thine is the blame.
51:55
But teach (thy Message) for teaching benefits the Believers.

Surah 52

52:31
Say thou: "Await ye!- I too will wait along with you!"
9:5
Verse of the Sword

52:45
So leave them alone until they encounter that Day of theirs, wherein they shall (perforce) swoon (with terror),-
9:5
Verse of the Sword

52:48
Now await in patience the command of thy Lord: for verily thou art in Our eyes: ...
9:5
Verse of the Sword

Surah 53

53:29
Therefore shun those who turn away from Our Message and desire nothing but the life of this world.
9:5
Verse of the Sword

53:39
That man can have nothing but what he strives for;
52:21

And those who believe and whose families follow them in Faith,- to them shall We join their families: Nor shall We deprive them (of the fruit) of aught of their works: (Yet) is each individual in pledge for his deeds.

Surah 54

54:6
Therefore, (O prophet,) turn away from them. The Day that the Caller will call (them) to a terrible affair,
9:5
Verse of the Sword

Surah 56

56:13 - 56:14
A number of people from those of old,
And a few from those of later times.
56:39 - 56 : 40
A (goodly) number from those of old,
And a (goodly) number from those of later times.

Surah 58

58:12

O ye who believe! When ye consult the Messenger in private, spend something in charity before your private consultation. That will be best for you, and most conducive to purity (of conduct). ...
58:13
Is it that ye are afraid of spending sums in charity before your private consultation (with him)? If, then, ye do not so, and Allah forgives you, then (at least) establish regular prayer; practise regular charity; and obey Allah and His Messenger. ...

Surah 60

60:8
Allah forbids you not, with regard to those who fight you not for (your) Faith nor drive you out of your homes, from dealing kindly and justly with them: for Allah loveth those who are just.
60:9
Allah only forbids you, with regard to those who fight you for (your) Faith, and drive you out of your homes, and support (others) in driving you out, from turning to them (for friendship and protection). It is such as turn to them (in these circumstances), that do wrong.

60:10 (A)
O ye who believe! When there come to you believing women refugees, examine (and test) them: Allah knows best as to their Faith
...
60:10 (B)
send them not back to the Unbelievers. ...
(Note: The entire verse was not written at one time. The second half came later and cancels out a section of the first part.)

60:11
And if any of your wives deserts you to the Unbelievers, and ye have an accession (by the coming over of a woman from the other side), then pay to those whose wives have deserted the equivalent

of what they had spent (on their dower). And fear Allah, in Whom
ye believe.
9:5
Verse of the Sword

Surah 68

68:44

Then leave Me alone with such as reject this Message: by degrees
shall We punish them from directions they perceive not.
9:5
Verse of the Sword

68:48

So wait with patience for the Command of thy Lord, and be not like
the Companion of the Fish,- when he cried out in agony.
9:5
Verse of the Sword

Surah 70

70:5

Therefore do thou hold Patience,- a Patience of beautiful
(contentment).
9:5
Verse of the Sword

70:42
So leave them to plunge in vain talk and play about, until they
encounter that Day of theirs which they have been promised
9:5
Verse of the Sword

Surah 73

73:1 - 73:2
O thou folded in garments!
Stand (to prayer) by night, but not all night,-...
73:2 - 73:3 - 73:4
Stand (to prayer) by night, but not all night,-
Half of it,- or a little less,
Or a little more; ...

73:5
Soon shall We send down to thee a weighty Message.
4:32
Allah doth wish to lighten your (difficulties): For man was created
Weak (in flesh).

73:10
And have patience with what they say, and leave them with noble
(dignity).
9:5
Verse of the Sword

73:11
And leave Me (alone to deal with) those in possession of the good
things of life, who (yet) deny the Truth; and bear with them for a
little while.
9:5
Verse of the Sword

73:19

Verily this is an Admonition: therefore, whoso will, let him take a (straight) path to his Lord!

76:30

But ye will not, except as Allah wills; for Allah is full of Knowledge and Wisdom.

Surah 74

74:11

Leave Me alone, (to deal) with the (creature) whom I created (bare and) alone!-

9:5

Verse of the Sword

Surah 75

75:16

Move not thy tongue concerning the (Quran) to make haste therewith.

87:6

By degrees shall We teach thee to declare (the Message), so thou shalt not forget,

Surah 76

76:8
And they feed, for the love of Allah, the indigent, the orphan, and the captive,-
9:5
Verse of the Sword

76:24
Therefore be patient with constancy to the Command of thy Lord, and hearken not to the sinner or the ingrate among them.
9:5
Verse of the Sword

76:29
This is an admonition: Whosoever will, let him take a (straight) Path to his Lord.
9:5
Verse of the Sword

Surah 80

80:12
Therefore let whoso will, keep it in remembrance.
81:29
But ye shall not will except as Allah wills,- the Cherisher of the Worlds.

Surah 81

81:28

(With profit) to whoever among you wills to go straight:
81:29
But ye shall not will except as Allah wills,- the Cherisher of the Worlds.

Surah 86

86:17
Therefore grant a delay to the Unbelievers: Give respite to them gently (for awhile).
9:5
Verse of the Sword

Surah 88

88:21 - 88:22 - 88:23
Therefore do thou give admonition, for thou art one to admonish.
Thou art not one to manage (men's) affairs.
But if any turn away and reject Allah,-
9:5
Verse of the Sword

Surah 95

95:8
Is not Allah the wisest of judges?
9:5
Verse of the Sword

Surah 103

103:2
Verily Man is in loss,
103:3
Except such as have Faith, and do righteous deeds,...

Surah 109

109:6
To you be your Way, and to me mine.
9:5 Verse of the Sword

This view, if understood, explains the actions and beliefs of fundamental Muslims. The prophet went from being a peaceful leader and devoted married man in the first half of his life but progressed to his final state of a warlord who took many wives, some as young as six years of age. So went the trajectory of the religion. Since the prophet's words were the last revelation and his life was to be used as a template of goodness and righteousness, all laws, judgments, and worldviews ceased to evolve and left the fundamentalists firmly planted in the barbarism of the 7th century with all its injustice and cruelty.

Appendix "B"
Mohammed's Wives

This list of Mohammed is provided by the Muslim scholar Ali Dashti, based on The History of al-Tabari vol.9 p.126-241. Scholars do not agree on the the number of wives. Some hadiths (not Bukhari or Sahih Muslim) mention wives Mohammed had divorced. Status of many women are uncertain.

1. Khadija/Khadijah bint Khuwailid/Khywaylid - died – his first wife.
2. Sauda/Sawda bint Zam'a
3. 'Aisha/Aesha/'A'ishah – (9 yreas old)
4. Omm Salama/Salamah
5. Hafsa/Hafsah
6. Zaynab/Zainab of Jahsh (his cousin)
7. Juwairiya/Jowayriya bint Harith (Slave/captive)
8. Umm Habiba
9. Safiya/Safiyya bint Huyai/Huyayy bint Akhtab (Slave/captive)
10. Maymuna/Maimuna of Hareth
11. Fatima/Fatema/Fatimah (married briefly)
12. Hend/Hind (She was widowed)
13. Asma of Saba (Sana bint Asma')
14. Zaynab of Khozayma
15. Habla?
16. Divorced Asma of Noman / bint al-Nu'man

slaves / concubines
17. Mary the Copt/Christian (some source say they married when she had Mohammed's son.)
18. Rayhana/Raihana/Rayhanah bint Zayd/Zaid

uncertain relationship
19. Divorced Omm Sharik
20. Maymuna/Maimuna (slave girl?)
21. Zaynab/Zainab the third?
22. Khawla / Khawlah
23. Divorced Mulaykah bint Dawud (13 years old)
24. Divorced al-Shanba' bint 'Amr

25. Divorced al-'Aliyyah
26. Divorced 'Amrah bint Yazid
27. Divorced an Unnamed Woman
28. Qutaylah bint Qays (died right away)
29. Sana bint Sufyan
30. Sharaf bint Khalifah

Mohammed married 15 women and consummated his marriages with 13. (al-Tabari vol.9 p.126-127)

Bukhari vol.1 Book 5 ch.25 no.282 p.172-173 said that the maximum number of wives at any time was nine wives.

Joseph Lumpkin

Appendix "C"
Letters From Osama Bin Laden
An al-Qaeda Manifesto

Letter from Bin Laden
Supplied by World News – November, 2002

In the Name of Allah, the Most Gracious, the Most Merciful,
"Permission to fight (against disbelievers) is given to those (believers) who are fought against, because they have been wronged and surely, Allah is Able to give them (believers) victory" [Quran 22:39]

"Those who believe, fight in the Cause of Allah, and those who disbelieve, fight in the cause of Taghut (anything worshipped other than Allah e.g. Satan). So fight you against the friends of Satan; ever feeble is indeed the plot of Satan."[Quran 4:76]

Some American writers have published articles under the title 'On what basis are we fighting?' These articles have generated a number of responses, some of which adhered to the truth and were based on Islamic Law, and others which have not. Here we wanted to outline the truth - as an explanation and warning - hoping for Allah's reward, seeking success and support from Him.

While seeking Allah's help, we form our reply based on two questions directed at the Americans:

(Q1) Why are we fighting and opposing you?
Q2)What are we calling you to, and what do we want from you?

As for the first question: Why are we fighting and opposing you? The answer is very simple:

(1) Because you attacked us and continue to attack us.

a) You attacked us in Palestine:

(i) Palestine, which has sunk under military occupation for more than 80 years. The British handed over Palestine, with your help and your support, to the Jews, who have occupied it for more than 50 years; years overflowing with oppression, tyranny, crimes, killing, expulsion, destruction and devastation. The creation and continuation of Israel is one of the greatest crimes, and you are the leaders of its criminals. And of course there is no need to explain and prove the degree of American support for Israel. The creation of Israel is a crime which must be erased. Each and every person whose hands have become polluted in the contribution towards this crime must pay its*price, and pay for it heavily.

(ii) It brings us both laughter and tears to see that you have not yet tired of repeating your fabricated lies that the Jews have a historical right to Palestine, as it was promised to them in the Torah. Anyone who disputes with them on this alleged fact is accused of anti-semitism. This is one of the most fallacious, widely-circulated fabrications in history. The people of Palestine are pure Arabs and original Semites. It is the Muslims who are the inheritors of Moses (peace be upon him) and the inheritors of the real Torah that has not been changed. Muslims believe in all of the Prophets, including Abraham, Moses, Jesus and Muhammad, peace and blessings of Allah be upon them all. If the followers of Moses have been promised a right to Palestine in the Torah, then the Muslims are the most worthy nation of this.

When the Muslims conquered Palestine and drove out the Romans, Palestine and Jerusalem returned to Islaam, the religion of all the Prophets peace be upon them. Therefore, the call to a historical right to Palestine cannot be raised against the Islamic Ummah that believes in all the Prophets of Allah (peace and blessings be upon them) - and we make no distinction between them.

(iii) The blood pouring out of Palestine must be equally revenged. You must know that the Palestinians do not cry alone; their women are not widowed alone; their sons are not orphaned alone.

(b) You attacked us in Somalia; you supported the Russian atrocities against us in Chechnya, the Indian oppression against us in Kashmir, and the Jewish aggression against us in Lebanon.

(c) Under your supervision, consent and orders, the governments of our countries which act as your agents, attack us on a daily basis;

(i) These governments prevent our people from establishing the Islamic Shariah, using violence and lies to do so.

(ii) These governments give us a taste of humiliation, and places us in a large prison of fear and subdual.

(iii) These governments steal our Ummah's wealth and sell them to you at a paltry price.

(iv) These governments have surrendered to the Jews, and handed them most of Palestine, acknowledging the existence of their state over the dismembered limbs of their own people.

(v) The removal of these governments is an obligation upon us, and a necessary step to free the Ummah, to make the Shariah the supreme law and to regain Palestine. And our fight against these governments is not separate from out fight against you.

(d) You steal our wealth and oil at paltry prices because of you international influence and military threats. This theft is indeed the biggest theft ever witnessed by mankind in the history of the world.

(e) Your forces occupy our countries; you spread your military bases throughout them; you corrupt our lands, and you besiege our sanctities, to protect the security of the Jews and to ensure the continuity of your pillage of our treasures.

(f) You have starved the Muslims of Iraq, where children die every day. It is a wonder that more than 1.5 million Iraqi children have died as a result of your sanctions, and you did not show concern. Yet when 3000 of your people died, the entire world rises and has not yet sat down.

(g) You have supported the Jews in their idea that Jerusalem is their eternal capital, and agreed to move your embassy there. With your help and under your protection, the Israelis are planning to destroy the Al-Aqsa mosque. Under the protection of your weapons, Sharon entered the Al-Aqsa mosque, to pollute it as a preparation to capture and destroy it.

(2) These tragedies and calamities are only a few examples of your oppression and aggression against us. It is commanded by our religion and intellect that the oppressed have a right to return the aggression. Do not await anything from us but Jihad, resistance and revenge. Is it in any way rational to expect that after America has attacked us for more than half a century, that we will then leave her to live in security and peace?!!

(3) You may then dispute that all the above does not justify aggression against civilians, for crimes they did not commit and offenses in which they did not partake:

(a) This argument contradicts your continuous repetition that America is the land of freedom, and its leaders in this world. Therefore, the American people are the ones who choose their government by way of their own free will; a choice which stems from their agreement to its policies. Thus the American people have chosen, consented to, and affirmed their support for the Israeli oppression of the Palestinians, the occupation and usurpation of their land, and its continuous killing, torture, punishment and expulsion of the Palestinians. The American people have the ability and choice to refuse the policies of their Government and even to change it if they want.

(b) The American people are the ones who pay the taxes which fund the planes that bomb us in Afghanistan, the tanks that strike and destroy our homes in Palestine, the armies which occupy our lands in the Arabian Gulf, and the fleets which ensure the blockade of Iraq. These tax dollars are given to Israel for it to continue to attack us and penetrate our lands. So the American people are the ones who fund the attacks against us, and they are the ones who oversee the expenditure of these monies in the way they wish, through their elected candidates.

(c) Also the American army is part of the American people. It is this very same people who are shamelessly helping the Jews fight against us.

(d) The American people are the ones who employ both their men and their women in the American Forces which attack us.

(e) This is why the American people cannot be not innocent of all the crimes committed by the Americans and Jews against us.

(f) Allah, the Almighty, legislated the permission and the option to take revenge. Thus, if we are attacked, then we have the right to attack back. Whoever has destroyed our villages and towns, then we have the right to destroy their villages and towns. Whoever has stolen our wealth, then we have the right to destroy their economy. And whoever has killed our civilians, then we have the right to kill theirs.

The American Government and press still refuses to answer the question:

Why did they attack us in New York and Washington?

If Sharon is a man of peace in the eyes of Bush, then we are also men of peace!!! America does not understand the language of manners and principles, so we are addressing it using the language it understands.

(Q2) As for the second question that we want to answer: What are we calling you to, and what do we want from you?

(1) The first thing that we are calling you to is Islam.

(a) The religion of the Unification of God; of freedom from associating partners with Him, and rejection of this; of complete love of Him, the Exalted; of complete submission to His Laws; and of the discarding of all the opinions, orders, theories and religions which contradict with the religion He sent down to His Prophet Muhammad (peace be upon him). Islam is the religion of all the prophets, and makes no distinction between them - peace be upon them all.

It is to this religion that we call you; the seal of all the previous religions. It is the religion of Unification of God, sincerity, the best of manners, righteousness, mercy, honour, purity, and piety. It is the religion of showing kindness to others, establishing justice between them, granting them their rights, and defending the oppressed and the persecuted. It is the religion of enjoining the good and forbidding the evil with the hand, tongue and heart. It is the religion of Jihad in the way of Allah so that Allah's Word and religion reign Supreme. And it is the religion of unity and agreement on the obedience to Allah, and total equality between all people, without regarding their colour, sex, or language.

(b) It is the religion whose book - the Quran - will remained preserved and unchanged, after the other Divine books and messages have been changed. The Quran is the miracle until the Day of Judgment. Allah has challenged anyone to bring a book like the Quran or even ten verses like it.

(2) The second thing we call you to, is to stop your oppression, lies, immorality and debauchery that has spread among you.

(a) We call you to be a people of manners, principles, honour, and purity; to reject the immoral acts of fornication, homosexuality, intoxicants, gambling's, and trading with interest.

We call you to all of this that you may be freed from that which you have become caught up in; that you may be freed from the deceptive lies that you are a great nation, that your leaders spread amongst you to conceal from you the despicable state to which you have reached.

(b) It is saddening to tell you that you are the worst civilization witnessed by the history of mankind:

(i) You are the nation who, rather than ruling by the Shariah of Allah in its Constitution and Laws, choose to invent your own laws as you will and desire. You separate religion from your policies, contradicting the pure nature which affirms Absolute Authority to the Lord and your Creator. You flee from the embarrassing question posed to you: How is it possible for Allah the Almighty to create His creation, grant them power over all the creatures and land, grant them all the amenities of life, and then deny them that which they are most in need of: knowledge of the laws which govern their lives?

(ii) You are the nation that permits Usury, which has been forbidden by all the religions. Yet you build your economy and investments on Usury. As a result of this, in all its different forms and guises, the Jews have taken control of your economy, through which they have then taken control of your media, and now control all aspects of your life making you their servants and achieving their aims at your expense; precisely what Benjamin Franklin warned you against.

(iii) You are a nation that permits the production, trading and usage of intoxicants. You also permit drugs, and only forbid the trade of them, even though your nation is the largest consumer of them.

(iv) You are a nation that permits acts of immorality, and you consider them to be pillars of personal freedom. You have continued to sink down this abyss from level to level until incest has spread amongst you, in the face of which neither your sense of honour nor your laws object.

Who can forget your President Clinton's immoral acts committed in the official Oval office? After that you did not even bring him to account, other than that he 'made a mistake', after which everything passed with no punishment. Is there a worse kind of event for which your name will go down in history and remembered by nations?

(v) You are a nation that permits gambling in its all forms. The companies practice this as well, resulting in the investments becoming active and the criminals becoming rich.

(vi) You are a nation that exploits women like consumer products or advertising tools calling upon customers to purchase them. You use women to serve passengers, visitors, and strangers to increase your profit margins. You then rant that you support the liberation of women.

(vii) You are a nation that practices the trade of sex in all its forms, directly and indirectly. Giant corporations and establishments are established on this, under the name of art, entertainment, tourism and freedom, and other deceptive names you attribute to it.

(viii) And because of all this, you have been described in history as a nation that spreads diseases that were unknown to man in the past. Go ahead and boast to the nations of man, that you brought them AIDS as a Satanic American Invention.

(xi) You have destroyed nature with your industrial waste and gases more than any other nation in history. Despite this, you refuse to sign the Kyoto agreement so that you can secure the profit of your greedy companies and*industries.

(x) Your law is the law of the rich and wealthy people, who hold sway in their political parties, and fund their election campaigns with their gifts. Behind them stand the Jews, who control your policies, media and economy.

(xi) That which you are singled out for in the history of mankind, is that you have used your force to destroy mankind more than any other nation in history; not to defend principles and values, but to hasten to secure your interests and profits. You who dropped a nuclear bomb on Japan, even though Japan was ready to negotiate an end to the war. How many acts of oppression, tyranny and injustice have you carried out, O callers to freedom?

(xii) Let us not forget one of your major characteristics: your duality in both manners and values; your hypocrisy in manners and principles. All*manners, principles and values have two scales: one for you and one for the others.

(a)The freedom and democracy that you call to is for yourselves and for white race only; as for the rest of the world, you impose upon them your monstrous, destructive policies and Governments, which you call the 'American friends'. Yet you prevent them from establishing democracies. When the Islamic party in Algeria wanted to practice democracy and they won the election, you unleashed your agents in the Algerian army onto them, and to attack them with tanks and guns, to imprison them and torture them - a new lesson from the 'American book of democracy'!!!

(b)Your policy on prohibiting and forcibly removing weapons of mass destruction to ensure world peace: it only applies to those countries which you do not permit to possess such weapons. As for the countries you consent to, such as Israel, then they are allowed to keep and use such weapons to defend their security. Anyone else who you suspect might be manufacturing or keeping these kinds of weapons, you call them criminals and you take military action against them.

(c)You are the last ones to respect the resolutions and policies of International Law, yet you claim to want to selectively punish anyone else who does the same. Israel has for more than 50 years been pushing UN resolutions and rules against the wall with the full support of America.

(d)As for the war criminals which you censure and form criminal courts for - you shamelessly ask that your own are granted immunity!! However, history will not forget the war crimes that you committed against the Muslims and the rest of the world; those you have killed in Japan, Afghanistan, Somalia, Lebanon and Iraq will remain a shame that you will never be able to escape. It will suffice to remind you of your latest war crimes in Afghanistan, in which densely populated innocent civilian villages were destroyed, bombs were dropped on mosques causing the roof of the mosque to come crashing down on the heads of the Muslims praying inside. You are the ones who broke the agreement with the Mujahideen when they left Qunduz, bombing them in Jangi fort, and killing more than 1,000 of your prisoners through suffocation and thirst. Allah alone knows how many people have died by torture at the hands of you and your agents. Your planes remain in the Afghan skies, looking for anyone remotely suspicious.

(e)You have claimed to be the vanguards of Human Rights, and your Ministry of Foreign affairs issues annual reports containing statistics of those countries that violate any Human Rights. However, all these things vanished when the Mujahideen hit you, and you then implemented the methods of the same documented governments that you used to curse. In America, you captured thousands the Muslims and Arabs, took them into custody with neither reason, court trial, nor even disclosing their names. You issued newer, harsher laws.

What happens in Guatanamo is a historical embarrassment to America and its values, and it screams into your faces - you hypocrites, "What is the value of your signature on any agreement or treaty?"

(3) What we call you to thirdly is to take an honest stance with yourselves - and I doubt you will do so - to discover that you are a nation without principles or manners, and that the values and principles to you are

something which you merely demand from others, not that which you yourself must adhere to.

(4) We also advise you to stop supporting Israel, and to end your support of the Indians in Kashmir, the Russians against the Chechens and to also cease supporting the Manila Government against the Muslims in Southern Philippines.

(5) We also advise you to pack your luggage and get out of our lands. We desire for your goodness, guidance, and righteousness, so do not force us to send you back as cargo in coffins.

(6) Sixthly, we call upon you to end your support of the corrupt leaders in our countries. Do not interfere in our politics and method of education. Leave us alone, or else expect us in New York and Washington.

(7) We also call you to deal with us and interact with us on the basis of mutual interests and benefits, rather than the policies of sub dual, theft and occupation, and not to continue your policy of supporting the Jews because this will result in more disasters for you.

If you fail to respond to all these conditions, then prepare for fight with the Islamic Nation. The Nation of Monotheism, that puts complete trust on Allah and fears none other than Him. The Nation which is addressed by its Quran with the words: "Do you fear them? Allah has more right that you should fear Him if you are believers. Fight against them so that Allah will punish them by your hands and disgrace them and give you victory over them and heal the breasts of believing people. And remove the anger of their (believers') hearts. Allah accepts the repentance of whom He wills. Allah is All-Knowing, All-Wise." [Quran9:13-1]

The Nation of honour and respect:
"But honour, power and glory belong to Allah, and to His Messenger (Muhammad- peace be upon him) and to the believers." [Quran 63:8]

"So do not become weak (against your enemy), nor be sad, and you will be*superior (in victory)if you are indeed (true) believers" [Quran 3:139]

The Nation of Martyrdom; the Nation that desires death more than you desire life:

"Think not of those who are killed in the way of Allah as dead. Nay, they are alive with their Lord, and they are being provided for. They rejoice in what Allah has bestowed upon them from His bounty and rejoice for the sake of those who have not yet joined them, but are left behind (not yet martyred) that on them no fear shall come, nor shall they grieve. They rejoice in a grace and a bounty from Allah, and that Allah will not waste the reward of the believers." [Quran 3:169-171]

The Nation of victory and success that Allah has promised:

"It is He Who has sent His Messenger (Muhammad peace be upon him) with guidance and the religion of truth (Islam), to make it victorious over all other religions even though the Polytheists hate it." [Quran 61:9]

"Allah has decreed that 'Verily it is I and My Messengers who shall be victorious.' Verily Allah is All-Powerful, All-Mighty." [Quran 58:21]

The Islamic Nation that was able to dismiss and destroy the previous evil Empires like yourself; the Nation that rejects your attacks, wishes to remove your evils, and is prepared to fight you. You are well aware that the Islamic Nation, from the very core of its soul, despises your haughtiness and arrogance.

If the Americans refuse to listen to our advice and the goodness, guidance and righteousness that we call them to, then be aware that you will lose this Crusade Bush began, just like the other previous Crusades in which you were humiliated by the hands of the Mujahideen, fleeing to your home in great silence and disgrace. If the Americans do not respond, then their fate will be that of the Soviets who fled from Afghanistan to deal with their military defeat, political breakup, ideological downfall, and economic bankruptcy.

This is our message to the Americans, as an answer to theirs. Do they now know why we fight them and over which form of ignorance, by the permission of Allah, we shall be victorious?

A Letter To The American People
Recovered in 2011

(Fully Translated)

In the name of Allah, the Compassionate, the Merciful. FromUsama Bin Muhammad Bin Ladin to the American people, I speak to you about the subject of the ongoing war between you and us. Even though the consensus of your wise thinkers and others is that your time (TN: of defeat) will come, compassion for the women and children who are being unjustly killed, wounded, and displaced in Iraq, Afghanistan, and Pakistan motivates me to speak to you. First of all, I would like to say that your war with us is the longest war in your history and the most expensive for you financially. As for us, we see it as being only halfway finished. If you were to ask your wise thinkers, they would tell you that there is no way to win it because the indications are against it. How will you win a war whose leaders are pessimistic and whose soldiers are committing suicide? If fear enters the hearts of men, winning the war becomes impossible. How will you win a war whose cost is like a hurricane blowing violently at your economy and weakening your dollar? The Bush administration got you into these wars on the premise that they were vital to your security. He promised that it would be a quick war, won within six days or six weeks; however, six years have passed, and they are still promising you victory and not achieving it. Then Obama came and delayed the withdrawal that he had promised you by 16 more months. He promised you victory in Afghanistan and set a date for withdrawal fromthere. Six months later, Petraeus came to you once again with the number six, requesting that the withdrawal be delayed six months beyond the date that had been set. All the while you continue to bleed in Iraq and Afghanistan. You are wading into a war with no end in sight on the horizon and which has no connection to your security, which was confirmed by the operation of 'Umar al-Faruq (Var.: Umar Farouk), which was not launched fromthe battlefield and could have been launched fromany place in the world. As for us, jihad against the tyrants and the aggressors is a formof great worship in our religion. It is more precious to us than our fathers and sons. Thus, our jihad against you is worship,

Page 2 and your killing us is a testimony. Thanks to God, Almighty, we have been waging jihad for 30 years, against the Russians and then against you. Not a single one of our men has committed suicide, whereas every 30 days 30 of your men commit suicide. Continue the war if you will. (TN: Two lines of poetry that say the Mujahidin will not stop fighting until the United States leaves their land.) Peace be upon those who follow right guidance. We are defending our right. Jihad against the aggressors is a formof great worship in our religion, and killing us means a high status with our Lord. Thanks to God, we have been waging jihad for 30 years, against the Russians and then against you. Not a single one of our men has committed suicide, whereas every 30 days 30 of your men commit suicide. Continue the war if you will. Justice is the strongest army, and security is the best way of life, but it slipped out of your grasp the day you made the Jews victorious in occupying our land and killing our brothers in Palestine. The path to security is for you to lift your oppression from us.

Joseph Lumpkin

Appendix "D"
An ISIS Manifesto

Translation provided by Shoebat.com
September 22, 2014

An ISIS spokesman posted a call to arms for Muslims around the world to kill American, Canadian and European citizens for their governments' role in a coalition against ISIS. In a 42-minute speech released on social media ISIS made a call to arms for Muslims to kill all non-Muslims. The manifesto stated in part:

"If you can kill a disbelieving American or European – especially the spiteful and filthy French – or an Australian, or a Canadian, or any other disbeliever ... including the citizens of the countries that entered into a coalition against the Islamic State, then rely upon Allah, and kill him in any manner or way however it may be,"

He added:

"You will not be safe, even in your own bedrooms while you sleep. Your Crusader campaign will fail. You will pay the price and we will hit you on your home front in a way that will cripple you to never extend your long arm ever again." (see minute 18:50)

"Peace, mercy and blessings of God. It is no secret what was published in the media about the intention to hit America with weapons of mass Destruction. So what is the Fatwa ruling for the Mujahideen to use these? Is it permissible at all? Is it the Mother of necessity? ... This issue, needs a complete message; and gathering from evidence and scholarly sources to the question regarding The House of War and how to practice Jihad-u-Dafi' (Repulse Jihad) and the meaning of destruction of crops including reproduction of life (children) religiously, and so on which I will collect what was given by Allah's will".

"If the infidels cannot be repulsed from the Muslims except by resorting to using such weapons, then it may be used even if it killed and wiped them out completely including decimating their crops and their

305

descendants. I will include the details in my letter I mentioned. Therefore the question is asked and the answer is given and the matter is closed and concluded.

"It was shown in Sahih … the Prophet said "Allah wrote everything we need to know about Ihsan (kindness) so if you kill perfect your killing and if you slaughter, perfect your slaughter and sharpen your blade and comfort your sacrifice" (also see Hadith Muslim 107/13)

"Ibn Rajab said regarding Allah's mercy in his collection on science and governance, p 112: "in charity it is permissible to kill people and animals in the easiest way and do not increase in the torture and the easiest method to kill a human being is to strike off the neck with the sword of violence in accordance to the Quran when "you meet the unbelievers then strike off their necks"(Quran) and it also said: "I will spread horror/terror in the hearts of the unbelievers, smite above their necks and smite there fingertips thereof"

Section I: evidence for an age to use specific weapons for a particular enemy:
And so like if America at this time; the issue to hit with these weapons [mass destruction] is permissible without mentioning the evidence of the second section the following (evidence of general legality); because Allah Almighty says "to punish in similar fashion as you were afflicted", and the Almighty says "Attack who attacks you in similar ways as you were attacked," and the Almighty says "Pay evil with evil," so the observer sees American aggression on Muslims and their lands during the past decades concludes the permission to use aggression with reciprocity only as has been collected by some of the brothers the number of dead from amongst the Muslims with their weapons of direct and indirect, methods to bring the number close to ten million. And as for the lands that [America] burned with their bombs and their explosives and rockets not one can enumerate except Allah, and whatever else happened in Afghanistan and Iraq, and this is what caused the wars on many of the Muslims causing homelessness. So if bomb is launched at them that will kill ten million of them, and it will burn their land as much as they burned the Muslim lands this is therefore permissible without the need to mention any other evidence, but other evidence may be needed if we are to perish of them more than this number!

"And so it is allowed to throw at them, that is the Kafirs [unbelievers] with fire, snakes, scorpions while using the catapults. It is also permissible to smoke them, open water on them in order to drown them, destroy their buildings on top of them. Since in the meaning of Tabyeet is that if you kill, do it well ...And it is permissible to kill them therefore even if amongst them are women and children since this is included in Tabyeet"

"Sarkhasi said, quoting Muhammad ibn al-Hasan in his "The Explanation of the Major Hadith" #4111/1:
He said: **"There is nothing wrong for Muslims to burn the infidels fortresses with fire, or to drown them with water and poison them and cut off their water, and to make their water bitter by pouring blood and menstrual blood and poison until they spoil it for them because we were ordered to belittle them and to break their unity"**

Recommended Reading
Bibliography

The Great Transformation: The Beginning of Our Religious Traditions
Karen Armstrong (Author)
Anchor; Reprint edition (April 10, 2007)
ISBN-13: 978-0385721240

The Origin and Goal of History
Karl Jaspers (Author)
Routledge (April 11, 2011)
ISBN-13: 978-0415578806

The Translation of the Meanings of Summarized Sahih Al-Bukhari: Arabic-English
Mohammed M. Khan (Translator)
Kazi Pubns Inc (January 1995)
ISBN-13: 978-1567445190

The Book of Hadith: Sayings of the prophet Mohammed from the Mishkat al Masabih
Charles Le Gai Eaton (Author), Jeremy Henzell-Thomas (Introduction)
Publisher: The Book Foundation (November 1, 2008)
ISBN-13: 978-1904510178

The life of Mohammad from original sources
William Muir (Author), Thomas Hunter Weir (Author)
Publisher: Book on Demand Ltd. (April 1, 2013)
ISBN-13: 978-5518464780

The Life of Mohammed
I. Ishaq (Author), A. Guillaume (Translator)
Oxford University Press (July 18, 2002)
ISBN-13: 978-0196360331

The War of the End of Times: What the Islamic State Wants
Kindle Edition
Graeme Wood (Author)

Islam and the Infidels: The Politics of Jihad, Dawah, and Hijrah
David Bukay (Author)
Transaction Publishers (March 31, 2016)
ISBN-13: 978-1412862950

Essence Of Life: A Translation Of AIN ALHAYAT [Print Replica]
Mohammed Baqir Majlisi (Author), Sayed Tahir Bilgrami (Translator)
Kindle Edition September 14, 2015

Taliban
Alhem Rashid (Author)
Yale University Press (2001)
ISBN-10: 03000089023

The Islamic Antichrist
Joel Richardson (Author)
WorldNetDaily Publishing (2009)
ISBN-13: 9781935071129

Recommended Websites

Fbi.gov
The atlantic.com
Answering-islam.org
Beilefnet.com
Sunnah.com
Nationalreview.com
Americanthinker.com
Wikiislam.net
Theguardian.com
Questionislam.com
Religionfacts.com
Breitbart.com

Joseph Lumpkin